C-5010 CAREER EXAMINATION SERIES

This is your
PASSBOOK for...

Director Social Work (LCSW)

Test Preparation Study Guide
Questions & Answers

NATIONAL LEARNING CORPORATION®

COPYRIGHT NOTICE

This book is SOLELY intended for, is sold ONLY to, and its use is RESTRICTED to individual, bona fide applicants or candidates who qualify by virtue of having seriously filed applications for appropriate license, certificate, professional and/or promotional advancement, higher school matriculation, scholarship, or other legitimate requirements of education and/or governmental authorities.

This book is NOT intended for use, class instruction, tutoring, training, duplication, copying, reprinting, excerption, or adaptation, etc., by:

1) Other publishers
2) Proprietors and/or Instructors of "Coaching" and/or Preparatory Courses
3) Personnel and/or Training Divisions of commercial, industrial, and governmental organizations
4) Schools, colleges, or universities and/or their departments and staffs, including teachers and other personnel
5) Testing Agencies or Bureaus
6) Study groups which seek by the purchase of a single volume to copy and/or duplicate and/or adapt this material for use by the group as a whole without having purchased individual volumes for each of the members of the group
7) Et al.

Such persons would be in violation of appropriate Federal and State statutes.

PROVISION OF LICENSING AGREEMENTS – Recognized educational, commercial, industrial, and governmental institutions and organizations, and others legitimately engaged in educational pursuits, including training, testing, and measurement activities, may address request for a licensing agreement to the copyright owners, who will determine whether, and under what conditions, including fees and charges, the materials in this book may be used them. In other words, a licensing facility exists for the legitimate use of the material in this book on other than an individual basis. However, it is asseverated and affirmed here that the material in this book CANNOT be used without the receipt of the express permission of such a licensing agreement from the Publishers. Inquiries re licensing should be addressed to the company, attention rights and permissions department.

All rights reserved, including the right of reproduction in whole or in part, in any form or by any means, electronic or mechanical, including photocopying, recording, or by any information storage and retrieval system, without permission in writing from the Publisher.

Copyright © 2025 by
National Learning Corporation

212 Michael Drive, Syosset, NY 11791
(516) 921-8888 • www.passbooks.com
E-mail: info@passbooks.com

PASSBOOK® SERIES

THE *PASSBOOK® SERIES* has been created to prepare applicants and candidates for the ultimate academic battlefield – the examination room.

At some time in our lives, each and every one of us may be required to take an examination – for validation, matriculation, admission, qualification, registration, certification, or licensure.

Based on the assumption that every applicant or candidate has met the basic formal educational standards, has taken the required number of courses, and read the necessary texts, the *PASSBOOK® SERIES* furnishes the one special preparation which may assure passing with confidence, instead of failing with insecurity. Examination questions – together with answers – are furnished as the basic vehicle for study so that the mysteries of the examination and its compounding difficulties may be eliminated or diminished by a sure method.

This book is meant to help you pass your examination provided that you qualify and are serious in your objective.

The entire field is reviewed through the huge store of content information which is succinctly presented through a provocative and challenging approach – the question-and-answer method.

A climate of success is established by furnishing the correct answers at the end of each test.

You soon learn to recognize types of questions, forms of questions, and patterns of questioning. You may even begin to anticipate expected outcomes.

You perceive that many questions are repeated or adapted so that you can gain acute insights, which may enable you to score many sure points.

You learn how to confront new questions, or types of questions, and to attack them confidently and work out the correct answers.

You note objectives and emphases, and recognize pitfalls and dangers, so that you may make positive educational adjustments.

Moreover, you are kept fully informed in relation to new concepts, methods, practices, and directions in the field.

You discover that you are actually taking the examination all the time: you are preparing for the examination by "taking" an examination, not by reading extraneous and/or supererogatory textbooks.

In short, this PASSBOOK®, used directedly, should be an important factor in helping you to pass your test.

DIRECTOR SOCIAL WORK
(LICENSED CLINICAL SOCIAL WORKER)

DUTIES
As a Director Social Work (Licensed Clinical Social Worker), you would direct a social work program or department by establishing and/or monitoring social work program policies and practices that are consistent with standards required by the Joint Commission, Centers for Medicare and Medicaid Services (CMS), and the social work profession; serving as a senior staff member to treatment teams by providing case consultation to inpatient and outpatient Treatment Teams; developing competency-based assessment tools for the social work discipline; leading and managing professional and paraprofessional social work staff; and performing the full range of supervisory responsibilities. In addition, you may perform all the duties and activities of a Social Work Supervisor I (Licensed Clinical Social Worker).

SCOPE OF THE EXAMINATION
The multiple-choice test will cover knowledge, skills and abilities in such areas as:

1. **Administrative supervision** - These questions test for knowledge of the principles and practices involved in directing the activities of a large subordinate staff, including subordinate supervisors. Questions relate to the personal interactions between an upper-level supervisor and their subordinate supervisors in the accomplishment of objectives. These questions cover such areas as assigning work to and coordinating the activities of several units, establishing and guiding staff development programs, evaluating the performance of subordinate supervisors, and maintaining relationships with other organizational sections;
2. **Developing and implementing treatment in a social work program** - These questions test for knowledge, understanding, and ability to apply social work concepts, theories, standards, principles, and practices in various settings. Questions may cover such topics as assessment, development, implementation, monitoring and evaluation of treatment for individuals and families; coordination of services; advocacy and counseling for individuals and families of all backgrounds; and crisis intervention;
3. **Organizing and administering social work services programs** - These questions test for the knowledge and ability to develop, oversee and administer social work services programs in a variety of settings. Questions may cover such topics as developing and administering policies and procedures, planning, implementing, monitoring and evaluating program services and staff, and representing agency programs to community agencies, individuals, and groups; and
4. **Preparing written material** - These questions test for the ability to present information clearly and accurately, and to organize paragraphs logically and comprehensibly. For some questions, you will be given information in two or three sentences followed by four restatements of the information. You must then choose the best version. For other questions, you will be given paragraphs with their sentences out of order. You must then choose, from four suggestions, the best order for the sentences.

HOW TO TAKE A TEST

I. YOU MUST PASS AN EXAMINATION

A. *WHAT EVERY CANDIDATE SHOULD KNOW*

Examination applicants often ask us for help in preparing for the written test. What can I study in advance? What kinds of questions will be asked? How will the test be given? How will the papers be graded?

As an applicant for a civil service examination, you may be wondering about some of these things. Our purpose here is to suggest effective methods of advance study and to describe civil service examinations.

Your chances for success on this examination can be increased if you know how to prepare. Those "pre-examination jitters" can be reduced if you know what to expect. You can even experience an adventure in good citizenship if you know why civil service exams are given.

B. *WHY ARE CIVIL SERVICE EXAMINATIONS GIVEN?*

Civil service examinations are important to you in two ways. As a citizen, you want public jobs filled by employees who know how to do their work. As a job seeker, you want a fair chance to compete for that job on an equal footing with other candidates. The best-known means of accomplishing this two-fold goal is the competitive examination.

Exams are widely publicized throughout the nation. They may be administered for jobs in federal, state, city, municipal, town or village governments or agencies.

Any citizen may apply, with some limitations, such as the age or residence of applicants. Your experience and education may be reviewed to see whether you meet the requirements for the particular examination. When these requirements exist, they are reasonable and applied consistently to all applicants. Thus, a competitive examination may cause you some uneasiness now, but it is your privilege and safeguard.

C. *HOW ARE CIVIL SERVICE EXAMS DEVELOPED?*

Examinations are carefully written by trained technicians who are specialists in the field known as "psychological measurement," in consultation with recognized authorities in the field of work that the test will cover. These experts recommend the subject matter areas or skills to be tested; only those knowledges or skills important to your success on the job are included. The most reliable books and source materials available are used as references. Together, the experts and technicians judge the difficulty level of the questions.

Test technicians know how to phrase questions so that the problem is clearly stated. Their ethics do not permit "trick" or "catch" questions. Questions may have been tried out on sample groups, or subjected to statistical analysis, to determine their usefulness.

Written tests are often used in combination with performance tests, ratings of training and experience, and oral interviews. All of these measures combine to form the best-known means of finding the right person for the right job.

II. HOW TO PASS THE WRITTEN TEST

A. NATURE OF THE EXAMINATION

To prepare intelligently for civil service examinations, you should know how they differ from school examinations you have taken. In school you were assigned certain definite pages to read or subjects to cover. The examination questions were quite detailed and usually emphasized memory. Civil service exams, on the other hand, try to discover your present ability to perform the duties of a position, plus your potentiality to learn these duties. In other words, a civil service exam attempts to predict how successful you will be. Questions cover such a broad area that they cannot be as minute and detailed as school exam questions.

In the public service similar kinds of work, or positions, are grouped together in one "class." This process is known as *position-classification*. All the positions in a class are paid according to the salary range for that class. One class title covers all of these positions, and they are all tested by the same examination.

B. FOUR BASIC STEPS

1) Study the announcement

How, then, can you know what subjects to study? Our best answer is: "Learn as much as possible about the class of positions for which you've applied." The exam will test the knowledge, skills and abilities needed to do the work.

Your most valuable source of information about the position you want is the official exam announcement. This announcement lists the training and experience qualifications. Check these standards and apply only if you come reasonably close to meeting them.

The brief description of the position in the examination announcement offers some clues to the subjects which will be tested. Think about the job itself. Review the duties in your mind. Can you perform them, or are there some in which you are rusty? Fill in the blank spots in your preparation.

Many jurisdictions preview the written test in the exam announcement by including a section called "Knowledge and Abilities Required," "Scope of the Examination," or some similar heading. Here you will find out specifically what fields will be tested.

2) Review your own background

Once you learn in general what the position is all about, and what you need to know to do the work, ask yourself which subjects you already know fairly well and which need improvement. You may wonder whether to concentrate on improving your strong areas or on building some background in your fields of weakness. When the announcement has specified "some knowledge" or "considerable knowledge," or has used adjectives like "beginning principles of…" or "advanced … methods," you can get a clue as to the number and difficulty of questions to be asked in any given field. More questions, and hence broader coverage, would be included for those subjects which are more important in the work. Now weigh your strengths and weaknesses against the job requirements and prepare accordingly.

3) Determine the level of the position

Another way to tell how intensively you should prepare is to understand the level of the job for which you are applying. Is it the entering level? In other words, is this the position in which beginners in a field of work are hired? Or is it an intermediate or advanced level? Sometimes this is indicated by such words as "Junior" or "Senior" in the class title. Other jurisdictions use Roman numerals to designate the level – Clerk I, Clerk II, for example. The word "Supervisor" sometimes appears in the title. If the level is not indicated by the title, check the description of duties. Will you be working under very close supervision, or will you have responsibility for independent decisions in this work?

4) Choose appropriate study materials

Now that you know the subjects to be examined and the relative amount of each subject to be covered, you can choose suitable study materials. For beginning level jobs, or even advanced ones, if you have a pronounced weakness in some aspect of your training, read a modern, standard textbook in that field. Be sure it is up to date and has general coverage. Such books are normally available at your library, and the librarian will be glad to help you locate one. For entry-level positions, questions of appropriate difficulty are chosen – neither highly advanced questions, nor those too simple. Such questions require careful thought but not advanced training.

If the position for which you are applying is technical or advanced, you will read more advanced, specialized material. If you are already familiar with the basic principles of your field, elementary textbooks would waste your time. Concentrate on advanced textbooks and technical periodicals. Think through the concepts and review difficult problems in your field.

These are all general sources. You can get more ideas on your own initiative, following these leads. For example, training manuals and publications of the government agency which employs workers in your field can be useful, particularly for technical and professional positions. A letter or visit to the government department involved may result in more specific study suggestions, and certainly will provide you with a more definite idea of the exact nature of the position you are seeking.

III. KINDS OF TESTS

Tests are used for purposes other than measuring knowledge and ability to perform specified duties. For some positions, it is equally important to test ability to make adjustments to new situations or to profit from training. In others, basic mental abilities not dependent on information are essential. Questions which test these things may not appear as pertinent to the duties of the position as those which test for knowledge and information. Yet they are often highly important parts of a fair examination. For very general questions, it is almost impossible to help you direct your study efforts. What we can do is to point out some of the more common of these general abilities needed in public service positions and describe some typical questions.

1) General information

Broad, general information has been found useful for predicting job success in some kinds of work. This is tested in a variety of ways, from vocabulary lists to questions about current events. Basic background in some field of work, such as sociology or economics, may be sampled in a group of questions. Often these are principles which have become familiar to most persons through exposure rather than through formal training. It is difficult to advise you how to study for these questions; being alert to the world around you is our best suggestion.

2) Verbal ability

An example of an ability needed in many positions is verbal or language ability. Verbal ability is, in brief, the ability to use and understand words. Vocabulary and grammar tests are typical measures of this ability. Reading comprehension or paragraph interpretation questions are common in many kinds of civil service tests. You are given a paragraph of written material and asked to find its central meaning.

3) Numerical ability

Number skills can be tested by the familiar arithmetic problem, by checking paired lists of numbers to see which are alike and which are different, or by interpreting charts and graphs. In the latter test, a graph may be printed in the test booklet which you are asked to use as the basis for answering questions.

4) Observation

A popular test for law-enforcement positions is the observation test. A picture is shown to you for several minutes, then taken away. Questions about the picture test your ability to observe both details and larger elements.

5) Following directions

In many positions in the public service, the employee must be able to carry out written instructions dependably and accurately. You may be given a chart with several columns, each column listing a variety of information. The questions require you to carry out directions involving the information given in the chart.

6) Skills and aptitudes

Performance tests effectively measure some manual skills and aptitudes. When the skill is one in which you are trained, such as typing or shorthand, you can practice. These tests are often very much like those given in business school or high school courses. For many of the other skills and aptitudes, however, no short-time preparation can be made. Skills and abilities natural to you or that you have developed throughout your lifetime are being tested.

Many of the general questions just described provide all the data needed to answer the questions and ask you to use your reasoning ability to find the answers. Your best preparation for these tests, as well as for tests of facts and ideas, is to be at your physical and mental best. You, no doubt, have your own methods of getting into an exam-taking mood and keeping "in shape." The next section lists some ideas on this subject.

IV. KINDS OF QUESTIONS

Only rarely is the "essay" question, which you answer in narrative form, used in civil service tests. Civil service tests are usually of the short-answer type. Full instructions for answering these questions will be given to you at the examination. But in case this is your first experience with short-answer questions and separate answer sheets, here is what you need to know:

1) Multiple-choice Questions

Most popular of the short-answer questions is the "multiple choice" or "best answer" question. It can be used, for example, to test for factual knowledge, ability to solve problems or judgment in meeting situations found at work.

A multiple-choice question is normally one of three types—
- It can begin with an incomplete statement followed by several possible endings. You are to find the one ending which *best* completes the statement, although some of the others may not be entirely wrong.
- It can also be a complete statement in the form of a question which is answered by choosing one of the statements listed.

- It can be in the form of a problem – again you select the best answer.

Here is an example of a multiple-choice question with a discussion which should give you some clues as to the method for choosing the right answer:

When an employee has a complaint about his assignment, the action which will *best* help him overcome his difficulty is to
- A. discuss his difficulty with his coworkers
- B. take the problem to the head of the organization
- C. take the problem to the person who gave him the assignment
- D. say nothing to anyone about his complaint

In answering this question, you should study each of the choices to find which is best. Consider choice "A" – Certainly an employee may discuss his complaint with fellow employees, but no change or improvement can result, and the complaint remains unresolved. Choice "B" is a poor choice since the head of the organization probably does not know what assignment you have been given, and taking your problem to him is known as "going over the head" of the supervisor. The supervisor, or person who made the assignment, is the person who can clarify it or correct any injustice. Choice "C" is, therefore, correct. To say nothing, as in choice "D," is unwise. Supervisors have and interest in knowing the problems employees are facing, and the employee is seeking a solution to his problem.

2) True/False Questions

The "true/false" or "right/wrong" form of question is sometimes used. Here a complete statement is given. Your job is to decide whether the statement is right or wrong.

SAMPLE: A roaming cell-phone call to a nearby city costs less than a non-roaming call to a distant city.

This statement is wrong, or false, since roaming calls are more expensive.

This is not a complete list of all possible question forms, although most of the others are variations of these common types. You will always get complete directions for answering questions. Be sure you understand *how* to mark your answers – ask questions until you do.

V. RECORDING YOUR ANSWERS

Computer terminals are used more and more today for many different kinds of exams.
For an examination with very few applicants, you may be told to record your answers in the test booklet itself. Separate answer sheets are much more common. If this separate answer sheet is to be scored by machine – and this is often the case – it is highly important that you mark your answers correctly in order to get credit.
An electronic scoring machine is often used in civil service offices because of the speed with which papers can be scored. Machine-scored answer sheets must be marked with a pencil, which will be given to you. This pencil has a high graphite content which responds to the electronic scoring machine. As a matter of fact, stray dots may register as answers, so do not let your pencil rest on the answer sheet while you are pondering the correct answer. Also, if your pencil lead breaks or is otherwise defective, ask for another.

Since the answer sheet will be dropped in a slot in the scoring machine, be careful not to bend the corners or get the paper crumpled.

The answer sheet normally has five vertical columns of numbers, with 30 numbers to a column. These numbers correspond to the question numbers in your test booklet. After each number, going across the page are four or five pairs of dotted lines. These short dotted lines have small letters or numbers above them. The first two pairs may also have a "T" or "F" above the letters. This indicates that the first two pairs only are to be used if the questions are of the true-false type. If the questions are multiple choice, disregard the "T" and "F" and pay attention only to the small letters or numbers.

Answer your questions in the manner of the sample that follows:

32. The largest city in the United States is
    A. Washington, D.C.
    B. New York City
    C. Chicago
    D. Detroit
    E. San Francisco

1) Choose the answer you think is best. (New York City is the largest, so "B" is correct.)
2) Find the row of dotted lines numbered the same as the question you are answering. (Find row number 32)
3) Find the pair of dotted lines corresponding to the answer. (Find the pair of lines under the mark "B.")
4) Make a solid black mark between the dotted lines.

VI. BEFORE THE TEST

Common sense will help you find procedures to follow to get ready for an examination. Too many of us, however, overlook these sensible measures. Indeed, nervousness and fatigue have been found to be the most serious reasons why applicants fail to do their best on civil service tests. Here is a list of reminders:

- Begin your preparation early – Don't wait until the last minute to go scurrying around for books and materials or to find out what the position is all about.
- Prepare continuously – An hour a night for a week is better than an all-night cram session. This has been definitely established. What is more, a night a week for a month will return better dividends than crowding your study into a shorter period of time.
- Locate the place of the exam – You have been sent a notice telling you when and where to report for the examination. If the location is in a different town or otherwise unfamiliar to you, it would be well to inquire the best route and learn something about the building.
- Relax the night before the test – Allow your mind to rest. Do not study at all that night. Plan some mild recreation or diversion; then go to bed early and get a good night's sleep.
- Get up early enough to make a leisurely trip to the place for the test – This way unforeseen events, traffic snarls, unfamiliar buildings, etc. will not upset you.
- Dress comfortably – A written test is not a fashion show. You will be known by number and not by name, so wear something comfortable.

- Leave excess paraphernalia at home – Shopping bags and odd bundles will get in your way. You need bring only the items mentioned in the official notice you received; usually everything you need is provided. Do not bring reference books to the exam. They will only confuse those last minutes and be taken away from you when in the test room.
- Arrive somewhat ahead of time – If because of transportation schedules you must get there very early, bring a newspaper or magazine to take your mind off yourself while waiting.
- Locate the examination room – When you have found the proper room, you will be directed to the seat or part of the room where you will sit. Sometimes you are given a sheet of instructions to read while you are waiting. Do not fill out any forms until you are told to do so; just read them and be prepared.
- Relax and prepare to listen to the instructions
- If you have any physical problem that may keep you from doing your best, be sure to tell the test administrator. If you are sick or in poor health, you really cannot do your best on the exam. You can come back and take the test some other time.

VII. AT THE TEST

The day of the test is here and you have the test booklet in your hand. The temptation to get going is very strong. Caution! There is more to success than knowing the right answers. You must know how to identify your papers and understand variations in the type of short-answer question used in this particular examination. Follow these suggestions for maximum results from your efforts:

1) Cooperate with the monitor

The test administrator has a duty to create a situation in which you can be as much at ease as possible. He will give instructions, tell you when to begin, check to see that you are marking your answer sheet correctly, and so on. He is not there to guard you, although he will see that your competitors do not take unfair advantage. He wants to help you do your best.

2) Listen to all instructions

Don't jump the gun! Wait until you understand all directions. In most civil service tests you get more time than you need to answer the questions. So don't be in a hurry. Read each word of instructions until you clearly understand the meaning. Study the examples, listen to all announcements and follow directions. Ask questions if you do not understand what to do.

3) Identify your papers

Civil service exams are usually identified by number only. You will be assigned a number; you must not put your name on your test papers. Be sure to copy your number correctly. Since more than one exam may be given, copy your exact examination title.

4) Plan your time

Unless you are told that a test is a "speed" or "rate of work" test, speed itself is usually not important. Time enough to answer all the questions will be provided, but this does not mean that you have all day. An overall time limit has been set. Divide the total time (in minutes) by the number of questions to determine the approximate time you have for each question.

5) Do not linger over difficult questions

If you come across a difficult question, mark it with a paper clip (useful to have along) and come back to it when you have been through the booklet. One caution if you do this – be sure to skip a number on your answer sheet as well. Check often to be sure that you have not lost your place and that you are marking in the row numbered the same as the question you are answering.

6) Read the questions

Be sure you know what the question asks! Many capable people are unsuccessful because they failed to *read* the questions correctly.

7) Answer all questions

Unless you have been instructed that a penalty will be deducted for incorrect answers, it is better to guess than to omit a question.

8) Speed tests

It is often better NOT to guess on speed tests. It has been found that on timed tests people are tempted to spend the last few seconds before time is called in marking answers at random – without even reading them – in the hope of picking up a few extra points. To discourage this practice, the instructions may warn you that your score will be "corrected" for guessing. That is, a penalty will be applied. The incorrect answers will be deducted from the correct ones, or some other penalty formula will be used.

9) Review your answers

If you finish before time is called, go back to the questions you guessed or omitted to give them further thought. Review other answers if you have time.

10) Return your test materials

If you are ready to leave before others have finished or time is called, take ALL your materials to the monitor and leave quietly. Never take any test material with you. The monitor can discover whose papers are not complete, and taking a test booklet may be grounds for disqualification.

VIII. EXAMINATION TECHNIQUES

1) Read the general instructions carefully. These are usually printed on the first page of the exam booklet. As a rule, these instructions refer to the timing of the examination; the fact that you should not start work until the signal and must stop work at a signal, etc. If there are any *special* instructions, such as a choice of questions to be answered, make sure that you note this instruction carefully.

2) When you are ready to start work on the examination, that is as soon as the signal has been given, read the instructions to each question booklet, underline any key words or phrases, such as *least, best, outline, describe* and the like. In this way you will tend to answer as requested rather than discover on reviewing your paper that you *listed without describing*, that you selected the *worst* choice rather than the *best* choice, etc.

3) If the examination is of the objective or multiple-choice type – that is, each question will also give a series of possible answers: A, B, C or D, and you are called upon to select the best answer and write the letter next to that answer on your answer paper – it is advisable to start answering each question in turn. There may be anywhere from 50 to 100 such questions in the three or four hours allotted and you can see how much time would be taken if you read through all the questions before beginning to answer any. Furthermore, if you come across a question or group of questions which you know would be difficult to answer, it would undoubtedly affect your handling of all the other questions.

4) If the examination is of the essay type and contains but a few questions, it is a moot point as to whether you should read all the questions before starting to answer any one. Of course, if you are given a choice – say five out of seven and the like – then it is essential to read all the questions so you can eliminate the two that are most difficult. If, however, you are asked to answer all the questions, there may be danger in trying to answer the easiest one first because you may find that you will spend too much time on it. The best technique is to answer the first question, then proceed to the second, etc.

5) Time your answers. Before the exam begins, write down the time it started, then add the time allowed for the examination and write down the time it must be completed, then divide the time available somewhat as follows:
   - If 3-1/2 hours are allowed, that would be 210 minutes. If you have 80 objective-type questions, that would be an average of 2-1/2 minutes per question. Allow yourself no more than 2 minutes per question, or a total of 160 minutes, which will permit about 50 minutes to review.
   - If for the time allotment of 210 minutes there are 7 essay questions to answer, that would average about 30 minutes a question. Give yourself only 25 minutes per question so that you have about 35 minutes to review.

6) The most important instruction is to *read each question* and make sure you know what is wanted. The second most important instruction is to *time yourself properly* so that you answer every question. The third most important instruction is to *answer every question*. Guess if you have to but include something for each question. Remember that you will receive no credit for a blank and will probably receive some credit if you write something in answer to an essay question. If you guess a letter – say "B" for a multiple-choice question – you may have guessed right. If you leave a blank as an answer to a multiple-choice question, the examiners may respect your feelings but it will not add a point to your score. Some exams may penalize you for wrong answers, so in such cases *only*, you may not want to guess unless you have some basis for your answer.

7) Suggestions
   a. Objective-type questions
      1. Examine the question booklet for proper sequence of pages and questions
      2. Read all instructions carefully
      3. Skip any question which seems too difficult; return to it after all other questions have been answered
      4. Apportion your time properly; do not spend too much time on any single question or group of questions

5. Note and underline key words – *all, most, fewest, least, best, worst, same, opposite*, etc.
6. Pay particular attention to negatives
7. Note unusual option, e.g., unduly long, short, complex, different or similar in content to the body of the question
8. Observe the use of "hedging" words – *probably, may, most likely,* etc.
9. Make sure that your answer is put next to the same number as the question
10. Do not second-guess unless you have good reason to believe the second answer is definitely more correct
11. Cross out original answer if you decide another answer is more accurate; do not erase until you are ready to hand your paper in
12. Answer all questions; guess unless instructed otherwise
13. Leave time for review

b. Essay questions
1. Read each question carefully
2. Determine exactly what is wanted. Underline key words or phrases.
3. Decide on outline or paragraph answer
4. Include many different points and elements unless asked to develop any one or two points or elements
5. Show impartiality by giving pros and cons unless directed to select one side only
6. Make and write down any assumptions you find necessary to answer the questions
7. Watch your English, grammar, punctuation and choice of words
8. Time your answers; don't crowd material

8) Answering the essay question

Most essay questions can be answered by framing the specific response around several key words or ideas. Here are a few such key words or ideas:

M's: manpower, materials, methods, money, management
P's: purpose, program, policy, plan, procedure, practice, problems, pitfalls, personnel, public relations

a. Six basic steps in handling problems:
1. Preliminary plan and background development
2. Collect information, data and facts
3. Analyze and interpret information, data and facts
4. Analyze and develop solutions as well as make recommendations
5. Prepare report and sell recommendations
6. Install recommendations and follow up effectiveness

b. Pitfalls to avoid
1. *Taking things for granted* – A statement of the situation does not necessarily imply that each of the elements is necessarily true; for example, a complaint may be invalid and biased so that all that can be taken for granted is that a complaint has been registered

2. *Considering only one side of a situation* – Wherever possible, indicate several alternatives and then point out the reasons you selected the best one
3. *Failing to indicate follow up* – Whenever your answer indicates action on your part, make certain that you will take proper follow-up action to see how successful your recommendations, procedures or actions turn out to be
4. *Taking too long in answering any single question* – Remember to time your answers properly

IX. AFTER THE TEST

Scoring procedures differ in detail among civil service jurisdictions although the general principles are the same. Whether the papers are hand-scored or graded by machine we have described, they are nearly always graded by number. That is, the person who marks the paper knows only the number – never the name – of the applicant. Not until all the papers have been graded will they be matched with names. If other tests, such as training and experience or oral interview ratings have been given, scores will be combined. Different parts of the examination usually have different weights. For example, the written test might count 60 percent of the final grade, and a rating of training and experience 40 percent. In many jurisdictions, veterans will have a certain number of points added to their grades.

After the final grade has been determined, the names are placed in grade order and an eligible list is established. There are various methods for resolving ties between those who get the same final grade – probably the most common is to place first the name of the person whose application was received first. Job offers are made from the eligible list in the order the names appear on it. You will be notified of your grade and your rank as soon as all these computations have been made. This will be done as rapidly as possible.

People who are found to meet the requirements in the announcement are called "eligibles." Their names are put on a list of eligible candidates. An eligible's chances of getting a job depend on how high he stands on this list and how fast agencies are filling jobs from the list.

When a job is to be filled from a list of eligibles, the agency asks for the names of people on the list of eligibles for that job. When the civil service commission receives this request, it sends to the agency the names of the three people highest on this list. Or, if the job to be filled has specialized requirements, the office sends the agency the names of the top three persons who meet these requirements from the general list.

The appointing officer makes a choice from among the three people whose names were sent to him. If the selected person accepts the appointment, the names of the others are put back on the list to be considered for future openings.

That is the rule in hiring from all kinds of eligible lists, whether they are for typist, carpenter, chemist, or something else. For every vacancy, the appointing officer has his choice of any one of the top three eligibles on the list. This explains why the person whose name is on top of the list sometimes does not get an appointment when some of the persons lower on the list do. If the appointing officer chooses the second or third eligible, the No. 1 eligible does not get a job at once, but stays on the list until he is appointed or the list is terminated.

X. HOW TO PASS THE INTERVIEW TEST

The examination for which you applied requires an oral interview test. You have already taken the written test and you are now being called for the interview test – the final part of the formal examination.

You may think that it is not possible to prepare for an interview test and that there are no procedures to follow during an interview. Our purpose is to point out some things you can do in advance that will help you and some good rules to follow and pitfalls to avoid while you are being interviewed.

What is an interview supposed to test?

The written examination is designed to test the technical knowledge and competence of the candidate; the oral is designed to evaluate intangible qualities, not readily measured otherwise, and to establish a list showing the relative fitness of each candidate – as measured against his competitors – for the position sought. Scoring is not on the basis of "right" and "wrong," but on a sliding scale of values ranging from "not passable" to "outstanding." As a matter of fact, it is possible to achieve a relatively low score without a single "incorrect" answer because of evident weakness in the qualities being measured.

Occasionally, an examination may consist entirely of an oral test – either an individual or a group oral. In such cases, information is sought concerning the technical knowledges and abilities of the candidate, since there has been no written examination for this purpose. More commonly, however, an oral test is used to supplement a written examination.

Who conducts interviews?

The composition of oral boards varies among different jurisdictions. In nearly all, a representative of the personnel department serves as chairman. One of the members of the board may be a representative of the department in which the candidate would work. In some cases, "outside experts" are used, and, frequently, a businessman or some other representative of the general public is asked to serve. Labor and management or other special groups may be represented. The aim is to secure the services of experts in the appropriate field.

However the board is composed, it is a good idea (and not at all improper or unethical) to ascertain in advance of the interview who the members are and what groups they represent. When you are introduced to them, you will have some idea of their backgrounds and interests, and at least you will not stutter and stammer over their names.

What should be done before the interview?

While knowledge about the board members is useful and takes some of the surprise element out of the interview, there is other preparation which is more substantive. It *is* possible to prepare for an oral interview – in several ways:

1) Keep a copy of your application and review it carefully before the interview

This may be the only document before the oral board, and the starting point of the interview. Know what education and experience you have listed there, and the sequence and dates of all of it. Sometimes the board will ask you to review the highlights of your experience for them; you should not have to hem and haw doing it.

2) Study the class specification and the examination announcement

Usually, the oral board has one or both of these to guide them. The qualities, characteristics or knowledges required by the position sought are stated in these documents. They offer valuable clues as to the nature of the oral interview. For example, if the job involves supervisory responsibilities, the announcement will usually indicate that knowledge of modern supervisory methods and the qualifications of the candidate as a supervisor will be tested. If so, you can expect such questions, frequently in the form of a hypothetical situation which you are expected to solve. NEVER go into an oral without knowledge of the duties and responsibilities of the job you seek.

3) Think through each qualification required

Try to visualize the kind of questions you would ask if you were a board member. How well could you answer them? Try especially to appraise your own knowledge and background in each area, *measured against the job sought*, and identify any areas in which you are weak. Be critical and realistic – do not flatter yourself.

4) Do some general reading in areas in which you feel you may be weak

For example, if the job involves supervision and your past experience has NOT, some general reading in supervisory methods and practices, particularly in the field of human relations, might be useful. Do NOT study agency procedures or detailed manuals. The oral board will be testing your understanding and capacity, not your memory.

5) Get a good night's sleep and watch your general health and mental attitude

You will want a clear head at the interview. Take care of a cold or any other minor ailment, and of course, no hangovers.

What should be done on the day of the interview?

Now comes the day of the interview itself. Give yourself plenty of time to get there. Plan to arrive somewhat ahead of the scheduled time, particularly if your appointment is in the fore part of the day. If a previous candidate fails to appear, the board might be ready for you a bit early. By early afternoon an oral board is almost invariably behind schedule if there are many candidates, and you may have to wait. Take along a book or magazine to read, or your application to review, but leave any extraneous material in the waiting room when you go in for your interview. In any event, relax and compose yourself.

The matter of dress is important. The board is forming impressions about you – from your experience, your manners, your attitude, and your appearance. Give your personal appearance careful attention. Dress your best, but not your flashiest. Choose conservative, appropriate clothing, and be sure it is immaculate. This is a business interview, and your appearance should indicate that you regard it as such. Besides, being well groomed and properly dressed will help boost your confidence.

Sooner or later, someone will call your name and escort you into the interview room. *This is it.* From here on you are on your own. It is too late for any more preparation. But remember, you asked for this opportunity to prove your fitness, and you are here because your request was granted.

What happens when you go in?

The usual sequence of events will be as follows: The clerk (who is often the board stenographer) will introduce you to the chairman of the oral board, who will introduce you to the other members of the board. Acknowledge the introductions before you sit down. Do not be surprised if you find a microphone facing you or a stenotypist sitting by. Oral interviews are usually recorded in the event of an appeal or other review.

Usually the chairman of the board will open the interview by reviewing the highlights of your education and work experience from your application – primarily for the benefit of the other members of the board, as well as to get the material into the record. Do not interrupt or comment unless there is an error or significant misinterpretation; if that is the case, do not hesitate. But do not quibble about insignificant matters. Also, he will usually ask you some question about your education, experience or your present job – partly to get you to start talking and to establish the interviewing "rapport." He may start the actual questioning, or turn it over to one of the other members. Frequently, each member undertakes the questioning on a particular area, one in which he is perhaps most competent, so you can expect each member to participate in the examination. Because time is limited, you may also expect some rather abrupt switches in the direction the questioning takes, so do not be upset by it. Normally, a board member will not pursue a single line of questioning unless he discovers a particular strength or weakness.

After each member has participated, the chairman will usually ask whether any member has any further questions, then will ask you if you have anything you wish to add. Unless you are expecting this question, it may floor you. Worse, it may start you off on an extended, extemporaneous speech. The board is not usually seeking more information. The question is principally to offer you a last opportunity to present further qualifications or to indicate that you have nothing to add. So, if you feel that a significant qualification or characteristic has been overlooked, it is proper to point it out in a sentence or so. Do not compliment the board on the thoroughness of their examination – they have been sketchy, and you know it. If you wish, merely say, "No thank you, I have nothing further to add." This is a point where you can "talk yourself out" of a good impression or fail to present an important bit of information. Remember, *you close the interview yourself*.

The chairman will then say, "That is all, Mr. _____, thank you." Do not be startled; the interview is over, and quicker than you think. Thank him, gather your belongings and take your leave. Save your sigh of relief for the other side of the door.

How to put your best foot forward

Throughout this entire process, you may feel that the board individually and collectively is trying to pierce your defenses, seek out your hidden weaknesses and embarrass and confuse you. Actually, this is not true. They are obliged to make an appraisal of your qualifications for the job you are seeking, and they want to see you in your best light. Remember, they must interview all candidates and a non-cooperative candidate may become a failure in spite of their best efforts to bring out his qualifications. Here are 15 suggestions that will help you:

1) Be natural – Keep your attitude confident, not cocky

If you are not confident that you can do the job, do not expect the board to be. Do not apologize for your weaknesses, try to bring out your strong points. The board is interested in a positive, not negative, presentation. Cockiness will antagonize any board member and make him wonder if you are covering up a weakness by a false show of strength.

2) Get comfortable, but don't lounge or sprawl

Sit erectly but not stiffly. A careless posture may lead the board to conclude that you are careless in other things, or at least that you are not impressed by the importance of the occasion. Either conclusion is natural, even if incorrect. Do not fuss with your clothing, a pencil or an ashtray. Your hands may occasionally be useful to emphasize a point; do not let them become a point of distraction.

3) Do not wisecrack or make small talk

This is a serious situation, and your attitude should show that you consider it as such. Further, the time of the board is limited – they do not want to waste it, and neither should you.

4) Do not exaggerate your experience or abilities

In the first place, from information in the application or other interviews and sources, the board may know more about you than you think. Secondly, you probably will not get away with it. An experienced board is rather adept at spotting such a situation, so do not take the chance.

5) If you know a board member, do not make a point of it, yet do not hide it

Certainly you are not fooling him, and probably not the other members of the board. Do not try to take advantage of your acquaintanceship – it will probably do you little good.

6) Do not dominate the interview

Let the board do that. They will give you the clues – do not assume that you have to do all the talking. Realize that the board has a number of questions to ask you, and do not try to take up all the interview time by showing off your extensive knowledge of the answer to the first one.

7) Be attentive

You only have 20 minutes or so, and you should keep your attention at its sharpest throughout. When a member is addressing a problem or question to you, give him your undivided attention. Address your reply principally to him, but do not exclude the other board members.

8) Do not interrupt

A board member may be stating a problem for you to analyze. He will ask you a question when the time comes. Let him state the problem, and wait for the question.

9) Make sure you understand the question

Do not try to answer until you are sure what the question is. If it is not clear, restate it in your own words or ask the board member to clarify it for you. However, do not haggle about minor elements.

10) Reply promptly but not hastily

A common entry on oral board rating sheets is "candidate responded readily," or "candidate hesitated in replies." Respond as promptly and quickly as you can, but do not jump to a hasty, ill-considered answer.

11) Do not be peremptory in your answers

A brief answer is proper – but do not fire your answer back. That is a losing game from your point of view. The board member can probably ask questions much faster than you can answer them.

12) Do not try to create the answer you think the board member wants

He is interested in what kind of mind you have and how it works – not in playing games. Furthermore, he can usually spot this practice and will actually grade you down on it.

13) Do not switch sides in your reply merely to agree with a board member

Frequently, a member will take a contrary position merely to draw you out and to see if you are willing and able to defend your point of view. Do not start a debate, yet do not surrender a good position. If a position is worth taking, it is worth defending.

14) Do not be afraid to admit an error in judgment if you are shown to be wrong

The board knows that you are forced to reply without any opportunity for careful consideration. Your answer may be demonstrably wrong. If so, admit it and get on with the interview.

15) Do not dwell at length on your present job

The opening question may relate to your present assignment. Answer the question but do not go into an extended discussion. You are being examined for a *new* job, not your present one. As a matter of fact, try to phrase ALL your answers in terms of the job for which you are being examined.

Basis of Rating

Probably you will forget most of these "do's" and "don'ts" when you walk into the oral interview room. Even remembering them all will not ensure you a passing grade. Perhaps you did not have the qualifications in the first place. But remembering them will help you to put your best foot forward, without treading on the toes of the board members.

Rumor and popular opinion to the contrary notwithstanding, an oral board wants you to make the best appearance possible. They know you are under pressure – but they also want to see how you respond to it as a guide to what your reaction would be under the pressures of the job you seek. They will be influenced by the degree of poise you display, the personal traits you show and the manner in which you respond.

ABOUT THIS BOOK

This book contains tests divided into Examination Sections. Go through each test, answering every question in the margin. We have also attached a sample answer sheet at the back of the book that can be removed and used. At the end of each test look at the answer key and check your answers. On the ones you got wrong, look at the right answer choice and learn. Do not fill in the answers first. Do not memorize the questions and answers, but understand the answer and principles involved. On your test, the questions will likely be different from the samples. Questions are changed and new ones added. If you understand these past questions you should have success with any changes that arise. Tests may consist of several types of questions. We have additional books on each subject should more study be advisable or necessary for you. Finally, the more you study, the better prepared you will be. This book is intended to be the last thing you study before you walk into the examination room. Prior study of relevant texts is also recommended. NLC publishes some of these in our Fundamental Series. Knowledge and good sense are important factors in passing your exam. Good luck also helps. So now study this Passbook, absorb the material contained within and take that knowledge into the examination. Then do your best to pass that exam.

EXAMINATION SECTION

EXAMINATION SECTION
TEST 1

DIRECTIONS: Each question or incomplete statement is followed by several suggested answers or completions. Select the one that BEST answers the question or completes the statement. *PRINT THE LETTER OF THE CORRECT ANSWER IN THE SPACE AT THE RIGHT.*

1. The MAJOR responsibility of a director is to
   A. make certain that his line supervisors keep proper control of staff activity
   B. see that training is given to his staff according to individual needs
   C. insure that his total organization is coordinated toward agency goals and objectives
   D. work constructively with groups so that programs will reflect their needs

    1.____

2. A good organizational chart of a department is an IMPORTANT instrument because it can
   A. make it easier to understand the mission of the department
   B. help new employees become acquainted with department personnel
   C. clarify relationships and responsibilities of the various department components
   D. simplify the task of *going to the top*

    2.____

3. Unnecessary and obsolete forms can be eliminated MOST effectively by
   A. appointing a representative committee to review and evaluate all forms in relation to operating procedures
   B. discarding all forms which have not been used during the past year
   C. assembling all forms and destroying those which are duplicates or obsolete
   D. directing office managers to review the forms to determine which should be revised or abolished

    3.____

4. The director must adopt methods and techniques to insure that his budgeted allowances are properly spent and that organizational objectives are being reached.
   These responsibilities can be fulfilled BEST by
   A. controlling operations with electronic data processing equipment
   B. shifting caseload controls from caseworkers to clerical staff
   C. installing a work simplification program and establishing controls for crucial areas of operation
   D. assigning employees with special skills and training to perform the more important and specialized jobs

    4.____

5. The MOST appropriate technique for making the staff thoroughly familiar with department policies would be to
   A. maintain an up-to-date loose-leaf binder of written policies in a central point in the office
   B. issue copies of all policy directives to the unit supervisors
   C. distribute copies of policy directives to the entire staff and arrange for follow-up discussion on a unit basis
   D. discuss all major policy directives at an office-wide staff meeting

5.____

6. When a proposed change in a departmental procedure is being evaluated, the factor which should be considered MOST important in reaching the decision is the
   A. extent of resistance anticipated from members of the staff
   B. personnel needed to execute the proposed change
   C. time required for training staff in the revised procedure
   D. degree of organizational dislocation compared with gains expected from the change

6.____

7. A director anticipates that certain aspects of a new departmental procedure will be distasteful to many staff members.
   Assuming that the procedure is basically sound in spite of this drawback, the BEST approach for the director to take with his staff is to
   A. advise them to accept the procedure since it has the support of the highest authorities in the department
   B. point out that other procedures which were resisted initially have come to be accepted in time
   C. challenge staff members to suggest another procedure which will accomplish the same purpose better
   D. ask the staff members to discuss the *pros* and *cons* of the procedure and suggest how it can be improved

7.____

8. At a staff meeting at which a basic change in departmental procedure is to be announced, a director begins the discussion by asking the participants for criticisms of the existing procedure. He then describes the new procedure to be employed and explains the improvements that are anticipated.
   The director's method of introducing the change is
   A. *good*, mainly because the participants would be more receptive to the new procedure is they understood the inadequacies of the old one
   B. *good*, mainly because the participants' comments on the old procedure will provide the basis for evaluation of the feasibility of the new one
   C. *bad*, mainly because the participants will realize that the decision for change has been made before the meeting, without consideration of the participants' comments
   D. *bad*, mainly because the discussion is focused on the old procedure, rather than on the procedure being introduced

8.____

3 (#1)

9. Assume that you are conducting a staff conference to discuss the development of a procedure implementing a change in state policy. There are twelve participants whose office titles range from unit supervisor to senior supervisor, each of whom has responsibility for some aspect of the program affected by the policy change.
After some introductory remarks, the BEST procedure for you to follow is to call upon the participants in the order of their
   A. titles, with the highest titles first because they are likely to have the most experience and knowledge of the subject
   B. titles, with the lower titles first because they are likely to be less inhibited if they are permitted to give their views before the senior participants speak
   C. places around the table, to promote informality and democratic procedure
   D. specialized knowledge of the subject so that those with the most knowledge and competence may lead the discussion

9.____

10. A staff member has suggested a way of reducing the time required to prepare a monthly report by combining several items of information, separating one item into two part, and generally revising definitions of terms.
The CHIEF disadvantage of such a revision is that
   A. comparison of present with past periods will be more difficult
   B. subordinates who prepare the report will require retraining
   C. forms currently in use will have to be discarded
   D. employees using the records will be confused by the changes

10.____

11. Assume that a director happens to be present at a regular staff conference conducted by a senior supervisor. During the course of the conference, the director frequently takes over the discussion in order to amplify remarks made by the supervisor, to impart information about departmental policies, and to modify or correct possible misinterpretations of the supervisor's remarks.
The director's actions in this situation are
   A. *proper*, mainly because the conference members were given the latest and most accurate information concerning departmental policies
   B. *proper*, mainly because the director has an obligation to assist and support the supervisor
   C. *improper*, mainly because the director did not completely take over the conference
   D. *improper*, mainly because the supervisor was put in a difficult position in the presence of his staff

11.____

12. A center has a serious staff morale problem because of rumors that it will probably be abolished. To handle this situation, the direct adopts a policy of promptly corroborating rumors that he knows to be true and denying false ones.
Although this method of dealing with the situation should have some good results, its CHIEF weakness is that
   A. it chases the rumors instead of forestalling them by giving correct information concerning the center's future

12.____

B. the director may not have the necessary information at hand
C. status is given to the rumors as a result of the attention paid to them
D. the director may inadvertently divulge confidential information

13. Realizing the importance of harmonious staff relationships, one of your supervisors makes a practice of unobtrusively intervening in any conflict situation among staff members. Whenever friction seems to be developing, he attempts to soothe ruffled feelings and remove the source of difficulty by such methods as rescheduling, reassigning personnel, etc. His efforts are always behind the scenes and unknown to the personnel involved.
    This practice may produce some good results, but the CHIEF drawback is that it
    A. permits staff to engage in unacceptable practices without correction
    B. violates the principle of chain of command
    C. involves the supervisor in personal relationships which are not properly his concern
    D. requires confidential sources of information about personal relationships within the center

14. Assume that the department adopts a policy of transferring administrative personnel from one center to another after stated periods of service in a center, or in a central office.
    Of the following, the MAIN advantage of such a policy is that it helps
    A. prevent the formation of cliques among staff members
    B. key staff members keep abreast of new developments
    C. effect a greater utilization of staff members' special talents
    D. develop a broader outlook and loyalty to the department as a whole, rather than to one center

15. A delegation of union members meets with you in your role as director to discuss obtaining assistance for a group of strikers who live in the neighborhood covered by the center. In the course of discussion, you learn that the strike has been called by the local union against the explicit directive of the national union's leadership.
    The MOST appropriate course of action for you to take in this instance is to advise the union committee
    A. of your sympathy and assure them that individual applications from the strikers for assistance will receive priority
    B. that if the strikers are in need, they will be able to receive assistance as long as they are on strike
    C. that since the strike is illegal, none of the workers will be eligible for assistance
    D. that there is no bar to an of the strikers receiving assistance provided they are in need and are ready and willing to accept other employment if offered

16. The quality control system is a management tool used to test the validity of the eligibility caseload.
    This system can be helpful to a director in the following ways, with the EXCEPTION of
    A. obtaining objective data to use in evaluating the performance of specific staff members
    B. identifying the need for policy changes
    C. sorting out the source of errors in determining eligibility
    D. setting up training objectives for his staff

16._____

17. As director, you observe that there has been a sharp rise in the number of fair hearings. The increase seems to coincide with the intensified activities of the local recipients' organization.
    The MOST appropriate action under the circumstances is to
    A. determine whether the fair hearing requests result from weaknesses in the center's operation, and remedy the causes, if feasible
    B. disregard the matter for the time being because complaints have been stirred up by an organized client group
    C. emphasize to your staff the importance of meeting client needs promptly in order to avoid fair hearing requests
    D. resolve the grievances with the leaders of the recipients' organization

17._____

18. As director, you receive notice of a fair hearing decision from the State Commissioner ordering you to restore assistance to a family. You are appalled by the order because the facts cited by the hearing officer are at complete variance with what actually occurred, according to your personal knowledge of the case.
    Of the following, the MOST appropriate course of action for you to take FIRST is to
    A. point out to central office that the decision should be reconsidered and appropriately modified
    B. comply with the decision under protest because it is patently wrong
    C. recommend to central office that it consider court action through an Article 78 proceeding to correct the erroneous decision
    D. comply with the decision, although an order of the State Commissioner has no force and effect of law

18._____

19. In your capacity as director, you have received a copy of the monthly statistical report issued by the department. In reviewing the report, you note that your center is showing a rise in caseload which is substantially higher than the average rise throughout the city.
    Which of the alternatives listed below would be MOST appropriate in order to deal with this situation?
    A. Make plans to discuss the situation with central office so that appropriate corrective action can be taken on the basis of your consultation
    B. Collect necessary information and data about the operations of your center and the area it serves to determine the cause of the trend, and plan appropriate action on the basis of your findings

19._____

C. Call a meeting of your unit supervisors in order to impress upon them the importance of more diligent efforts to assist clients
D. Assume that the rise in caseload is an inevitable result of the substantial increase in unemployment, and take no immediate action

20. Of the following phases of a training program for administrative personnel, the one which is usually the MOST difficult to formulate is the
    A. selection of training methods for the program
    B. obtaining of frank opinions of the participants as to the usefulness of the program
    C. chief executive officer's judgment as to the need for such a program
    D. evaluation of the effectiveness of the program

21. Assume that you are conducting a conference dealing with problems of the center of which you are the director. The problem being discussed is one with which you have had no experience. However, two of the participants, who have had considerable experience with it, carry on an extended discussion, showing that they understand the problem thoroughly. The others are very much interested in the discussion and are taking notes on the material presented.
To permit the two staff members to continue for the length of time allowed for discussion of the problem is
    A. *desirable*, chiefly because introduction of the material by the two participants themselves may encourage others to contribute their work experience
    B. *desirable*, chiefly because their discussion may be more meaningful to the others than a discussion which is not based on work experience
    C. *undesirable*, chiefly because they are discussing material only in light of their own experience rather than in general terms
    D. *undesirable*, chiefly because it would reveal your own lack of experience with the problem and undermine your authority with the staff

22. In dealing with staff members, it is a commonly accepted principle that individual differences exist, suggesting that employees should be treated in an unlike manner in order to achieve maximum results from their work assignments.
This statement means MOST NEARLY that
    A. supervisors should be aware of the personal problems of their subordinates and make allowances for poor performance because of such problems
    B. standardized work rules are ineffective because of the different capabilities of employees to maintain such work rules
    C. employees' individual needs should be considered by their supervisors to the greatest extent possible, within the practical limitations of the work situation
    D. knowledge of general principles of human behavior is generally of little use to a supervisor in assisting him to supervise his subordinates effectively

23. A supervisor under your jurisdiction reports to you that one of his subordinates has been taking unusually long lunch hours, has been absent from work frequently, and has been doing poorer work than previously.
The BEST procedure for you to follow FIRST is to advise the supervisor to
    A. prefer charges against the employee
    B. arrange for a psychological consultation for the employee
    C. ascertain whether the employee is ill and, if so, arrange a medical examination for him
    D. have a private conversation with the employee to obtain more information about the reasons for his behavior

23._____

24. If the term *executive development* is defined as the continuous, ongoing, on-the-job process of constructing plans to improve individuals in specific positions, both for the purpose of present improvement as well as for any future advancement which is envisaged for the employee, it follows that the emphasis in an executive development program should
    A. provide learning experiences through formal or informal classes, seminars, or conferences, for which the focus is on the function of the position
    B. be oriented to the individual participant and may include a host of planned activities, such as appraisal, coaching, counseling, and job rotation
    C. attempt to create needs, to awaken, enlarge, and stimulate the individual so as to broaden his outlook and potentialities as a human being
    D. insure that the individual is able to plan, organize, direct, and control operations in the bureau, division, or agency

24._____

25. Most psychologists agree that employees have a need for recognition for the work they perform.
Therefore, it can be concluded that
    A. employees should be praised every time they complete a job satisfactorily
    B. praise is a more effective incentive to good performance than is punishment
    C. administrative personnel should be aware that subordinates do not have needs similar to their own
    D. a formalized system of rewards and punishment is better than no system at all, as long as there is a built-in consistency in its administration

25._____

KEY (CORRECT ANSWERS)

1.	C	11.	D
2.	C	12.	A
3.	A	13.	A
4.	C	14.	D
5.	C	15.	D
6.	D	16.	A
7.	D	17.	A
8.	C	18.	A
9.	D	19.	B
10.	A	20.	D

21.	B
22.	C
23.	D
24.	B
25.	B

TEST 2

DIRECTIONS: Each question or incomplete statement is followed by several suggested answers or completions. Select the one that BEST answers the question or completes the statement. *PRINT THE LETTER OF THE CORRECT ANSWER IN THE SPACE AT THE RIGHT.*

1. Studies have shown that the MOST effective kind of safety training program is one in which the
    A. training is conducted by consultants who are expert in the nature of the work performed
    B. lectures are given by the top executives in an agency
    C. employees participate in all phases of the program
    D. supervisors are responsible for the safety training

    1._____

2. Of the following, the MOST effective method of selecting potential top executives would be
    A. situational testing which simulates actual conditions
    B. a written test which covers the knowledge required to perform the job
    C. an oral test which requires candidate to discuss significant aspects of the job
    D. a confidential interview with his former employee

    2._____

3. With regard to staff morale, MOST evidence shows that
    A. employees with positive job attitudes always outproduce those with negative job attitudes
    B. morale always relates to the employee's attitude toward his working conditions and his job
    C. low morale always results in poor job performance
    D. high morale has a direct relationship to effective union leadership

    3._____

4. Of the following groups of factors, the group which has been shown to be related to the incidence of job accidents is
    A. personality characteristics, intelligence, defective vision
    B. experience, fatigue, motor and perceptual speed
    C. coordination, fatigue, intelligence
    D. defective vision, motor and perceptual speed, intelligence

    4._____

5. Executives who have difficulty making decisions when faced with a number of choices USUALLY
    A. have domestic problems which interfere with the decision-making process
    B. can be trained to improve their ability to make decisions
    C. are production-oriented rather than employee-centered
    D. do not know their jobs well enough to act decisively

    5._____

6. Studies of disciplinary dismissals of workers reveal that
   A. the majority of employees were dismissed because of lack of technical competence
   B. the supervisors were unusually demanding of employee competence
   C. most employees were dismissed because of inability to work with their co-workers
   D. the chief executive set unrealistic standards of performance

7. One philosophy of assigning workers to a specific job is that the worker and his job are an integral unit.
   This means MOST NEARLY that the
   A. employee and the job may both require adjustment
   B. employee must meet all the specifications of the job as a prerequisite for employment
   C. employee's morale will be affected by his salary
   D. employee's job satisfaction has a direct effect on his emotional health

8. The statement that the supervisor and the administrator are the *primary personnel men* means MOST NEARLY that
   A. supervisors and administrators are more skilled in personnel techniques than are professional personnel technicians
   B. they are in the best position to implement personnel policies and procedures
   C. employees have more confidence in their supervisors and administrators than in the professional personnel administrator
   D. personnel administration is most effective when it combines both centralized and decentralized approaches

9. Administrators frequently have to interview people in order to obtain information. Although the interview is a legitimate fact-gathering technique, it has limitations which should not be overlooked.
   The one of the following which is an IMPORTANT limitation is that
   A. individuals generally hesitate to give information orally which they would usually answer in writing
   B. the material derived from the interview can usually be obtained at lower cost from existing records
   C. the emotional attitudes of individuals during an interview often affect the accuracy of the information given
   D. the interview is a poor technique for discovering how well clients understand departmental policies

10. Leadership styles have frequently been categorized as authoritarian, laissez-faire, and democratic.
    In general, management's reliance on leadership to produce desired results would be MOST effectively implemented through
    A. the laissez-faire approach when group results are desired
    B. the authoritarian approach in a benevolent manner when quick decisions are required

C. the democratic approach, when quick decisions are unimportant
D. all three approaches, depending upon circumstances

11. As director, you are responsible for enforcing a recently established regulation which has aroused antagonism among many clients.
You should deal with this situation by
    A. explaining to the clients that you are not responsible for making regulations
    B. enforcing the regulation but reporting to your superior the number and kind of complaints against it
    C. carrying out your duty of enforcing the regulation as well as you can without comment
    D. suggesting to your clients that you may overlook violations of the regulation

11.____

12. One of the observations made in a recent psychological study of leadership is that the behavior of a new employee in a leadership position can be predicted more accurately on the basis of the behavior of the previous incumbent in the post than on the behavior of the new employee in his previous job.
The BEST explanation for this observation is that there is a tendency
    A. for a newly appointed executive to avoid making basic changes in operational procedures
    B. to choose similar types of personalities to fill the same type of position
    C. for a given organizational structure and set of duties and responsibilities to produce similar patterns of behavior
    D. for executives to develop more mature patterns of behavior as a result of increased responsibility

12.____

13. A director finds that reports submitted by him to his subordinates tend to emphasize the favorable and minimize the unfavorable aspects of situations.
The MOST valid reason for this is that
    A. subordinates usually hesitate to give their supervisors an honest picture of a situation
    B. the director may not have been sufficiently critical of previous reports submitted by his subordinates
    C. subordinates have a normal tendency to represent themselves and their actions in the best possible light
    D. many subordinates in the field have developed a tendency to understatement in the depiction of unfavorable situations

13.____

14. Effective delegation of authority and responsibility to subordinates is essential for the proper administration of a center. However, the director should retain some activities under his direct control.
Of the following activities, the one for which there is LEAST justification for delegation by the director to a subordinate is one involving
    A. relationships with client groups
    B. physical danger to clients
    C. policies which are unpopular with staff
    D. matters for which there are no established policies

14.____

15. According to the principle of *span of control*, there should be a limited number of subordinates reporting to one supervisor.
    Of the following, the CHIEF disadvantage which may result from the application of this principle is a reduction in the
    A. contact between lower ranking staff members and higher ranking administrative personnel
    B. freedom of action of subordinates
    C. authority and responsibility of subordinates
    D. number of organizational levels through which a matter must pass before action is taken

16. The CHIEF objection to a practice of decentralizing the preparation and distribution of memoranda by bureaus, rather than controlling distribution through central office is that it is LIKELY to result in
    A. overloading bureaus with a multiplicity of communications
    B. limited and specialized rather than broad and general viewpoints in the memoranda
    C. violation of the principle of unit of command
    D. unimportant information being communicated to all bureaus

17. A report has been completed by members of your staff. As director, you have reviewed the report and feel that the information revealed could be damaging to the department. You find yourself in conflict in your multiple role as director, as a professional, and as a citizen.
    The one of the following actions which would be MOST desirable for you to take FIRST would be to
    A. send a copy of the report to your supervisor and request an immediate conference with him
    B. instruct staff to re-check the report and defer issuance of the report until the findings are confirmed
    C. immediately share the report with your supervisors and your advisory committee
    D. file the report until your advisory committee makes a request for it

18. In order for employees to function effectively, they should have a feeling of being treated fairly by management.
    Which of the following general policies is MOST likely to give employees such a feeling?
    A. An employee publication should be mailed directly to the home of each employee.
    B. Employee attitude surveys should be conducted at regular intervals.
    C. Employees should be consulted and kept informed on all matters that affect them.
    D. Employees should be informed when the press publishes statements of policy.

19. In order to give employees greater job satisfaction, some management experts advocate a policy of job enrichment.
The one of the following which would be the BEST example of job enrichment is to
    A. allow an aide to decide which portion of his normal duties and responsibilities he prefers
    B. increase the fringe benefits currently available to paraprofessional employees
    C. add variety to the duties of an employee
    D. permit more flexible working schedules for professional employees

20. Management of large organizations has often emphasized high salaries and fringe benefits as the most important means of motivating employees.
The one of the following which is NOT an argument used to support this approach is
    A. most people endure work mainly in order to collect the rewards and to have the opportunity to enjoy them
    B. material incentives have proved to be the best means of stimulating creative capacity and the will to work
    C. the majority of employees place little emphasis on work-centered motivation to perform
    D. numerous research studies have shown that pay ranks first on a scale of factors motivating employees in government and industry in the United States

21. Some organizations provide psychologists or other professionally trained persons with whom employees can consult on a confidential basis regarding personal problems.
Of the following, which is MOST likely to be a benefit management can derive from such a practice?
    A. Increase in the authority of management
    B. Disclosure of the corrupt practices of those handling money
    C. Receipt of new ideas and approaches to organizational problems
    D. Obtaining tighter control on employees' private behavior

22. Authorities agree that it is generally most desirable for an employee experiencing mental health problems to seek competent professional help without being required or forced to do so by another person.
They view self-referral as a most desirable action PRIMARILY because
    A. it shows that the employee probably is more aware of the problem and more highly motivated to solve his problems
    B. the employee's right to privacy in his personal affairs is maintained
    C. another person cannot be blamed in the event the outcome of the referral is not successful
    D. the employee knows best his problems and will do what is necessary to serve his own best interests

Questions 23-25.

DIRECTIONS: Questions 23 through 25 consist of three excerpts each. Consider an excerpt correct if all the statements in the excerpt are correct. Mark your answer as follows:
A. if only excerpts I and II are correct
B. if only excerpts II and III are correct
C. if only excerpt I is correct
D. if only excerpt II is correct

23. I. Many executive decisions are based on assumptions. They may be assumptions supported by sketchy data about future needs for services; assumptions about the attitudes and future behavior of employees, perhaps based on reports of staff members or hearsay evidence; or assumptions about agency values that are as much a reflection of personal desires as of agency goals.
    II. A good pattern of well-conceived plans is only a first step in administration. The administrator must also create an organization to formulate and carry out such plans. Resources must be assembled; supervision of actual operations is necessary; and before the executive's task is completed, he must exercise control.
    III. When a problem is well defined, good alternatives identified, and the likely consequences of each alternative forecast as best we can, one can assume that the final choice of action to be taken would be easy, if not obvious.

23.____

24. I. Principles of motivation are not difficult to establish because human behavior is not complex and is easily understood; individual differences in human beings are substantial; and people are continuously learning and changing.
    II. What gives employees satisfaction or dissatisfaction indicates the nature of the motivation problem and provides positive guidance to the administrator who faces the problem of trying to get people to carry out a set of plans.
    III. The administrator's job of motivation can be described as that of creating a situation in which actions that provide net satisfaction to individual members of the enterprise are at the same time actions that make appropriate contributions toward the objectives of the enterprise.

24.____

25. I. Administrative organization is primarily concerned with legal, technical, or ultimate authority; the operational authority relationships that may be created by organization are of major significance.
    II. Accountability is not removed by delegation. Appraisal of results should be tempered by the extent to which an administrator must rely on subordinates.
    III. In delegations to operating subordinate, authority to plan exceeds authority to do, inasmuch as the executive typically reserves some of the planning for himself.

25.____

KEY (CORRECT ANSWERS)

1. C
2. A
3. B
4. B
5. B

6. C
7. A
8. B
9. C
10. D

11. B
12. C
13. C
14. D
15. A

16. A
17. B
18. C
19. C
20. D

21. C
22. A
23. A
24. B
25. D

SUPERVISION, ADMINISTRATION, MANAGEMENT, AND ORGANIZATION

EXAMINATION SECTION

TEST 1

DIRECTIONS: Each question or incomplete statement is followed by several suggested answers or completions. Select the one that BEST answers the question or completes the statement. *PRINT THE LETTER OF THE CORRECT ANSWER IN THE SPACE AT THE RIGHT.*

1. In coaching a subordinate on the nature of decision-making, an executive would be right if he stated that the one of the following which is general the BEST definition of decision-making is:
   A. Choosing between alternatives
   B. Making diagnoses of feasible ends
   C. Making diagnoses of feasible means
   D. Comparing alternatives

   1.____

2. Of the following, which one would be LEAST valid as a purpose of an organizational policy statement?
   To
   A. keep personnel from performing improper actions and functions on routine matters
   B. prevent the mishandling of non-routine matters
   C. provide management personnel with a tool that precludes the need for their use of judgment
   D. provide standard decisions and approaches in handling problems of a recurrent nature

   2.____

3. Much has been written criticizing bureaucratic organizations. Current thinking on the subject is GENERALLY that
   A. bureaucracy is on the way out
   B. bureaucracy, though not perfect, is unlikely to be replaced
   C. bureaucratic organizations are most effective in dealing with constant change
   D. bureaucratic organizations are most effective when dealing with sophisticated customers or clients

   3.____

4. The development of alternate plans as a major step in planning will normally result in the planner having several possible courses of action available.
   GENERALLY, this is
   A. *desirable*, since such development helps to determine the most suitable alternative and to provide for the unexpected
   B. *desirable*, since such development makes the use of planning premises and constraints unnecessary

   4.____

C. *undesirable*, since the planners should formulate only one way of achieving given goals at a given time
D. *undesirable*, since such action restricts efforts to modify the planning to take advantage of opportunities

5. The technique of departmentation by task force includes the assigning of a team or task force to a definite project or block of work which extends from the beginning to the completing of a wanted and definite type and quantity of work. Of the following, the MOST important actor aiding the successful use of this technique *normally* is
   A. having the task force relatively large, at least one hundred members
   B. having a definite project termination date established
   C. telling each task force member what his next assignment will be only after the current project ends
   D. utilizing it only for projects that are regularly recurring

6. With respect to communication in small group settings such as may occur in business, government, and the military, it is generally TRUE that people usually derive more satisfaction and are usually more productive under conditions which
   A. permit communication only with superiors
   B. permit the minimum intragroup communication possible
   C. are generally restricted by management
   D. allow open communication among all group members

7. If an executive were asked to list some outstanding features of decentralization, which one of the following would NOT be such a feature?
   Decentralization
   A. provides decision-making experience for lower level managers
   B. promotes uniformity of policy
   C. is a relatively new concept in management
   D. is similar to the belief in encouragement of free enterprise

8. Modern management experts have emphasized the importance of the informal organization in motivating employees to increase productivity.
   Of the following, the characteristic which would have the MOST direct influence on employee motivation is the tendency of members of the informal organization to
   A. resist change
   B. establish their own norms
   C. have similar outside interests
   D. set substantially higher goals than those of management

9. According to leading management experts, the decision-making process contains separate and distinct steps that must be taken in an orderly sequence.
   Of the following arrangements, which one is in CORRECT order?

A. I. Search for alternatives; II. diagnosis; III. comparison; IV. choice
B. I. Diagnose; II. comparison; III. search for alternatives; IV. choice
C. I. Diagnose; II. search for alternatives; III. comparison; IV. choice
D. I. Diagnose; II. search for alternatives; III. choice; IV. comparison

10. Of the following, the growth of professionalism in large organizations can PRIMARILY be expected to result in
    A. greater equalization of power
    B. increased authoritarianism
    C. greater organizational disloyalty
    D. increased promotion opportunities

11. Assume an executive carries out his responsibilities to his staff according to what is now known about managerial leadership.
    Which of the following statements would MOST accurately reflect his assumptions about proper management?
    A. Efficiency in operations results from allowing the human element to participate in a minimal way.
    B. Efficient operation result from balancing work considerations with personnel considerations.
    C. Efficient operation results from a workforce committed to its self-interest.
    D. Efficient operation results from staff relationships that produce a friendly work climate.

12. Assume that an executive is called upon to conduct a management audit. To do this properly, he would have to take certain steps in a specific sequence.
    Of the following steps, which step should this manager take FIRST?
    A. Managerial performance must be surveyed.
    B. A method of reporting must be established.
    C. Management auditing procedures and documentation must be developed.
    D. Criteria for the audit must be considered.

13. If a manager is required to conduct a scientific investigation of an organizational problem, the FIRST step he should take is to
    A. state his assumptions about the problem
    B. carry out a search for background information
    C. choose the right approach to investigate the validity of his assumptions
    D. define and state the problem

14. An executive would be right to assert that the principle of delegation states that decisions should be made PRIMARILY
    A. by persons in an executive capacity qualified to make them
    B. by persons in a non-executive capacity
    C. at as low an organization level of authority as practicable
    D. by the next lower level of authority

15. Of the following, which one is NOT regarded by management authorities as a FUNDAMENTAL characteristic of an *ideal* bureaucracy?
    A. Division of labor and specialization
    B. An established hierarchy
    C. Decentralization of authority
    D. A set of operating rules and regulations

16. As the number of subordinates in a manager's span of control increases, the ACTUAL number of possible relationships
    A. increases disproportionately to the number of subordinates
    B. increases in equal number to the number of subordinates
    C. reaches a stable level
    D. will first increase then slowly decrease

17. An executive's approach to controlling the activities of his subordinates concentrated on ends rather than means, and was diagnostic rather than punitive.
    This manager may MOST properly be characterized as using the managerial technique of management-by-
    A. exception   B. objectives   C. crisis   D. default

18. In conducting a training session on the administrative control process, which of the following statements would be LEAST valid for an executive to make?
    Controlling
    A. requires checking upon assignments to see what is being done
    B. involves comparing what is being done to what ought to be done
    C. requires corrective action when what is being done does not meet expectations
    D. occurs after all the other managerial processes have been performed

19. The "brainstorming" technique for creative solutions of management problems MOST generally consists of
    A. bringing staff together in an exchange of a quantity of freewheeling ideas
    B. isolating individual staff members to encourage thought
    C. developing improved office procedures
    D. preparation of written reports on complex problems

20. Computer systems hardware MOST often operates in relation to which one of the following steps in solving a data-processing problem?
    A. Determining the problem
    B. Defining and stating the problem
    C. Implementing the programmed solution
    D. Completing the documentation of every unexplored solution

21. There is a tendency in management to upgrade objectives.
    This trend is generally regarded as
    A. *desirable*; the urge to improve is demonstrated by adopting objectives that have been adjusted to provide improved service

B. *undesirable*; the typical manager searches for problems which obstruct his objectives
   C. *desirable*; it is common for a manager to find that the details of an immediate operation have occupied so much of his time that he has lost sight of the basic overall objective
   D. *undesirable*; efforts are wasted when they are expended on a mass of uncertain objectives, since the primary need of most organizations is a single target or several major ones

22. Of the following, it is generally LEAST effective for an executive to delegate authority where working conditions involve
    A. rules establishing normal operating procedures
    B. consistent methods of operation
    C. rapidly changing work standards
    D. complex technology

23. If an executive was explaining the difficulty of making decisions under *risk* conditions, he would be MOST accurate if he said that such decisions would be difficult to make when the decision maker has _____ information and experience and can expect _____ outcomes for each action.
    A. limited; many
    B. much; many
    C. much; few
    D. limited; few

24. If an executive were asked to list some outstanding features of centralized organization, which one of the following would be INCORRECT?
    Centralized organization
    A. lessens risks of errors by unskilled subordinates
    B. utilizes the skills of specialized experts at a central location
    C. produces uniformity of policy and non-uniformity of action
    D. enables closer control of operations than a decentralized set-up

25. It is possible for an organization's management to test whether or not the organization has a sound structure.
    Of the following, which one is NOT a test of soundness in an organization's structure?
    The
    A. ability to replace key personnel with minimum loss of effectiveness
    B. ability of information and decisions to flow more freely through the *grapevine* than through formal channels
    C. provision for orderly organizational growth with the ability to handle change as the need arises.

KEY (CORRECT ANSWERS)

1.	A	11.	B
2.	C	12.	D
3.	B	13.	D
4.	A	14.	C
5.	B	15.	C
6.	D	16.	A
7.	B	17.	B
8.	B	18.	D
9.	C	19.	A
10.	A	20.	C

21. A
22. C
23. A
24. C
25. B

TEST 2

DIRECTIONS: Each question or incomplete statement is followed by several suggested answers or completions. Select the one that BEST answers the question or completes the statement. *PRINT THE LETTER OF THE CORRECT ANSWER IN THE SPACE AT THE RIGHT.*

1. Management experts generally believe that computer-based management information systems (MIS) have greater potential for improving the process of management than any other development in recent decades.
   The one of the following which MOST accurately describes the objectives of MIS is to
   A. provide information for decision-making on planning, initiating, and controlling the operations of the various units of the organization
   B. establish mechanization of routine functions such as clerical records, payroll, inventory, and accounts receivable in order to promote economy and efficiency
   C. computerize decision-making on planning, initiative, organizing, and controlling the operations of an organization
   D. provide accurate facts and figures on the various programs of the organization to be used for purposes of planning and research

   1.____

2. The one of the following which is the BEST application on the *management-by-exception* principle is that this principle
   A. stimulates communication and aids in management of crisis situations, thus reducing the frequency of decision-making
   B. saves time and reserves top-management decisions only for crisis situations, thus reducing the frequency of decision-making
   C. stimulates communication, saves time, and reduces the frequency of decision-making
   D. is limited to crisis-management situations

   2.____

3. It is generally recognized that each organization is dependent upon availability of qualified personnel.
   Of the following, the MOST important factor affecting the availability of qualified people to each organization is
   A. innovations in technology and science
   B. the general decline in the educational levels of our population
   C. the rise of sentiment against racial discrimination
   D. pressure by organized community groups

   3.____

4. A fundamental responsibility of all managers is to decide what physical facilities and equipment are needed to help attain basic goals.
   Good planning for the purchase and use of equipment is seldom easy to do and is complicated MOST by the fact that
   A. organizations rarely have stable sources of supply
   B. nearly all managers tend to be better at personnel planning than at equipment planning

   4.____

C. decisions concerning physical resources are made too often on a *crash basis* rather than under carefully prepared policies
D. legal rulings relative to depreciation fluctuate very frequently

5. In attempting to reconcile managerial objectives and an individual employee's goals, it is generally LEAST desirable for management to
   A. recognize the capacity of the individual to contribute toward realization of managerial goals
   B. encourage self-development of the employee to exceed minimum job performance
   C. consider an individual employee's work separately from other employees
   D. demonstrate that an employee advances only to the extent that he contributes directly to the accomplishment of stated goals

6. As a management tool for discovering individual training needs a job analysis would generally be of LEAST assistance in determining
   A. the performance requirements of individual jobs
   B. actual employee performance on the job
   C. acceptable standards of performance
   D. training needs for individual jobs

7. One of the major concerns of organizational managers today is how the spread of automation will affect them and the status of their positions. Realistically speaking, one can say that the MOST likely effect of our newer forms of highly automated technology on managers will be to
   A. make most top-level positions superfluous or obsolete
   B. reduce the importance of managerial work in general
   C. replace the work of managers with the work of technicians
   D. increase the importance of and demand for top managerial personnel

8. Which one of the following is LEAST likely to be an area or cause of trouble in the use of staff people (e.g., assistants to the administrator)?
   A. Misunderstanding of the role the staff people are supposed to play, as a result of vagueness of definition of their duties and authority
   B. Tendency of staff personnel almost always to be older than line personnel at comparable salary levels with who they must deal
   C. Selection of staff personnel who fail to have simultaneously both competence in their specialties and skill in staff work
   D. The staff person fails to understand mixed staff and operating duties

9. The one of the following which is the BEST measure of decentralization in an agency is the
   A. amount of checking required on decisions made at lower levels in the chain of command
   B. amount of checking required on decisions made at lower levels of the chain of command and the number of functions affected thereby
   C. number of functions affected by decisions made at higher levels
   D. number of functions affected by middle echelon decision-making

10. Which of the following is generally NOT a valid statement with respect to the supervisory process?
    A. General supervision is more effective than close supervision.
    B. Employee-centered supervisors lead more effectively than do production-centered supervisors.
    C. Employee satisfaction is directly related to productivity.
    D. Low-producing supervisors use techniques that are different from high-producing supervisors.

11. The one of the following which is the MOST essential element for proper evaluation of the performance of subordinate supervisors is a
    A. careful definition of each supervisor's specific job responsibilities and of his progress in meeting mutually agreed upon work goals
    B. system of rewards and penalties based on each supervisor's progress in meeting clearly defined performance standards
    C. definition of personality traits, such as industry, initiative, dependability, and cooperativeness, required for effective job performance
    D. breakdown of each supervisor's job into separate components and a rating of his performance on each individual task

12. The one of the following which is the PRINCIPAL advantage of specialization for the operating efficiency of a public service agency is that specialization
    A. reduces the amount of red tape in coordinating the activities of mutually dependent departments
    B. simplifies the problem of developing adequate job controls
    C. provides employees with a clear understanding of the relationship of their activities to the overall objectives of the agency
    D. reduces destructive competition for power between departments

13. Of the following, the group which generally benefits MOST from supervisory training programs in public service agencies are those supervisors who have
    A. accumulated a long period of total service to the agency
    B. responsibility for a large number of subordinate personnel
    C. been in the supervisory ranks for a long period of time
    D. a high level of formalized academic training

14. A list of conditions which encourages good morale inside a work group would NOT include a
    A. high rate of agreement among group members on values and objectives
    B. tight control system to minimize the risk of individual error
    C. good possibility that joint action will accomplish goals
    D. past history of successful group accomplishment

15. Of the following, the MOST important factor to be considered in selecting a training strategy or program is the
    A. requirements of the job to be performed by the trainees
    B. educational level or prior training of the trainees
    C. size of the training group
    D. quality and competence of available training specialists

16. Of the following, the one which is considered to be LEAST characteristic of the higher ranks of management is
    A. that higher levels of management benefit from modern technology
    B. that success is measured by the extent to which objectives are achieved
    C. the number of subordinates that directly report to an executive
    D. the de-emphasis of individual and specialized performance

16.____

17. Assume that an executive is preparing a training syllabus to be used in training members of his staff.
    Which of the following would NOT be a valid principle of the learning process for this manager to keep in mind in the preparation of the training syllabus?
    A. When a person has thoroughly learned a task, it takes a lot of effort to create a little more improvement.
    B. In complicated learning situations, there is a period in which an additional period of practice produces an equal amount of improvement in learning.
    C. The less a person knows about the task, the slower the initial progress.
    D. The more the person knows about the risk, the slower the initial progress.

17.____

18. Of the following, which statement BEST illustrates when collective bargaining agreements are working well?
    A. Executives strongly support subordinate managers.
    B. The management rights clause in the contract is clear and enforced.
    C. Contract provisions are competently interpreted.
    D. The provisions of the agreement are properly interpreted, communicated, and observed.

18.____

19. An executive who wishes to encourage subordinates to communicate freely with him about a job-related problem should FIRST
    A. state his own position on the problem before listening to the subordinates' ideas
    B. invite subordinates to give their own opinions on the problem
    C. ask subordinates for their reactions to his own ideas about the problem
    D. guard the confidentiality of management information about the problem

19.____

20. The ability to deal constructively with intra-organizational conflict is an essential attribute of the successful manager.
    The one of the following types of conflict which would be LEAST difficult to handle constructively is a situation in which there is
    A. agreement on objectives, but disagreement as to the probable results of adopting the various alternatives
    B. agreement on objectives, disagreement on alternative courses of action, and relative certainty as to the outcome of one of the alternatives
    C. disagreement on objectives and on alternate courses of action, but relative certainty as to the outcome of the alternatives
    D. disagreement on objectives and on alternative course of action, but uncertainty as to the outcome of the alternatives

20.____

5 (#2)

21. Which of the following statements is LEAST accurate in describing formal job evaluation and wage and salary classification plans?   21.____
    A. Parties that disagree on wage matters can examine an established system rather than unsupported opinions.
    B. The use of such plans tends to overlook the effect of age and seniority of employees on job values in the plan.
    C. Such plans can eliminate salary controversies in organizations designing and using them properly.
    D. These plans are not particularly useful in checking on executive compensation.

22. In carrying out disciplinary action, the MOST important procedure for all managers to follow is to   22.____
    A. sell all levels of management on the need for discipline from the organization's viewpoint
    B. follow up on a disciplinary action and not assume that the action has been effective
    C. convince all executives that proper discipline is a legitimate tool for their use
    D. convince all executives that they need to display confidence in the organization's rules

Questions 23-25.

DIRECTIONS: Questions 23 through 25 are to be answered on the basis of the following situation. Richard Ford, a top administrator, is responsible for output in his organization. Because productivity had been lagging for two periods in a row, Ford decided to establish a committee of his subordinate managers to investigate the reasons for the poor performance and to make recommendations for improvements. After two meetings, the committee came to the conclusions and made the recommendations that follow:

Output forecasts had been handed down from the top without prior consultation with middle management and first level supervision. Lines of authority and responsibility had been unclear. The planning and control process should be decentralized.
After receiving the committee's recommendations, Ford proceeded to take the following actions:
Ford decided he would retain final authority to establish quotas but would delegate to the middle managers the responsibility for meeting quotas.
After receiving Ford's decision, the middle managers proceeded to delegate to the first-line supervisors the authority to establish their own quotas. The middle managers eventually received and combined the first-line supervisors' quotas so that these conformed with Ford's.

23. Ford's decision to delegate responsibility for meeting quotas to the middle managers is INCONSISTENT with sound management principles because of which one of the following?   23.____
    A. Ford shouldn't have involved himself in the first place.
    B. Middle managers do not have the necessary skills.

C. Quotas should be established by the chief executive.
D. Responsibility should not be delegated.

24. The principle of co-extensiveness of responsibility and authority bears on Ford's decision.
   In this case, it IMPLIES that
   A. authority should exceed responsibility
   B. authority should be delegated to match the degree of responsibility
   C. both authority and responsibility should be retained and not delegated
   D. responsibility should be delegated but authority should be retained

25. The middle manager's decision to delegate to the first-line supervisors the authority to establish quotas was INCORRECTLY reasoned because
   A. delegation and control must go together
   B. first-line supervisors are in no position to establish quotas
   C. one cannot delegate authority that one does not possess
   D. the meeting of quotas should not be delegated

KEY (CORRECT ANSWERS)

1.	A	11.	A
2.	C	12.	B
3.	A	13.	D
4.	C	14.	B
5.	C	15.	A
6.	B	16.	C
7.	D	17.	D
8.	B	18.	D
9.	B	19.	B
10.	C	20.	B

21.	C
22.	B
23.	D
24.	B
25.	C

TEST 3

DIRECTIONS: Each question or incomplete statement is followed by several suggested answers or completions. Select the one that BEST answers the question or completes the statement. *PRINT THE LETTER OF THE CORRECT ANSWER IN THE SPACE AT THE RIGHT.*

1. A danger which exists in any organization as complex as that required for administration of a large public agency is that each department comes to believe that it exists for its own sake.
   The one of the following which has been attempted in some organizations as a cure for this condition is to
   A. build up the departmental esprit de corps
   B. expand the functions and jurisdictions of the various departments so that better integration is possible
   C. develop a body of specialists in the various subject matter fields which cut across departmental lines
   D. delegate authority to the lowest possible echelon
   E. systematically transfer administrative personnel from one department to another

   1.____

2. At best, the organization chart is ordinarily and necessarily an idealized picture of the intent of top management, a reflection of hopes and aims rather than a photograph of the operating facts within the organization.
   The one of the following which is the basic reason for this is that the organization chart
   A. does not show the flow of work within the organization
   B. speaks in terms of positions rather than of live employees
   C. frequently contains unresolved internal ambiguities
   D. is a record of past organization or proposed future organization and never a photograph of the living organization
   E. does not label the jurisdiction assigned to each component unit

   2.____

3. The drag of inadequacy is always downward. The need in administration is always for the reverse; for a department head to project his thinking to the city level, for the unit chief to try to see the problems of the department.
   The inability of a city administration to recruit administrators who can satisfy this need usually results in departments characterized by
   A. disorganization   B. poor supervision
   C. circumscribed viewpoints D. poor public relations
   E. a lack of programs

   3.____

4. When, as a result of a shift in public sentiment, the elective officers of a city are changed, is it desirable for career administrators to shift ground without performing any illegal or dishonest act in order to conform to the policies of the new elective officers?
   A. *No*; the opinions and beliefs of the career officials are the result of long experience in administration and are more reliable than those of politicians

   4.____

B. *Yes*; only in this way can citizens, political officials, and career administrators alike have confidence in the performance of their respective functions
C. *No*; a top career official who is so spineless as to change his views or procedures as a result of public opinion is of little value to the public service
D. *Yes*; legal or illegal, it is necessary that a city employee carry out the orders of his superior officers
E. *No*; shifting ground with every change in administration will preclude the use of a constant overall policy

5. Participation in developing plans which will affect levels in the organization in addition to his own, will contribute to an individual's understanding of the entire system. When possible, this should be encouraged.
This policy is, in general,
    A. *desirable*; the maintenance of any organization depends upon individual understanding
    B. *undesirable*; employees should participate only in these activities which affect their own level, otherwise conflicts in authority may arise
    C. *desirable*; an employee's will to contribute to the maintenance of an organization depends to a great extent on the level which he occupies
    D. *undesirable*; employees can be trained more efficiently and economically in an organized training program than by participating in plan development
    E. *desirable*; it will enable the employee to make intelligent suggestions for adjustment of the plan in the future

6. Constant study should be made of the information contained in reports to isolate those elements of experience which are static, those which are variable and repetitive, and those which are variable and due to chance.
Knowledge of those elements of experience in his organization which are static or constant will enable the operating official to
    A. fix responsibility for their supervisor at a lower level
    B. revise the procedure in order to make the elements variable
    C. arrange for follow-up and periodic adjustment
    D. bring related data together
    E. provide a frame of reference within which detailed standards for measurement can be installed

7. A chief staff officer, serving as one of the immediate advisors to the department head, has demonstrated a special capacity for achieving internal agreements and for sound judgment. As a result he has been used more and more as a source of counsel and assistance by the department head. Other staff officers and line officials as well have discovered that it is wise for them to check with this colleague in advance on all problematical matters handed up to the department head.

Developments such as this are
- A. *undesirable*; they disrupt the normal lines for flow of work in an organization
- B. *desirable*; they allow an organization to make the most of its strength wherever such strength resides
- C. *undesirable*; they tend to undermine the authority of the department head and put it in the hands of a staff officer who does not have the responsibility
- D. *desirable*; they tend to resolve internal ambiguities in organization
- E. *undesirable*; they make for bad morale by causing *cutthroat* competition

8. A common difference among executives is that some are not content unless they are out in front of everything that concerns their organization, while others prefer to run things by pulling strings, by putting others out in front and by stepping into the breach only when necessary.
Generally speaking, an advantage this latter method of operation has over the former is that it
    - A. results in a higher level of morale over a sustained period of time
    - B. gets results by exhortation and direct stimulus
    - C. makes it unnecessary to calculate integrated moves
    - D. makes the personality of the executive felt further down the line
    - E. results in the executive getting the reputation for being a good fellow

8.____

9. Administrators frequently have to get facts by interviewing people. Although the interview is a legitimate fact gathering technique, it has definite limitations which should not be overlooked.
The one of the following which is an important limitation is that
    - A. people who are interviewed frequently answer questions with guesses rather than admit their ignorance
    - B. it is a poor way to discover the general attitude and thinking of supervisors interviewed
    - C. people sometimes hesitate to give information during an interview which they will submit in written form
    - D. it is a poor way to discover how well employees understand departmental policies
    - E. the material obtained from the interview can usually be obtained at lower cost from existing records

9.____

10. It is desirable and advantageous to leave a maximum measure of planning responsibility to operating agencies or units, rather than to remove the responsibility to a central planning staff agency.
Adoption of the former policy (decentralized planning) would lead to
    - A. *less effective planning*; operating personnel do not have the time to make long-term plans
    - B. *more effective planning*; operating units are usually better equipped technically than any staff agency and consequently are in a better position to set up valid plans
    - C. *less effective planning*; a central planning agency has a more objective point of view than any operating agency can achieve

10.____

D. *more effective planning*; plans are conceived in terms of the existing situation and their execution is carried out with the will to succeed
E. *less effective planning*; there is little or no opportunity to check deviation from plans in the proposed set-up

Questions 11-15.

DIRECTIONS: The following sections appeared in a report on the work production of two bureaus of a department. Base your answers to Questions 11 through 15 on this information. Throughout the report, assume that each month has 4 weeks.

Each of the two bureaus maintains a chronological file. In Bureau A, every 9 months on the average, this material fills a standard legal size cabinet sufficient for 12,000 work units. In Bureau B the same type of cabinet is filled in 18 months. Each bureau maintains three complete years of information plus a current file. When the current file cabinet is filled, the cabinet containing the oldest material is emptied, the contents disposed of, and the cabinet used for current material. The similarity of these operations makes it possible to consolidate these files with little effort.

Study of the practice of using typists as filing clerks for periods when there is no typing work showed: (1) Bureau A has for the past 6 months completed a total of 1,500 filing work units a week using on the average 100 man-hours of trained file clerk time and 20 man-hours of typist time; (2) Bureau B has in the same period completed a total of 2,000 filing work units a week using on the average 125 man-hours of trained file clerk time and 60 hours of typist time. This includes all work in chronological files. Assuming that all clerks work at the same speed and that all typists work at the same speed, this indicates that work other than filing should be found for typists or that they should be given some training in the filing procedures used. It should be noted that Bureau A has not been producing the 1,600 units of technical (not filing) work per 30-day period required by Schedule K, but is at present 200 units behind. The Bureau should be allowed 3 working days to get on schedule.

11. What percentage (approximate) of the total number of filing work units completed in both units consists of the work involved in the maintenance of the chronological files?
    A. 5%   B. 10%   C. 15%   D. 20%   E. 25%

12. If the two chronological files are consolidated, the number of months which should be allowed for filling a cabinet is
    A. 2   B. 4   C. 6   D. 8   E. 14

13. The MAXIMUM number of file cabinets which can be released for other uses as a result of the consolidation recommended is
    A. 0
    B. 1
    C. 2
    D. 3
    E. not determinable on the basis of the data given

14. If all the filing work for both units is consolidated without diminution in the amount to be done and all filing work is done by trained file clerks, the number of clerks required (35-hour work week) is
    A. 4   B. 5   C. 6   D. 7   E. 8

    14.____

15. In order to comply with the recommendation with respect to Schedule K, the present work production of Bureau A must be increased by
    A. 50%
    B. 100%
    C. 150%
    D. 200%
    E. an amount which is not determinable

    15.____

16. A certain training program during World War II resulted in the training of thousands of supervisors in industry. The methods of this program were later successfully applied in various government agencies. The program was based upon the assumption that there is an irreducible minimum of three supervisory skills.
    The one of these skills among the following is
    A. to know how to perform the job at hand well
    B. to be able to deal personally with workers, especially face-to-face
    C. to be able to imbue workers with the will to perform the job well
    D. to know the kind of work that is done by one's unit and the policies and procedures of one's agency
    E. the *know-how* of administrative and supervisory processes

    16.____

17. A comment made by an employee about a training course was, "*We never have any idea how we ae getting along in that course.*"
    The fundamental error in training methods to which this criticism points is
    A. insufficient student participation
    B. failure to develop a feeling of need or active want for the material being presented
    C. the training sessions may be too long
    D. no attempt may have been made to connect the new material with what was already known
    E. no goals have been set for the students

    17.____

18. Assume that you are attending a departmental conference on efficiency ratings at which it is proposed that a man-to-man rating scale be introduced.
    You should point out that, of the following, the CHIEF weakness of the man-to-man rating scale is that
    A. it involves abstract numbers rather than concrete employee characteristics
    B. judges are unable to select their own standards for comparison
    C. the standard for comparison shifts from man-to-man for each person rated
    D. not every person rated is given the opportunity to serve as a standard for comparison
    E. standards for comparison will vary from judge to judge

    18.____

19. Assume that you are conferring with a supervisor who has assigned to his subordinates efficiency ratings which you believe to be generally too low. The supervisor argues that his ratings are generally low because his subordinates are generally inferior.
Of the following, the evidence MOST relevant to the point at issue can be secured by comparing efficiency ratings assigned by the supervisor
    A. with ratings assigned by other supervisors in the same agency
    B. this year with ratings assigned by him in previous years
    C. to men recently transferred to his unit with ratings previously earned by these men
    D. with the general city average of ratings assigned by all supervisors to all employees
    E. with the relative order of merit of his employees as determined independently by promotion test marks

19.____

20. The one of the following which is NOT among the most common of the compensable factors used in wage evaluation studies is
    A. initiative and ingenuity required
    B. physical demand
    C. responsibility for the safety of others
    D. working conditions
    E. presence of avoidable hazards

20.____

21. If independent functions are separated, there is an immediate gain in conserving special skills. If we are to make optimum use of the abilities of our employees, these skills must be conserved.
Assuming the correctness of this statement, it follows that
    A. if we are not making optimum use of employee abilities, independent functions have not been separated
    B. we are making optimum uses of employee abilities if we conserve special skills
    C. we are making optimum use of employee abilities if independent functions have been separated
    D. we are not making optimum use of employee abilities if we do not conserve special skills
    E. if special skills are being conserved, independent functions need not be separated

21.____

22. A reorganization of the bureau to provide for a stenographic pool instead of individual unit stenographers will result in more stenographic help being available to each unit when it is required, and consequently will result in greater productivity for each unit. An analysis of the space requirements shows that setting up a stenographic pool will require a minimum of 400 square feet of good space. In order to obtain this space, it will be necessary to reduce the space available for technical personnel, resulting in lesser productivity for each unit.

22.____

On the basis of the above discussion, it can be stated that, in order to obtain greater productivity for each unit,
   A. a stenographic pool should be set up
   B. further analysis of the space requirement should be made
   C. it is not certain as to whether or not a stenographic pool should be set up
   D. the space available for each technician should be increased in order to compensate for the absence of a stenographic pool
   E. a stenographic pool should not be set up

23. The adoption of single consolidated form will mean that most of the form will not be used in any one operation. This would create waste and confusion. This conclusion is based upon the unstated hypothesis that
   A. if waste and confusion are to be avoided, a single consolidated form should be used
   B. if a single consolidated form is constructed, most of it can be used in each operation
   C. if waste and confusion are to be avoided, most of the form employed should be used
   D. most of a single consolidation form is not used
   E. a single consolidated form should not be used

23.____

KEY (CORRECT ANSWERS)

1.	E	11.	C
2.	B	12.	C
3.	C	13.	B
4.	B	14.	D
5.	E	15.	E
6.	A	16.	B
7.	B	17.	E
8.	A	18.	E
9.	A	19.	C
10.	D	20.	E

21.	D
22.	C
23.	C

EXAMINATION SECTION
TEST 1

DIRECTIONS: Each question or incomplete statement is followed by several suggested answers or completions. Select the one that BEST answers the question or completes the statement. *PRINT THE LETTER OF THE CORRECT ANSWER IN THE SPACE AT THE RIGHT.*

1. Professional staff members in large organizations are sometimes frustrated by a lack of vital work-related information because of the failure of some middle-management supervisors to pass along unrestricted information from top management.
   All of the following are considered to be reasons for such failure to pass along information EXCEPT the supervisors'
    A. belief that information affecting procedures will be ignored unless they are present to supervise their subordinates
    B. fear that specific information will require explanation or justification
    C. inclination to regard the possession of information as a symbol of higher status
    D. tendency to treat information a private property

1.____

2. Increasingly in government, employees' records are being handled by automated data processing systems. However, employees frequently doubt a computer's ability to handle their records properly.
   Which of the following is the BEST way for management to overcome such doubts?
    A. Conduct a public relations campaign to explain the savings certain to result from the use of computers
    B. Use automated data processing equipment made by the firm which has the best repair facilities in the industry
    C. Maintain a clerical force to spot check on the accuracy of the computer's recordkeeping
    D. Establish automated data processing systems that are objective, impartial, and take into account individual factors as far as possible

2.____

3. Some management experts question the usefulness of offering cash to individual employees for their suggestions.
   Which of the following reasons for opposing cash awards is MOST valid?
    A. Emphasis on individual gain deters cooperative effort.
    B. Money spent on evaluating suggestions may outweigh the value of the suggestions.
    C. Awards encourage employees to think about unusual methods of doing work.
    D. Suggestions too technical for ordinary evaluation are usually presented.

3.____

4. The use of outside consultants, rather than regular staff, in studying and recommending improvements in the operations of public agencies has been criticized.
Of the following, the BEST argument in favor of using regular staff is that such staff can better perform the work because they
   A. are more knowledgeable about operations and problems
   B. can more easily be organized into teams consisting of technical specialists
   C. may wish to gain additional professional experience
   D. will provide reports which will be more interesting to the public since they are more experienced

4._____

5. One approach to organizational problem-solving is to have all problem-solving authority centralized at the top of the organization.
However, from the viewpoint of providing maximum service to the public, this practice is UNWISE chiefly because it
   A. reduces the responsibility of the decision-makers
   B. produces delays
   C. reduces internal communications
   D. requires specialists

5._____

6. Research has shown that problem-solving efficiency is optimal when the motivation of the problem-solver is at a moderate rather than an extreme level.
Of the following, probably the CHIEF reason for this is that the problem-solver
   A. will cause confusion among his subordinates when his motivation is too high
   B. must avoid alternate solutions that tend to lead him up blind alleys
   C. can devote his attention to both the immediate problem as well as to other relevant problems in the general area
   D. must feel the need to solve the problem but not so urgently as to direct all his attention to the need and none to the means of solution

6._____

7. Don't be afraid to make mistakes. Many organizations are paralyzed from the fear of making mistakes. As a result, they don't do the things they should; they don't try new and different ideas.
For the effective supervisor, the MOST valid implication of this statement is that
   A. mistakes should not be encouraged, but there are some unavoidable risks in decision-making
   B. mistakes which stem from trying new and different ideas are usually not serious
   C. the possibility of doing things wrong is limited by one's organizational position
   D. the fear of making mistakes will prevent future errors

7._____

8. The duties of an employee under your supervision may be either routine, problem-solving, innovative, or creative.
Which of the following BEST describes duties which are both innovative and creative?

8._____

A. Checking to make sure that work is done properly
B. Applying principles in a practical matter
C. Developing new and better methods of meeting goals
D. Working at two or more jobs at the same time

9. According to modern management theory, a supervisor who uses as little authority as possible and as much as is necessary would be considered to be using a mode that is
    A. autocratic
    B. inappropriate
    C. participative
    D. directive

9._____

10. Delegation involves establishing and maintaining effective working arrangements between a supervisor and the persons who report to him.
    Delegation is MOST likely to have taken place when the
    A. entire staff openly discusses common problems in order to reach solutions satisfactory to the supervisor
    B. performance of specified work is entrusted to a capable person, and the expected results are mutually understood
    C. persons assigned to properly accomplish work are carefully evaluated and given a chance to explain shortcomings
    D. supervisor provides specific written instructions in order to prevent anxiety on the part of inexperienced persons

10._____

11. Supervisors often not aware of the effect that their behavior has on their subordinates.
    The one of the following training methods which would be BEST for changing such supervisory behavior is _____ training.
    A. essential skills
    B. off-the-job
    C. sensitivity
    D. developmental

11._____

12. A supervisor, in his role as a trainer, may have to decide on the length and frequency of training sessions.
    When the material to be taught is new, difficult, and lengthy, the trainer should be guided by the principle that for BEST results in such circumstances, sessions should be
    A. longer, relatively fewer in number, and held on successive days
    B. shorter, relatively greater in number, and spaced at intervals of several days
    C. of average length, relatively fewer in number, and held at intermittent intervals
    D. of random length and frequency, but spaced at fixed intervals

12._____

13. Employee training which is based on realistic simulation, sometimes known as *game play* or *role play*, is sometimes preferable to learning from actual experience on the job.
    Which of the following is NOT a correct statement concerning the value of simulation to trainees?

13._____

A. Simulation allows for practice in decision-making without any need for subsequent discussion.
B. Simulation is intrinsically motivating because it offers a variety of challenges.
C. Compared to other, more traditional training techniques, simulation is dynamic.
D. The simulation environment is nonpunitive as compared to real life.

14. Programmed instruction as a method of training has all of the following advantages EXCEPT:
    A. Learning is accomplished in an optimum sequence of distinct steps.
    B. Trainees have wide latitude in deciding what is to be learned within each program.
    C. The trainee takes an active part in the learning process.
    D. The trainee receives immediate knowledge of the results of his response.

14.____

15. In a work-study program, trainees were required to submit weekly written performance reports in order to insure that work assignments fulfilled the program objectives.
Such reports would also assist the administrator of the work-study program PRIMARILY to
    A. eliminate personal counseling for the trainees
    B. identify problems requiring prompt resolution
    C. reduce the amount of clerical work for all concerned
    D. estimate the rate at which budgeted funds are being expended

15.____

16. Which of the following would be MOST useful in order to avoid misunderstanding when preparing correspondence or reports?
    A. Use vocabulary which is at an elementary level
    B. Present each sentence as an individual paragraph
    C. Have someone other than the writer read the material for clarity
    D. Use general words which are open to interpretation

16.____

17. Which of the following supervisory methods would be MOST likely to train subordinates to give a prompt response to memoranda in an organizational setting where most transactions are informal?
    A. Issue a written directive setting forth a schedule of strict deadlines
    B. Let it be known, informally, that those who respond promptly will be rewarded
    C. Follow up each memorandum by a personal inquiry regarding the receiver's reaction to it
    D. Direct subordinates to furnish a precise explanation for ignoring memos

17.____

18. Conferences may fail for a number of reasons. Still, a conference that is an apparent failure may have some benefit.
Which of the following would LEAST likely be such a benefit?
It may
    A. increase for most participants their possessiveness about information they have

18.____

B. produce a climate of good will and trust among many of the participants
C. provide most participants with an opportunity to learn things about the others
D. serve as a unifying force to keep most of the individuals functioning as a group

19. Assume that you have been assigned to study and suggest improvements in an operating unit of a delegate agency whose staff has become overwhelmed with problems, has had inadequate resources, and has become accustomed to things getting worse. The staff is indifferent to cooperating with you because they see no hope of improvement.
Which of the following steps would be LEAST useful in carrying out your assignment?
    A. Encourage the entire staff to make suggestions to you for change
    B. Inform the staff that management is somewhat dissatisfied with their performance
    C. Let staff know that you are fully aware of their problems and stresses
    D. Look for those problem area where changes can be made quickly

20. Which of the following statements about employer-employee relations is NOT considered to be correct by leading managerial experts?
    A. An important factor in good employer-employee relations is treating workers respectfully.
    B. Employer-employee relations are profoundly influenced by the fundamentals of human nature.
    C. Good employer-employee relations must stem from top management and reach downward.
    D. Employee unions are usually a major obstacle to establishing good employer-employee relations.

21. In connection with labor relations, the term *management rights* GENERALLY refers to
    A. a managerial review system in a grievance system
    B. statutory prohibitions that bar monetary negotiations
    C. the impact of collective bargaining on government
    D. those subjects which management considers to be non-negotiable

22. Barriers may exist to the utilization of women in higher level positions. Some of these barriers are attitudinal in nature.
Which of the following is MOST clearly attitudinal in nature?
    A. Advancement opportunities which are vertical in nature and thus require seniority
    B. Experience which is inadequate or irrelevant to the needs of a dynamic and progressive organization
    C. Inadequate means of early identification of employees with talent and potential for advancement
    D. Lack of self-confidence on the part of some women concerning their ability to handle a higher position

23. Because a reader reacts to the meaning he associates with a word, we can neve be sure what emotional impact a word may carry or how it may affect our readers.
The MOST logical implication of this statement for employees who correspond with members of the public is that
   A. a writer should try to select a neutral word that will not bias his writing by its hidden emotional meaning
   B. simple language should be used in writing letters denying requests so that readers are not upset by the denial
   C. every writer should adopt a writing style which he finds natural and easy
   D. whenever there is doubt as to how a word is defined, the dictionary should be consulted

23.____

24. A public information program should be based on clear information about the nature of actual public knowledge and opinion. One way of learning about the views of the public is through the use of questionnaires.
Which of the following is of LEAST importance in designing a questionnaire?
   A. A respondent should be asked for his name and address.
   B. A respondent should be asked to choose from among several statements the one which expresses his views.
   C. Questions should ask for responses in a form suitable for processing.
   D. Questions should be stated in familiar language.

24.____

25. Assume that you have accepted an invitation to speak before an interested group about a problem. You have brought with you for distribution a number of booklets and other informational material.
Of the following, which would be the BEST way to use this material?
   A. Distribute it before you begin talking so that the audience may read it at their leisure.
   B. Distribute it during your talk to increase the likelihood that it will be read.
   C. Hold it until the end of your talk, then announce that those who wish may take or examine the material.
   D. Before starting the talk, leave it on a table in the back of the room so that people may pick it up as they enter.

25.____

KEY (CORRECT ANSWERS)

1.	A	11.	C
2.	D	12.	B
3.	A	13.	A
4.	A	14.	B
5.	B	15.	B
6.	D	16.	C
7.	A	17.	C
8.	C	18.	A
9.	C	19.	B
10.	B	20.	D

21.	D
22.	D
23.	A
24.	A
25.	C

TEST 2

DIRECTIONS: Each question or incomplete statement is followed by several suggested answers or completions. Select the one that BEST answers the question or completes the statement. *PRINT THE LETTER OF THE CORRECT ANSWER IN THE SPACE AT THE RIGHT.*

1. Of the following, the FIRST step in planning an operation is to 1.____
   A. obtain relevant information
   B. identify the goal to be achieved
   C. consider possible alternatives
   D. make necessary assignments

2. A supervisor who is extremely busy performing routine tasks is MOST likely making INCORRECT use of what basic principle of supervision? 2.____
   A. Homogeneous Assignment
   B. Span of Control
   C. Work Distribution
   D. Delegation of Authority

3. Controls help supervisors to obtain information from which they can determine whether their staffs are achieving planned goals.
Which one of the following would be LEAST useful as a control device? 3.____
   A. Employee diaries
   B. Organization charts
   C. Periodic inspections
   D. Progress charts

4. A certain employee has difficulty in effectively performing a particular portion of his routine assignments, but his overall productivity is average.
As the direct supervisor of his individual, your BEST course of action would be to 4.____
   A. attempt to develop the man's capacity to execute the problematic facets of his assignments
   B. diversify the employee's work assignments in order to build up his confidence
   C. reassign the man to less difficult tasks
   D. request in a private conversation that the employee improve his work output

5. A supervisor who uses persuasion as a means of supervising a unit would GENERALLY also use which of the following practices to supervise his unit? 5.____
   A. Supervise and control the staff with an authoritative attitude to indicate that he is a *take-charge* individual
   B. Make significant changes in the organizational operations so as to improve job efficiency
   C. Remove major communication barriers between himself, subordinates, and management
   D. Supervise everyday operations while being mindful of the problems of his subordinates

6. Whenever a supervisor in charge of a unit delegate a routine task to a capable subordinate, he tells him exactly how to do it. 6.____

This practice is GENERALLY
- A. *desirable*, chiefly because good supervisors should be aware of the traits of their subordinates and delegate responsibilities to them accordingly
- B. *undesirable*, chiefly because only non-routine tasks should be delegated
- C. *desirable*, chiefly because a supervisor should frequently test the willingness of his subordinates to perform ordinary tasks
- D. *undesirable*, chiefly because a capable subordinate should usually be allowed to exercise his own discretion in doing a routine job

7. The one of the following activities through which a supervisor BEST demonstrates leadership ability is by
   - A. arranging periodic staff meetings in order to keep his subordinates informed about professional developments in the field
   - B. frequently issuing definite orders and directives which will lessen the need for subordinates to make decisions in handling any tasks assigned to them
   - C. devoting the major part of his time to supervising subordinates so as to simulate continuous improvement
   - D. setting aside time for self-development and research so as to improve the skills, techniques, and procedures of his unit

8. The following three statements relate to the supervision of employees:
   I. The assignment of difficult tasks that offer a challenge is more conducive to good morale than the assignment of easy tasks.
   II. The same general principles of supervision that apply to men are equally applicable to women.
   III. The best retraining program should cover all phases of an employee's work in a general manner.
   Which of the following choices list ALL of the above statements that are generally correct?
   A. II, III   B. I   C. I, II   D. I, II, III

9. Which of the following examples BEST illustrates the application of the *exception principle* as a supervisory technique?
   - A. A complex job is divided among several employees who work simultaneously to complete the whole job in a shorter time.
   - B. An employee is required to complete any task delegated to him to such an extent that nothing is left for the superior who delegated the task except to approve it.
   - C. A superior delegates responsibility to a subordinate but retains authority to make the final decisions.
   - D. A superior delegates all work possible to his subordinates and retains that which requires his personal attention or performance

10. Assume that you are a supervisor. Your immediate superior frequently gives orders to your subordinates without your knowledge.
    Of the following, the MOST direct and effective way for you to handle this problem is to

A. tell our subordinates to take orders only from you
B. submit a report to higher authority in which you cite specific instances
C. discuss it with your immediate superior
D. find out to what extent your authority and prestige as a supervisor have been affected

11. In an agency which has as its primary purpose the protection of the public against fraudulent business practices, which of the following would GENERALLY be considered an *auxiliary* or *staff* rather than a *line* function?
    A. Interviewing victims of frauds and advising them about their legal remedies
    B. Daily activities directed toward prevention of fraudulent business practices
    C. Keeping records and statistics about business violations reported and corrected
    D. Follow-up inspections by investigators after corrective action has been taken

12. A supervisor can MOST effectively reduce the spread of false rumors through the *grapevine* by
    A. identifying and disciplining any subordinate responsible for initiating such rumors
    B. keeping his subordinates informed as much as possible about matters affecting them
    C. denying false rumors which might tend to lower staff morale and productivity
    D. making sure confidential matters are kept secure from access by unauthorized employees

13. A supervisor has tried to learn about the background, education, and family relationships of his subordinates through observation, personal contact, and inspection of their personnel records.
    These supervisor actions are GENERALLY
    A. *inadvisable*, chiefly because they may lead to charges of favoritism
    B. *advisable*, chiefly because they may make him more popular with his subordinates
    C. *inadvisable*, chiefly because his efforts may be regarded as an invasion of privacy
    D. *advisable*, chiefly because the information may enable him to develop better understanding of each of his subordinates

14. In an emergency situation, when action must be taken immediately, it is BEST for the supervisor to give orders in the form of
    A. direct commands which are brief and precise
    B. requests, so that his subordinates will not become alarmed
    C. suggestions which offer alternative courses of action
    D. implied directives, so that his subordinates may use their judgment in carrying them out

15. When demonstrating a new and complex procedure to a group of subordinates, it is ESSENTIAL that a supervisor
    A. go slowly and repeat the steps involved at least once
    B. show the employees common errors and the consequences of such errors
    C. go through the process at the usual speed so that the employees can see the rate at which they should work
    D. distribute summaries of the procedure during the demonstration and instruct his subordinates to refer to them afterwards

16. After a procedures manual has been written and distributed,
    A. continuous maintenance work is necessary to keep the manual current
    B. it is best to issue new manuals rather than make changes in the original manual
    C. no changes should be necessary
    D. only major changes should be considered

17. Of the following, the MOST important criterion of effective report writing is
    A. eloquence of writing style
    B. the use of technical language
    C. to be brief and to the point
    D. to cover all details

18. The use of electronic data processing
    A. has proven unsuccessful in most organizations
    B. has unquestionable advantages for all organizations
    C. is unnecessary in most organizations
    D. should be decided upon only after careful feasibility studies by individual organizations

19. The PRIMARY purpose of work measurement is to
    A. design and install a wage incentive program
    B. determine who should be promoted
    C. establish a yardstick to determine extent of progress
    D. set up a spirit of competition among employee

20. The action which is MOST effective in gaining acceptance of a study by the agency which is being studied is
    A. a directive from the agency head to install a study based on recommendations included in a report
    B. a lecture-type presentation following approval of the procedure
    C. a written procedure in narrative form covering the proposed system with visual presentations and discussions
    D. procedural charts showing the *before* situation, forms, steps, etc., to the employees affected

21. Which organization principle is MOST closely related to procedural analysis and improvement?
    A. Duplication, overlapping, and conflict should be eliminated.
    B. Managerial authority should be clearly defined.
    C. The objectives of the organization should be clearly defined.
    D. Top management should be freed of burdensome detail.

22. Which one of the following is the MAJOR objective of operational audits?
    A. Detecting fraud
    B. Determining organization problems
    C. Determining the number of personnel needed
    D. Recommending opportunities for improving operating and management practices

23. Of the following, the formalization of organization structure is BEST achieved by
    A. a narrative description of the plan of organization
    B. functional charts
    C. job descriptions together with organization charts
    D. multi-flow charts

24. Budget planning is MOST useful when it achieves
    A. cost control
    B. forecast of receipts
    C. performance review
    D. personnel reduction

25. GENERALLY, in applying the principle of delegation in dealing with subordinates, a supervisor
    A. allows his subordinates to set up work goals and to fix the limits within which they can work
    B. allows his subordinates to set up work goals and then gives detailed orders as to how they are to be achieved
    C. makes relatively few decisions by himself and frames his orders in broad, general terms
    D. provides externalized motivation for his subordinate

KEY (CORRECT ANSWERS)

1.	B	11.	C
2.	D	12.	B
3.	B	13.	D
4.	A	14.	A
5.	D	15.	A
6.	D	16.	A
7.	C	17.	C
8.	C	18.	D
9.	D	19.	C
10.	C	20.	C

21.	A
22.	D
23.	C
24.	A
25.	C

EXAMINATION SECTION
TEST 1

DIRECTIONS: Each question or incomplete statement is followed by several suggested answers or completions. Select the one that BEST answers the question or completes the statement. *PRINT THE LETTER OF THE CORRECT ANSWER IN THE SPACE AT THE RIGHT.*

1. Following are three statements concerning on-the-job training: 1.____
   I. On-the-job training is rarely used as a method of training employees.
   II. On-the-job training is often carried on with little or no planning.
   III. On-the-job training is often less expensive than other types.
   Which of the following BEST classifies the above statements into those that are correct and those that are not?
      A. I is correct, but II and III are not.   B. II is correct but I and III are not.
      C. I and II are correct, but III is not.   D. II and III are correct, but I is not.

2. The one of the following which is NOT a valid principle for a supervisor to keep in mind when talking to a subordinate about his performance is: 2.____
      A. People frequently know when they deserve criticism.
      B. Supervisors should be prepared to offer suggestions to subordinates about how to improve their work.
      C. Good points should be discussed before bad points.
      D. Magnifying a subordinate's faults will get him to improve faster.

3. In many organizations information travels quickly through the grapevine. 3.____
   Following are three statements concerning the *grapevine*:
   I. Information a subordinate does not want to tell her supervisor may reach the supervisor through the *grapevine*.
   II. A supervisor can often do her job better by knowing the information that travels through the *grapevine*.
   III. A supervisor can depend on the *grapevine* as a way to get accurate information from the employees on his staff.
   Which one of the following CORRECTLY classifies the above statements into those which are generally correct and those which are not?
      A. II is correct, but I and III are not.   B. III is correct, but I and II are not.
      C. I and II are correct, but III is not.   D. I and III are correct, but II is not.

4. Following are three statements concerning supervision: 4.____
   I. A supervisor knows he is doing a good job if his subordinates depend upon him to make every decision.
   II. A supervisor who delegates authority to his subordinates soon finds that his subordinates begin to resent him.
   III. Giving credit for good work is frequently an effective method of getting subordinates to work harder

Which one of the following CORRECTLY classifies the above statements into those that are correct and those that are not?
- A. I and II are correct, but III is not.
- B. II and III are correct, but I is not.
- C. II is correct, but I and III are not.
- D. III is correct, but I and II are not.

5. Of the following, the LEAST appropriate action for a supervisor to take in preparing a disciplinary case against a subordinate is to
   - A. keep careful records of each incident in which the subordinate has been guilty of misconduct or incompetency, even though immediate disciplinary action may not be necessary
   - B. discuss with the employee each incident of misconduct as it occurs so the employee knows where he stands
   - C. accept memoranda from any other employees who may have been witnesses to acts of misconduct
   - D. keep the subordinate's personnel file confidential so that he is unaware of the evidence being gathered against him

6. Praise by a supervisor can be an important element in motivating subordinates. Following are three statements concerning a supervisor's praise of subordinates:
   I. In order to be effective, praise must be lavish and constantly restated.
   II. Praise should be given in a manner which meets the needs of the individual subordinate.
   III. The subordinate whose work is praised should believe that the praise is earned.

   Which of the following CORRECTLY classifies the above statements into those that are correct and those that are not?
   - A. I is correct, but II and III are not.
   - B. II and III are correct, but I is not.
   - C. III is correct, but I and II are not.
   - D. I and II are correct, but III is not.

7. A supervisor feels that he is about to lose his temper while reprimanding a subordinate.
   Of the following, the BEST action for the supervisor to take is to
   - A. postpone the reprimand for a short time until his self-control is assured
   - B. continue the reprimand because a loss of temper by the supervisor will show the subordinate the seriousness of the error he made
   - C. continue the reprimand because failure to do so will show that the supervisor does not have complete self-control
   - D. postpone the reprimand until the subordinate is capable of understanding the reason for the supervisor's loss of temper

8. Following are three statements concerning various ways of giving orders to subordinates:
   I. An implied order or suggestion is usually appropriate for the inexperienced employee.
   II. A polite request is less likely to upset a sensitive subordinate than a direct order.
   III. A direct order is usually appropriate in an emergency situation.

Which of the following CORRECTLY classifies the above statements into those that are correct and those that are not?
- A. I is correct, but II and III are not.
- B. II and III are correct, but I is not.
- C. III is correct, but I and II are not.
- D. I and II are correct, but III is not.

9. The one of the following which is NOT an acceptable reason for taking disciplinary action against a subordinate guilty of serious violations of the rules is that
    - A. the supervisor can *let off steam* against subordinates who break rules frequently
    - B. a subordinate whose work continues to be unsatisfactory may be terminated
    - C. a subordinate may be encouraged to improve his work
    - D. an example is set for other employees

10. At the first meeting with your staff after appointment as a supervisor, you find considerable indifference and some hostility among the participants.
    Of the following, the MOST appropriate way to handle this situation is to
    - A. disregard the attitudes displayed and continue to make your presentation until you have completed it
    - B. discontinue your presentation but continue the meeting and attempt to find out the reasons for their attitudes
    - C. warm up your audience with some good-natured statements and anecdotes and then proceed with your presentation
    - D. discontinue the meeting and set up personal interviews with the staff members to try to find out the reason for their attitude

11. Use a written rather than oral communication to amend any previous written communication.
    Of the following, the BEST justification for this statement is that
    - A. oral changes will be considered more impersonal and thus less important
    - B. oral changes will be forgotten or recalled indifferently
    - C. written communications are clearer and shorter
    - D. written communications are better able to convey feeling tone

12. Assume that a certain supervisor, when writing important communications to his subordinates, often repeats certain points in different words.
    This technique is GENERALLY
    - A. *ineffective*; it tends to confuse rather than help
    - B. *effective*; it tends to improve understanding by the subordinates
    - C. *ineffective*; it unnecessarily increases the length of the communication and may annoy the subordinates
    - D. *effective*; repetition is always an advantage in communications

13. In preparing a letter or a report, a supervisor may wish to persuade the reader of the correctness of some idea or course of action.
    The BEST way to accomplish this is for the supervisor to
    - A. encourage the reader to make a prompt decision
    - B. express each idea in a separate paragraph

C. present the subject matter of the letter in the first paragraph
D. state the potential benefits for the reader

14. Effective communications, a basic necessity for successful supervision is a two-way street. A good supervisor needs to listen to, as well as disseminate, information and he must be able to encourage his subordinates to communicate with him.
Which of the following suggestions will contribute LEAST to improving the *listening power* of a supervisor?
    A. Don't assume anything; don't anticipate, and don't let a subordinate think you know what he is going to say
    B. Don't interrupt; let him have his full say even if it requires a second session that day to get the full story
    C. React quickly to his statements so that he knows you are interested, even if you must draw some conclusions prematurely
    D. Try to understand the real need for his talking to you even if it is quite different from the subject under discussion

14.____

15. Of the following, the MOST useful approach for the supervisor to take toward the informal employee communications network known as the *grapevine* is to
    A. remain isolated from it, but not take any active steps to eliminate it
    B. listen to it, but not depend on it for accurate information
    C. use it to disseminate confidential information
    D. eliminate it as diplomatically as possible

15.____

16. If a supervisor is asked to estimate the number of employees that he believes he will need in his unit in the coming fiscal year, the supervisor should FIRST attempt to learn the
    A. nature and size of the workload his unit will have during that time
    B. cost of hiring and training new employees
    C. average number of employee absences per year
    D. number of employees needed to indirectly support or assist his unit

16.____

17. An important supervisory responsibility is coordinating the operations of the unit. This may include setting work schedules, controlling work quality, establishing interim due dates, etc. In order to handle this task, it has been divided into the following five stages:
    I. Determine the steps or sequence required for the tasks to be performed.
    II. Give the orders, either written or oral, to begin work on the tasks.
    III. Check up by following each task to make sure it is proceeding according to plan.
    IV. Schedule the jobs by setting a time for each task of operation to begin and end.
    V. Control the process by correcting conditions which interfere with the plan.
    The MOST logical sequence in which these planning steps should be performed is:
    A. I, II, III, IV, V   B. II, I, V, III, IV   C. I, IV, II, III, V   D. IV, I, II, III, V

17.____

18. Assume that a supervisor calls a meeting with the staff under his supervision in order to discuss several proposals. After some discussion, he realizes that he strongly disagrees with one proposal that four of the staff have rather firmly favored.
    At this point, he could BEST handle the situation by saying:
    A. *I have the responsibility for this decision, and I must disagree.*
    B. *I am just reminding you that I have had a great deal more experience in these matters.*
    C. *You have presented some good points, but perhaps we could look at it another way.*
    D. *The only way that this proposal can be disposed of is to defer it for further discussion.*

18.____

19. As far as the social activities and groups of his subordinates are concerned, a supervisor in a large organization can BEST strengthen his tools of leadership by
    A. emphasizing the organization as a whole and forbidding the formation of groups
    B. ignoring the groups as much as possible and dealing with each subordinate as an individual
    C. learning about the status structure of employee groups and their values
    D. avoiding any relationship with groups

19.____

20. If a subordinate asks you, his superior, for advice in planning his career in the department, you should
    A. encourage him to feel that he can easily reach the top of his occupational ladder
    B. discourage him from setting his hopes too high
    C. discuss career opportunities realistically with him
    D. explain that you have no control over his opportunities for advancement

20.____

21. A supervisor's evaluation of an employee is usually based upon a combination of objective facts and subjective judgments or opinions.
    Which of the following aspects of an employee's work or performance is MOST likely to be subjectively evaluated?
    A. Quantity   B. Accuracy   C. Attitude   D. Attendance

21.____

22. Of the following possible characteristics of supervisors, the one MOST likely to lead to failure as a supervisor is
    A. a tendency to seek several opinions before making decisions in complex matters
    B. lack of a strong desire to advance to a top position in management
    C. little formal training in human relations skills
    D. poor relations with subordinates and other supervisory personnel

22.____

23. People who break rules do so for a number of reasons. However, employees will break rules LESS often if
    A. the supervisor uses his own judgment about work methods
    B. the supervisor pretends to act strictly, but isn't really serious about it
    C. they greatly enjoy their work
    D. they have completed many years of service

24. Assume that an employee under your supervision has become resentful and generally non-cooperative after his request for transfer to another office closer to his place of residence was denied. The request was denied primarily because of the importance of his current assignment. The employee has been a valued worker, but you are now worried that his resentful attitude will have a detrimental effect.
    Of the following, the MOST desirable way for you to handle this situation is to
    A. arrange for the employee's transfer to the office he originally requested
    B. arrange for the employee's transfer to another office, but not the one he originally requested
    C. attempt to re-focus the employee's attention on those aspects of his current assignment which will be most rewarding and satisfying to him
    D. explain to the employee that, while you are sympathetic to his request, department rules will not allow transfers for reasons of personal convenience

25. Of the following, it would be LEAST advisable for a supervisor to use his administrative authority to affect the behavior and activities of his subordinates when he is trying to
    A. change the way his subordinates perform a particular task
    B. establish a minimum level of conformity to established rules
    C. bring about change in the attitudes of his subordinates
    D. improve the speed with which his subordinates respond to his orders

26. Assume that a supervisor gives his subordinate instructions which are appropriate and clear. The subordinate thereupon refuses to follow these instructions.
    Of the following, it would then be MOST appropriate for the supervisor to
    A. attempt to find out what it is that the employee objects to
    B. take disciplinary action that same day
    C. remind the subordinate about supervisory authority and threaten him with discipline
    D. insist that the subordinate carry out the order immediately

27. Of the following, the MOST effective way to identify training needs resulting from gradual changes in procedure is to
    A. monitor on a continuous basis the actual jobs performed and the skills required
    B. periodically send out a written questionnaire asking personnel to identify their needs
    C. conduct interviews at regular intervals with selected employees
    D. consult employees' personnel records

28. Assume that you, as a supervisor, have had a new employee assigned to you. If the duties of his position can be broken into independent parts, which of the following is usually the BEST way to train this new employee?
Start with
   A. the easiest duties and progressively proceed to the most difficult
   B. something easy; move to something difficult; then back to something easy
   C. something difficult; move to something easy; then to something difficult
   D. the most difficult duties and progressively proceed to the easiest

28.____

29. The oldest and most commonly used training technique is on-the-job training. Instruction is given to the worker by his supervisor or by another employee. Such training is essential in most jobs, although it is not always effective when used alone.
This technique, however, can be effectively used alone if
   A. the skills involved can be learned quickly
   B. a large number of people are to be trained at one time
   C. other forms of training have not been previously used with the people involved
   D. the skills to be taught are mental rather than manual

29.____

30. It is generally agreed that the learning process is facilitated in proportion to the amount of feedback that the learner is given about his performance.
Following are three statements concerning the learning process:
   I. The more specific the learner's knowledge of how he performed, the more rapid his improvement and the higher his level of performance
   II. Giving the learner knowledge of his results does not affect his motivation to learn.
   III. Learners who are not given feedback will set up subjective criteria and evaluate their own performance.
Which of the following choices lists ALL of the above statements that are generally CORRECT?
   A. I and II only   B. I and III only   C. II and III only   D. I, II, and III

30.____

KEY (CORRECT ANSWERS)

1.	D	11.	B	21.	C
2.	D	12.	B	22.	D
3.	C	13.	D	23.	C
4.	D	14.	C	24.	C
5.	D	15.	B	25.	C
6.	B	16.	A	26.	A
7.	A	17.	C	27.	A
8.	B	18.	C	28.	A
9.	A	19.	C	29.	A
10.	D	20.	C	30.	B

TEST 2

DIRECTIONS: Each question or incomplete statement is followed by several suggested answers or completions. Select the one that BEST answers the question or completes the statement. *PRINT THE LETTER OF THE CORRECT ANSWER IN THE SPACE AT THE RIGHT.*

Questions 1-6.

DIRECTIONS: Questions 1 through 6 are to be answered SOLELY on the basis of the information given in the following paragraph.

The use of role-playing as a training technique was developed during the past decade by social scientists, particularly psychologists, who have been active in training experiments. Originally, this technique was applied by clinical psychologists who discovered that a patient appears to gain understanding of an emotionally disturbing situation when encouraged to act out roles in that situation. As applied in government and business organizations, the purpose of role-playing is to aid employees to understand certain work problems involving interpersonal relations and to enable observers to evaluate various reactions to them. Thus, for example, on the problem of handling grievances, two individuals from the group might be selected to act out extemporaneously the parts of subordinate and supervisor. When this situation is enacted by various pairs among the class and the techniques and results are discussed, the members of the group are presumed to reach conclusions about the most effective means of handling similar situations. Often the use of role reversal, where participants take parts different from their actual work roles, assists individuals to gain more insight into other people's problems and viewpoints. Although role-playing can be a rewarding training device, the trainer must be aware of his responsibilities. If this technique is to be successful, thorough briefing of both actors and observers as to the situation in question, the participants' roles, and what to look for, is essential.

1. The role-playing technique was FIRST used for the purpose of
   A. measuring the effectiveness of training programs
   B. training supervisors in business organizations
   C. treating emotionally disturbed patients
   D. handling employee grievances

2. When role-playing is used in private business as a training device, the CHIEF aim is to
   A. develop better relations between supervisor and subordinate in the handling of grievances
   B. come up with a solution to a specific problem that has arisen
   C. determine the training needs of the group
   D. increase employee understanding of the human relation factors in work situations

3. From the above passage, it is MOST reasonable to conclude that when role-playing is used, it is preferable to have the roles acted out by
   A. only one set of actors
   B. no more than 2 sets of actors
   C. several different sets of actors
   D. the trainer or trainers of the group

4. Based on the above passage, a trainer using the technique of role reversal in a problem of first-line supervision should assign a senior employee to play the part of a(n)
   A. new employee
   B. senior employee
   C. principal employee
   D. angry citizen

4._____

5. It can be inferred from the above passage that a limitation of role-play as a training method is that
   A. many work situations do not lend themselves to role-play
   B. employees are not experienced enough as actors to play the roles realistically
   C. only trainers who have psychological training can use it successfully
   D. participants who are observing and not acting do not benefit from it

5._____

6. To obtain good results from the use of role-playing in training, a trainer should give participants
   A. a minimum of information about the situation so that they can act spontaneously
   B. scripts which illustrate the best method for handling the situation
   C. a complete explanation of the problem and the roles to be acted out
   D. a summary of work problems which involve interpersonal relations

6._____

7. Of the following, the MOST important reason for a supervisor to prepare good written reports is that
   A. a supervisor is rated on the quality of his reports
   B. decisions are often made on the basis of the reports
   C. such reports take less time for superiors to review
   D. such reports demonstrate efficiency of department operations

7._____

8. Of the following, the BEST test of a good report is whether it
   A. provides the information needed
   B. shows the good sense of the writer
   C. is prepared according to a proper format
   D. is grammatical and neat

8._____

9. When a supervisor writes a report, he can BEST show that he has an understanding of the subject of the report by
   A. including necessary facts and omitting non-essential details
   B. using statistical data
   C. giving his conclusions but not the data on which they are based
   D. using a technical vocabulary

9._____

10. Suppose you and another supervisor on the same level are assigned to work together on a report. You disagree strongly with one of the recommendations the other supervisor wants to include in the report but you cannot change his views.
    Of the following, it would be BEST that
    A. you refuse to accept responsibility for the report
    B. you ask that someone else be assigned to this project to replace you

10._____

C. each of you state his own ideas about this recommendation in the report
D. you give in to the other supervisor's opinion for the sake of harmony

11. Standardized forms are often provided for submitting reports. Of the following, the MOST important advantage of using standardized forms for reports is that
    A. they take less time to prepare than individually written reports
    B. necessary information is less likely to be omitted
    C. the responsibility for preparing these reports can be delegated to subordinates
    D. the person making the report can omit information he considers unimportant

12. A report which may BEST be classed as a *periodic* report is one which
    A. requires the same type of information at regular intervals
    B. contains detailed information which is to be retained in permanent records
    C. is prepared whenever a special situation occurs
    D. lists information in graphic form

13. Which one of the following is NOT an important reason for keeping accurate records in an office?
    A. Facts will be on hand when decisions have to be made.
    B. The basis for past actions can be determined.
    C. Information needed by other bureaus can be furnished.
    D. Filing is easier when records are properly made out.

14. Suppose you are preparing to write a report recommending a change in a certain procedure. You learn that another supervisor made a report a few years ago suggesting a change in this same procedure, but that no action was taken.
    Of the following, it would be MOST desirable for you to
    A. avoid reading the other supervisor's report so that you will write with a more up-to-date point of view
    B. make no recommendation since management seems to be against any change in the procedure
    C. read the other report before you write your report to see what bearing it may have on your recommendations
    D. avoid including in your report any information that can be obtained by referring to the other report

15. If a report you are preparing to your superior is going to be a very long one, it would be DESIRABLE to include a summary of your basic conclusions
    A. at the end of the report
    B. at the beginning of the report
    C. in a separate memorandum
    D. right after you present the supporting data

16. Suppose that some bureau and department policies must be very frequently applied by your subordinates while others rarely come into use.
As a supervising employee, a GOOD technique for you to use in fulfilling your responsibility of seeing to it that policies are adhered to is to
    A. ask the director of the bureau to issue to all employees an explanation in writing of all policies
    B. review with your subordinates every week those policies which have daily application
    C. follow up on and explain at regular intervals the application of those policies which are not used very often by your subordinates
    D. recommend to your superiors that policies rarely used be changed or dropped

17. The BASIC purpose behind the principle of delegation of authority is to
    A. give the supervisor who is delegating a chance to acquire skills in higher level functions
    B. free the supervisor from routine tasks in order that he may do the important parts of his job
    C. prevent supervisors from overstepping the lines of authority which have been established
    D. place the work delegated in the hands of those employees who can perform it best

18. A district commander can BEST assist management in long-range planning by
    A. reporting to his superiors any changing conditions in the district
    B. maintaining a neat and efficiently run office
    C. scheduling work so that areas with a high rate of non-compliance get more intensive coverage
    D. properly training new personnel assigned to his district

19. Suppose that new quarters have been rented for your district office.
Of the following, the LEAST important factor to be considered in planning the layout of the office is the
    A. need for screening confidential activities from unauthorized persons
    B. relative importance of the various types of work
    C. areas of noise concentration
    D. convenience with which communication between sections of the office can be achieved

20. Of the following, the MOST basic effect of organizing a department so that lines of authority are clearly defined and duties are specifically assigned is to
    A. increase the need for close supervision
    B. decreases the initiative of subordinates
    C. lessen the possibility of duplication of work
    D. increase the responsibilities of supervisory personnel

21. An accepted management principle is that decisions should be delegated to the lowest point in the organization at which they can be made effectively.
The one of the following which is MOST likely to be a result of the application of this principle is that
    A. no factors will be overlooked in making decisions
    B. prompt action will follow the making of decisions
    C. decisions will be made more rapidly
    D. coordination of decisions that are made will be simplified

22. Suppose you are a supervisor and need some guidance from a higher authority. In which one of the following situations would it be PERMISSIBLE for you to bypass the regular upward channels of communication in the chain of command?
    A. In an emergency when your superior is not available
    B. When it is not essential to get a quick reply
    C. When you feel your immediate superior is not understanding of the situation
    D. When you want to obtain information that you think your superior does not have

23. Of the following, the CHIEF limitation of the organization chart as it is generally used in business and government is that the chart
    A. makes lines of responsibility and authority undesirably definite and formal
    B. is often out of date as soon as it is completed
    C. does not show human factors and informal working relationships
    D. is usually too complicated

24. The *span of control* for any supervisor is the
    A. number of tasks he is expected to perform himself
    B. amount of office space he and his subordinates occupy
    C. amount of work he is responsible for getting out
    D. number of subordinates he can supervise effectively

25. Of the following duties performed by a supervising employee, which would be considered a LINE function rather than a staff function?
    A. Evaluation of office personnel
    B. Recommendations for disciplinary action
    C. Initiating budget requests for replacement of equipment
    D. Inspections, at irregular times, of conditions and staff in the field

KEY (CORRECT ANSWERS)

1.	C		11.	B
2.	D		12.	A
3.	C		13.	D
4.	A		14.	C
5.	A		15.	B
6.	C		16.	C
7.	B		17.	B
8.	A		18.	A
9.	A		19.	B
10.	C		20.	C

21. B
22. A
23. C
24. D
25. D

EXAMINATION SECTION
TEST 1

DIRECTIONS: Each question or incomplete statement is followed by several suggested answers or completions. Select the one that BEST answers the question or completes the statement. *PRINT THE LETTER OF THE CORRECT ANSWER IN THE SPACE AT THE RIGHT.*

1. During an assessment interview, a practitioner attempts to determine a client's "executive functioning." This means mostly the degree to which a client is able to
    I. live without stress
    II. act in a leadership role
    III. organize and implement activities
    IV. deal with multiple responsibilities

    A. I and IV
    B. II only
    C. III and IV
    D. I, II, III and IV

2. Most likely, family therapy would be the primary intervention of choice for each of the following, EXCEPT

    A. borderline personality issues
    B. individual problems related to family transitions
    C. problems in relationships
    D. problems with children

3. About _____ of today's elderly population suffer from mental health problems.

    A. 1/8
    B. 1/4
    C. 1/2
    D. 3/4

4. In interpersonal communication, responses such as ignoring a client, cutting him off in mid-sentence, changing the subject, reacting ambiguously, or being condescending can cause the client to value himself less. These types of responses are described as

    A. low-context
    B. toxic
    C. polarizing
    D. disconfirming

5. Nearly all forms of therapeutic relationships involve
    I. a suspension of moral judgment
    II. constancy of the clinician's interest no matter how disturbing the subject
    III. the practitioner allowing him/herself to be used as a transference object without the interference of counter-transference
    IV. the client's opportunity to speak the unspeakable

    A. I and II
    B. II and IV

C. III and IV
D. I, II, III and IV

6. Personality assessments are most often categorized as either

   A. verbal and performance
   B. behavioral and psychodynamic
   C. projective or objective
   D. social or vocational

7. _____ theory holds that it is a person's own unrealistic beliefs that generate a fear of failure.

   A. Systematic desensitization
   B. Empowerment
   C. Performance visualization
   D. Cognitive restructuring

8. What is the psychoanalytic term for the release of emotional energy related to unconscious conflicts?

   A. Dam-breaking
   B. Projection
   C. Catharsis
   D. Transference

9. According to the model of Rational-Emotive Behavior Therapy (REBT), which of the following would be an example of a core irrational belief?

   A. One should keep the focus on the present
   B. One must have perfect and definite self-control.
   C. No matter how bad it is, it will be over shortly.
   D. Things could always be worse.

10. Regarding professional consultation with colleagues about clients, the NASW code of ethics establishes the rule of thumb that social workers should

    A. avoid consultation in cases where the client is known to be violent
    B. disclose the least amount of information to achieve the purposes of the consultation
    C. disclose no confidential or potentially sensitive information to consultants
    D. make sure consulting professionals know as much as they do about the client before offering input into the case

11. To help female clients understand the ecosystems that affect their well-being, social work practitioners should use

    A. gender role analysis, to help women understand their relations with men
    B. stereotypes, to consider male-female interactions
    C. an androcentric knowledge base, to assess the experiences of women
    D. female biology and endocrinology, to explain emotional and behavioral responses

12. The use of psychological tests in clinical social work should be governed by the idea that
    I. clients should be involved in the test-selection process whenever possible or feasible
    II. a client should be made aware that tests are only tools, and will not provide any answers to the client's problems in and of themselves
    III. test results, and not merely scores, should always be released and explained to the client
    IV. clients' reasons for wanting tests, as well as their past experiences with tests, should be explored before selecting any assessment

    A. I and II
    B. II only
    C. II and IV
    D. I, II, III and IV

13. In Adlerian therapy, client nonverbal behaviors are often used to assess

    A. ego states
    B. self-talk
    C. hidden purposes of behaviors
    D. conflicts or discrepancies

14. In the behavioral model, maladjustment results from

    A. personality defects
    B. flawed learning
    C. heredity
    D. environmental barriers

15. Despite broad-based application and compatibility with social work values, evidence-based practice approaches are not universally accepted in clinical settings. Each of the following is a significant reason for this, EXCEPT

    A. clinician reluctance
    B. clinician unfamiliarity with empirical data collection methods
    C. lack of organizational availability
    D. client concerns

16. Which of the following is a structured personality assessment?

    A. Thematic Apperception Test (TAT)
    B. Minnesota Multiphasic Personality Inventory (MMPI)
    C. Sentence Completion Test
    D. Rorschach

17. An client must provide informed consent for psychological treatment if
    I. treatment may have positive or negative effects
    II. one treatment is not superior to another
    III. treatment may be hazardous
    IV. full cooperation is required for success of therapy

    A. I and II
    B. II only
    C. II, III and IV

D. I, II, III and IV

18. According to Sullivan, dysfunctional families seek 18.____

    A. security rather than satisfaction
    B. gratification rather than democracy
    C. power rather than cohesion
    D. avoidance rather than engagement

19. During a client interview, a practitioner wants to transition from his own preliminary comments and prompt a response from the client. Which of the following is NOT generally recognized as a gesture that would signify "turn yielding?" 19.____

    A. Talking more loudly
    B. Asking a direct question
    C. Slowing the rate of speech
    D. Terminating body movements and gazing at the client

20. Among Asian Americans, mental illness is often expressed as 20.____

    A. adjustment disorder
    B. borderline personality disorder
    C. psychosomatic complaint
    D. depression

21. In the *Diagnostic and Statistical Manual of Mental Disorders* (DSM-IV), diagnoses are a process of elimination. This means that a clinician 21.____

    I. arrives at diagnoses by eliminating differential diagnoses
    II. must adopt an attitude of skepticism when making a tentative diagnosis
    III. starts with many possible diagnostic categories, and through multiple observations eliminates each of them until only one remains
    IV. arrives at a diagnosis by determining how many symptoms the person has in common with what's published for a particular DSM diagnosis

    A. I and II
    B. I and III
    C. II and IV
    D. IV only

22. The psychoanalytic perspective holds that the infant's emergent sense of self begins in the 22.____

    A. uterus
    B. first two months of life
    C. first year of life
    D. first two years of life

23. After a client's presenting problem has been diagnosed, a social worker begins planning for service delivery. The FIRST step in this process is typically to 23.____

    A. identify services
    B. develop a plan for services
    C. conduct additional interviews and tests
    D. revisit the assessment/diagnosis phase

24. When a clinician asks his client to lie down on a couch and talk about whatever comes to mind, he is using the technique of

   A. transference
   B. catharsis
   C. free association
   D. response shaping

25. Which of the following is NOT usually part of a process recording?

   A. Recorder's feelings and reactions
   B. Observations
   C. Quotations, to the extent that they can be remembered
   D. Diagnosis

26. A mildly retarded male client lives in a resident facility and is sexually active. He has impregnated two young women at the facility, and one of the resident clinicians is recommending that the client's family consider persuading him to get a vasectomy. This case will most likely involve the ethical and legal issue of

   A. duty to warn
   B. informed consent
   C. due process
   D. confidentiality

27. Which of the following is NOT developed during infancy?

   A. Telegraphic speech
   B. Transductive reasoning
   C. Separation anxiety
   D. Object permanence

28. A client tells a practitioner: "One of the reasons I quit my job was because my boss was always pushing me. I could never say no to her. Whatever she wanted, I always gave in. I think it's hard to say no to people until I reach a point where I can't take it any more." The practitioner responds with the following summary of the client's statement: "You're discovering that you tend to give in or not do what you'd like until you become angry and break things off—not just in your working relationships, but in other relationships as well." This is an example of a summary whose purpose is to

   A. tie together multiple elements of a message
   B. review progress
   C. identify a theme
   D. regulate the pace of the session

29. Each of the following is a common form of countertransference that can occur in the treatment of clients, EXCEPT the

   A. focus on feeling liked and appreciated by the client
   B. reluctance to give advice because of a fear of creating a sense of dependence
   C. strong reaction to certain clients who evoke negative emotions in the practitioner
   D. reluctance to challenge a client because it might result in resentment or other negative feelings

30. In Baumrind's model of parenting styles, the happiest and best-behaved children usually have parents who use _____ style of parenting.

    A. permissive
    B. authoritarian
    C. disciplinarian
    D. authoritative

31. During an assessment interview, a practitioner asks a client: "In what kind of situations do you find it easier to manage or control this reaction?" The practitioner is attempting to identify

    A. secondary gains associated with the presenting problem
    B. client resources and strengths
    C. consequences of the problem
    D. antecedents to the problem

32. Interpersonal psychotherapy has proven effective in the treatment of

    A. schizophrenia
    B. depression
    C. phobias
    D. bipolar disorder

33. In the social service system, collaboration
    I. may involve community planning
    II. is achieved both formally and informally
    III. is most prominently illustrated among the work of clinic teams
    IV. increases treatment effectiveness by combining competencies

    A. I and III
    B. I, II and IV
    C. II and IV
    D. I, II, III and IV

34. Dysthymia is considered to be associated with a greater risk of suicide when it occurs in

    A. women
    B. children
    C. older men
    D. in conjunction with a personality disorder

35. A clinician suspects that a ten-year-old boy may be suffering from neglect. For children of this age, common indicators of neglect include
    I. refusal to even attempt homework assignments
    II. crying easily when hurt even slightly
    III. falling asleep in class
    IV. consistently showing up early to school

    A. I and II
    B. I, II and III
    C. III only
    D. I, II, III and

36. Minor clients-those under the age of consent-are considered to have

   A. a legal right to privacy
   B. an ethical right to privacy
   C. both an ethical and legal right to privacy
   D. deferred their right to privacy to their parents, who deserve to know the details of the intervention process

37. The use of probes is often helpful for either expanding or narrowing the parameters of discussions with clients. The FIRST step in formulating an effective probe is often to

   A. determine the purpose of the probe
   B. decide what type of question will be most helpful
   C. use a paraphrase or reflection response
   D. determine what the client needs to know or do

38. In Watson and Tellegen's map of the human emotions, the emotions that are most closely related are

   A. pleasure and pain
   B. surprise and relaxation
   C. disappointment and relief
   D. anger and fear

39. Helping a client to recognize and mobilize her own coping resources and available supportive network of friends and family is an example of the _____ effect of social support

   A. buffering
   B. transactional
   C. direct
   D. indirect

40. A working alliance with a client is said to be necessarily composed of each of the following, EXCEPT

   A. an emotional bond between client and practitioner
   B. agreement on therapeutic goals
   C. agreement on the practitioner's leadership role in planning and conducting interventions
   D. agreement on therapeutic tasks

41. Cognitive therapy has proven to be effective in the treatmqent of
   I. major depression
   II. eating disorders
   III. anxiety disorders
   IV. panic disorders

   A. I and II
   B. II only
   C. II and III
   D. I, II, III and IV

42. De-institutionalization, as it applies to mental health practices, involves the concept of the "least restrictive alternative." This concepts basically means that

   A. professionals should only commit clients who are delusional
   B. at least one less restrictive alternative must be attempted before voluntary commitment is sought
   C. practitioners should select a mode of treatment that gives them the greatest possible latitude in making decisions about a clien's future
   D. treatment should be no more intrusive or harsher than necessary in order to achieve therapeutic aims and protect clients and others from physical harm

43. Post-traumatic stress disorder falls under the category _____ disorders.

   A. dissociative
   B. mood
   C. somatoform
   D. anxiety

44. The stereotypes that lock Americans into traditional gender activities are MOST likely to be broken by

   A. equal pay for equal work
   B. greater male participation in family-oriented, nurturing activities
   C. greater female participation in institutional decision-making
   D. more stringent anti-discrimination legislation

45. _____ theories of ethics claim that certain actions are simply right or wrong as a matter of fundamental principle.

   A. Teleological
   B. Consequentialist
   C. Deontological
   D. Utilitarian

46. Which of the following is an Axis II disorder?

   A. Major Depression
   B. Separation Anxiety Disorder
   C. Mental retardation
   D. Panic Disorder

47. One of the most common dysfunctions of the nuclear family is that it can create

   A. a generation gap
   B. institutional fragmentation
   C. a breakdown of authority
   D. emotional overload

48. The frequency with which a clinical social work practitioner receives supervision should depend on each of the following, EXCEPT the

   A. level of the practitioner's training and experience
   B. worker's activities

C. expectations of the supervisor
D. agreement in theoretical perspective between supervisor and practitioner

49. _____ personality theories are based on the premise that predispositions direct the behavior of a person in a consistent pattern.

   A. Psychodynamic
   B. Behavioral
   C. Trait
   D. Humanistic

49.____

50. When a communicative response is given that matches a client's previous communication, the _____ is established.

   A. halo effect
   B. valence
   C. norm of reciprocity
   D. boundary elimination

50.____

51. Which of the following standardized assessment tools is a Likert-type self-report measure that assesses overall health or pathology in a general score?

   A. *McMaster Family Assessment Device*
   B. *Parenting Stress Index*
   C. *Family Environment Scale*
   D. *Dyadic Cohesion Scale*

51.____

52. Which of the following theories are most relevant to the humanistic-experiential model of treatment?

   A. Rational-emotive behavior therapy (REBT) and choice theory
   B. Gestalt therapy and person-centered treatment
   C. Freudian and Jungian theory
   D. Cognitive theory and behavioral theory

52.____

53. The principle that two people in a continuing relationship—such as a social worker and a client—feel a strong obligation to repay their social debts to one another is the

   A. Hawthorne effect
   B. law of empathy
   C. norm of reciprocity
   D. law of effect

53.____

54. In a therapeutic encounter, which of the following client behaviors is most likely to be interpreted as a "retroflection" by a Gestalt therapist?

   A. Not making eye contact
   B. Laughing off important things
   C. Speaking abstractly or indirectly
   D. Holding the breath

54.____

55. Verbal means of conveying empathy to a client include
    I. using verbal responses that refer to the client's feelings
    II. using verbal responses that bridge or add on to implicit client messages
    III. placing the client's presenting problems in a clinical context
    IV. explaining the client's emotions

    A. I and II
    B. I, II and III
    C. II and III
    D. I, II, III and IV

56. Conflict theorists assert that unity that is present in society is the result of

    A. consensus
    B. competition
    C. contract
    D. coercion

57. Confrontation can be a useful tool with clients who are unable or unwilling to face up to the realities of their own thoughts or feelings, but it is also a response that requires great vigilance and judiciousness on the part of the clinician. In describing a distortion or a discrepancy to a client, a clinician should NOT

    A. use a confrontation to vent frustration with a client's behaviors
    B. cite a specific example of the behavior, rather than a generalized inference
    C. avoid confronting near the end of a therapy session
    D. attempt to determine the client's willingness to change before presenting a challenge

58. In family systems theory, "first-order" change occurs only when

    A. the family's own narrative about their behavior changes
    B. the rules of the system change
    C. a feedback loop becomes evident
    D. a specific behavior in within the system changes

59. One principle of human behavior is that when people are observed, or believe someone is paying close attention, they behave differently. This phenomenon is known as

    A. role ambiguity
    B. the Peter principle
    C. self-perception bias
    D. the Hawthorne effect

60. During the service delivery process, a referral can sometimes fail to result in a positive client outcome. Which of the following is LEAST likely to be a reason for this failure?

    A. Insufficient practitioner knowledge of resources
    B. Countertransference from referring practitioner
    C. Practitioner misjudgement of client's capability to follow through with referral
    D. Practitioner insensitivity to, or misjudgement of, client needs

61. For children, the factor with the highest predictive value for social problems is

    A. ethnicity
    B. poverty
    C. education
    D. substance abuse

62. A practitioner has administered two separate standardized psychological assessments to a client. When considering the release of this assessment data to third parties, the practitioner

    A. release the data only to those competent to interpret them
    B. may release the data to anyone who asks for it
    C. should keep in mind that other practitioners can release assessment data transferred to them by the practitioner
    D. are not obligated to monitor the release of assessment data

63. Each of the following is a typical function served by the family unit, EXCEPT to

    A. provide for children's basic needs
    B. indoctrinate children in the ways of society
    C. act as the primary agent of socialization
    D. provide a uniform plan for socializing children

64. Social work supervisors who are attempting to evaluate their own questioning techniques with supervisees should be sure they

    A. ensure thorough case knowledge before moving on to questions related to intervention strategies
    B. preface individual questions with introductory statements
    C. ask questions in a general way in order to receive general answers
    D. make sure that questions related to intervention strategies and techniques are more specific that questions about diagnostic understanding

65. In its formulations, the *Diagnostic and Statistical Manual of Mental Disorders* (DSM-IV) relies on
    I. a medical model of human development
    II. an empirical array of the opinions of many diagnosticians
    III. a strengths model of human development
    IV. the opinions of a designated board of diagnosticians who share similar theoretical perspectives

    A. I and II
    B. II only
    C. II and III
    D. IV only

66. A clinician and a client are in the middle phase of a task-centered intervention. At the beginning of each session, they will

    A. establish incentives and rationales for tasks
    B. identify obstacles to task accomplishment
    C. engage in guided practice and rehearsal
    D. review problems and tasks to determine progress

67. An adolescent boy, shortly after his release from a reformatory for juvenile delinquents, commits an act of vandalism. The boy feels it is in his nature to commit such acts, because he has been identified as a "juvenile delinquent" by society. His act of vandalism is an example of

    A. primary deviance
    B. secondary deviance
    C. stigmatization
    D. a cry for help

68. What is the immediate short-term effect of a tricyclic antidepressant?

    A. Increasing the availability of serotonin and norepinephrine in synapses
    B. Dampening the CNS arousal state
    C. Reducing intracranial pressure by reducing cerebrospinal fluid
    D. Increasing available lithium in the bloodstream for absorption

69. A practitioner needs to wrap up a 50-minute session with a client in order to prepare for her next session. Of the following, the BEST closing to a session is

    A. I'm sorry this divorce has been so difficult for you. Let's pick up with that feeling next week.
    B. I see we have about ten minutes left together. Let's try to come up with some strategies that you can work on for next week.
    C. I see we have about ten minutes remaining in this session. Let's see if we can't address your drug problem to some extent before we say goodbye.
    D. It's 2:50 and my next client is in the office. Let's see if we can wrap this up together.

70. Which of the following theoretical perspectives provides a kind of bridge between psychoanalysis and family therapy?

    A. Object relations
    B. Ego identity
    C. Self psychology
    D. Family dynamism

71. When giving feedback to a client, it is usually NOT advisable to

    A. claim clear ownership of the comment
    B. be specific
    C. focus on personality traits
    D. note a behavior

72. Society typically neutralizes deviant behaviors in each of the following ways, EXCEPT by

    A. denying responsibilities
    B. denying victimhood
    C. appealing to higher loyalties
    D. denying deviant labels

73. A client, referred to a clinician, is covered by her insurer for a total of eight treatment sessions. The client is an incest victim, and the clinician believes it will take more sessions than this to help her with her problems. He decides to offer the client his services pro bono. The practitioner's decision is an illustration of the principle of

A. self-determination
B. fidelity
C. justice
D. due process

74. Each of the following is true of psychiatric inpatient care, EXCEPT that it 74.____

    A. can be combined with social systems intervention
    B. is increasingly associated with legal mandates
    C. is usually appropriate only for medical problems
    D. can often be shortened by crisis intervention

75. During an interview, a client says: "My life is really boring. There's nothing new going on and all my friends are away. I wish I had enough money to make something happen." The clinician has decided that the Adlerian approach will be most useful with this client. Which of the following interpretations of the above statement is most in line with the Adlerian approach? 75.____

    A. "You seem to be saying you don't know how to enjoy yourself without having other people around. Maybe recognizing this will help you learn to be more self-reliant."
    B. "Sounds as if you need excitement, friends, and money to make your life seem worthwhile."
    C. "It seems as if you can only be happy when you're able to play and have fun. The child in you seems to be in control of a good part of your life."
    D. "You seem to think things are terrible because you have no friends around now, and no money. Is there any proof for that? I think your feelings of boredom might change if you could draw a different and more logical conclusion from your circumstances."

KEY (CORRECT ANSWERS)

1. C	16. B	31. B	46. C	61. B
2. A	17. D	32. B	47. D	62. A
3. B	18. A	33. D	48. D	63. D
4. D	19. A	34. B	49. C	64. A
5. D	20. C	35. D	50. C	65. A
6. C	21. B	36. B	51. A	66. D
7. D	22. B	37. C	52. B	67. B
8. C	23. D	38. D	53. C	68. A
9. B	24. C	39. A	54. D	69. B
10. B	25. D	40. C	55. A	70. A
11. A	26. B	41. D	56. D	71. C
12. D	27. B	42. D	57. A	72. D
13. C	28. C	43. D	58. D	73. C
14. B	29. B	44. C	59. D	74. C
15. B	30. D	45. C	60. B	75. B

TEST 2

DIRECTIONS: Each question or incomplete statement is followed by several suggested answers or completions. Select the one that BEST answers the question or completes the statement. *PRINT THE LETTER OF THE CORRECT ANSWER IN THE SPACE AT THE RIGHT.*

1. In which of the following cases is treatment considered to be "mandated?"
    I. The court orders a person to attend treatment sessions, with consequences for noncompliance
    II. Concerned neighbors insist that a child who is disruptive in the community be evaluated for a mental illness or disturbance
    III. Parents withhold college tuition if their child does not check into a drug rehabilitation facility
    IV. A spouse threatens to leave if a partner does not seek treatment

    A. I only
    B. I and II
    C. I, II, and III
    D. I, II, III and IV

    1.____

2. Two types of psychological tests that are the most commonly used in clinical practice are

    A. cognitive/ability and personality
    B. interest surveys and vocational skills
    C. conscious and unconscious
    D. speech perception and reaction time

    2.____

3. The emphasis of contemporary psychodynamic approaches to treatment tends to be

    A. interpersonal functioning
    B. repressed sexuality
    C. long-term treatment
    D. childhood events

    3.____

4. A significant concept in the contemporary psychoanalytic view of families is the idea of a family as a

    A. sociological dimension
    B. group of interconnected intrapsychic systems
    C. cacophony of competing ids
    D. single organic entity focused on self-preservation

    4.____

5. Assumptions associated with the practice of professional consultation include each of the following, EXCEPT

    A. Consultation may result in confirming the rightness of the clinician's current actions.
    B. The consultant has greater knowledge than the consultee in the areas of agency and worker needs.
    C. In order to work positively, consultation cannot be compelled
    D. Consultation is made more effective when the consultant provides feedback to the employer or agency about the consultee's skills..

    5.____

6. Together, practitioner and client have identified the client's needs and corresponding services. The practitioner then turns his attention to resource selection. Typically, the paramount decision-making concern in resource selection is the

   A. capacity of the practitioner to treat the presenting problem(s)
   B. information and referral system
   C. agency's policies and procedures
   D. client's values and preferences

7. Of the following concepts, the one that most clearly is derived from the theoretical intersection between dynamic psychiatry and the social sciences is that
   I. culture influences personality
   II. role performance is an effect of personality
   III. social class will affect a person's response to stress

   A. I only
   B. I and II
   C. II and III
   D. I, II and III

8. The most prominent model for budgeting within human services organizations includes each of the following categories, EXCEPT

   A. subcontracts
   B. distribution and control
   C. recording and reporting
   D. acquisitions

9. A schizophrenic client who _____ would be considered to be at an increased risk for suicide.

   A. is female
   B. recently discharged from a hospital
   C. is older
   D. has manic symptoms

10. The distinctive quality of antipsychotic drugs is their ability to

    A. calm clients down
    B. elevate dopamine levels
    C. reduce the intensity of delusions and hallucinations
    D. reduce feelings of anxiety

11. In the *Diagnostic and Statistical Manual of Mental Disorders* (DSM-IV), a diagnosis of alcohol dependency
    I. is less severe than a diagnosis of alcohol abuse
    II. requires that the person does not have control over use
    III. requires only that the person regularly drinks to excess
    IV. requires a disruption of socio-economic functionings

    A. I and II
    B. II and IV
    C. III only
    D. III and IV

12. The FACES II is a standardized assessment tool in which members rate their families on the dimensions of

    A. conflict and cohesion
    B. cohesion and adaptability
    C. crisis-orientation and resilience
    D. adaptability and dysfunction

13. Records of client and practitioner behavior that are clinically relevant-including interventions used, client responses to treatments, the evolution of the treatment plan, and any follow-up measures taken are usually referred to as

    A. screening data
    B. progress notes
    C. baseline data
    D. assessments

14. During a session with his clinician, a 68-year-old client, who has confessed to becoming more withdrawn in recent years, describes his life as a "list of vaguely worded goals, all unachieved." Which of Erikson's stages does the client illustrate?

    A. basic trust vs. mistrust
    B. intimacy vs. isolation
    C. integrity vs. despair
    D. generativity vs. stagnation

15. The definition of psychotherapy includes each of the following characteristics, EXCEPT that it

    A. is conducted by a trained professional
    B. relies on medical treatment methods
    C. is based on psychological theory
    D. uses psychological methods

16. _____ explanation of aggression involves the process of catharsis.

    A. The social learning
    B. The frustration-aggression
    C. Freud's
    D. Jung's

17. A diagnosis of dementia requires that a clinician examine a client for

    A. aphasia
    B. alogia
    C. ataxia
    D. encephalitis

18. For Americans older than 65, isolation becomes a problem, especially for

    A. women
    B. ethnic minorities
    C. immigrants
    D. the disabled

19. A practitioner is beginning to suspect that the multiple injuries she has observed over a twelve-week period with an eight-year-old client may be the result of abuse. Because the child's family is from another culture with which the practitioner is admittedly unfamiliar, she decides not to report her suspicions to the authorities, and instead decides to address the abuse as part of her family treatment plan. The practitioner has

    A. broken the law
    B. demonstrated cultural competency
    C. shown the proper respect for the family's right to self-determination
    D. unethically shifted the focus of her intervention

20. Which of the following is a contemporary neo-Freudian form of psychotherapy that ignores unconscious motivation?

    A. Interpersonal psychotherapy
    B. Systematic desensitization
    C. Assertiveness training
    D. Social skills training

21. Human services organizations tend to have a unique set of characteristics that represent significant challenges to manager, including
    I. a mixture of private benefits for services users and public benefits for society
    II. dependence on external constituencies over which members have little control
    III. a determinate set of technologies, with predictable outcomes
    IV. core activities that involve interactive transactions between staff members and users of services

    A. I only
    B. I, II and IV
    C. III and IV
    D. I, II, III and IV

22. Which of the following refers to the elements of a person's position in society that have exceptional significance to her social identity?

    A. Role
    B. Niche markers
    C. Posting
    D. Master status

23. During a client interview, a practitioner notices a consistent discrepancy between what a client is saying and her nonverbal behaviors. Pointing out this discrepancy is an example of a response known as

    A. reflecting feeling
    B. interpretation
    C. clarification
    D. confrontation

24. Systematic desensitization and graded exposure are two techniques that are used to treat

- A. bipolar disorder
- B. depression
- C. phobias
- D. schizophrenia

25. The perspective that attributes a person's place in the society as a function of innate ability is 25.____

    A. labeling theory
    B. cultural transmission
    C. social Darwinism
    D. conflict theory

26. The Gestalt model of therapy views awareness as 26.____

    A. healing
    B. impossible
    C. a schema
    D. an inherently inhibitory process

27. The goal of a projective assessment is to 27.____

    A. evaluate the way a person perceives ambiguous stimuli
    B. predict a person's behavior
    C. compare a person's responses to those of other persons with similar presenting problems or disorders
    D. evaluate the degree to which organic factors influence a person's thinking

28. In structural family therapy, the tool used by the clinician to observe and modify problematic family patterns is the 28.____

    A. family narrative
    B. ecomap
    C. differential diagnosis
    D. enactment

29. Without the expression of warmth in the clinician/client relationship, particular strategies and helping interventions are likely to be 29.____

    A. more in line with the client's expectations that with the practitioner's
    B. helpful only to clients from low-context cultures
    C. technically correct but therapeutically useless
    D. perceived as abstract challenges by the client

30. As described by Robert Merton, typically human responses to anomie include each of the following, EXCEPT 30.____

    A. rebellion
    B. conformity
    C. ritualism
    D. recidivism

31. A clinician in object relations practice encounters a client who was abused as a child. The client believes the only way she can improve her situation is to change herself. The client is likely to solve this object-related dilemma by

    A. openly contemplating the abuse and its implications
    B. unconsciously repressing the abuse
    C. dividing the object into good and bad parts and then internalizing the bad aspects
    D. lying to the clinician about the abuse

32. Clinical scales of the Minnesota Multiphasic Personality Inventory (MMPI) include each of the following, EXCEPT the _____ scale.

    A. marital distress
    B. depression
    C. paranoia
    D. hypochondriasis

33. For legal purposes, a practitioner's "records" include

    A. audiotapes of sessions
    B. case notes
    C. appointment books
    D. intake forms

34. According to the transactional analysis model, each of the following describes the adult ego state, in transactional analysis, EXCEPT

    A. calculating
    B. instructive
    C. unemotional
    D. rational

35. Evidence suggests that the largest source of human service delivery in the area of mental health is the

    A. self-help group
    B. clergy
    C. clinician
    D. inpatient facility

36. One of the most common criticisms of diagnosis is that it

    A. is not a systematic process
    B. follows a medical model
    C. places meaningless labels on clients
    D. is subjective

37. For social workers in managerial positions who engage in program development, it is MOST important to be competent in

    A. guiding consumers in developing self-help programs
    B. organizing data in a way that increases the likelihood of gaining program support
    C. educating clients, professionals, and the community about the design and implementation of social programs

D. coordinating staff efforts in government-authorized service delivery programs

38. During the social work process, clients sometimes attempt to conceal their weaknesses by emphasizing their more desirable traits. This is an ego defense mechanism known as

    A. identification
    B. compensation
    C. denial
    D. rationalization

39. In attempting to paraphrase clients' statements, a practitioner should FIRST

    A. select an appropriate beginning or sentence stem for the paraphrase
    B. identify the emotions that are conveyed by the client's messages
    C. identify any vague or confusing parts to the message
    D. covertly restate the client's message to herself

40. The _____ model of human services organization management places the greatest value on maintaining stable and dependable procedures within the organization.

    A. internal process
    B. human relations
    C. open-system
    D. rational goal

41. Which of the following is NOT one of the major categories covered in a mental status examination?

    A. Executive functioning
    B. Impulse control
    C. Mood and affect
    D. Level of consciousness

42. Multivariate methods of data analysis include
    I. factor analysis
    II. multiple regression
    III. descriptive statistics
    IV. cross-tabulation

    A. I and II
    B. II only
    C. II, III and IV
    D. I, II, III and IV

43. The human personality

    A. appears to be organized into patterns that are observable and measurable to some degree
    B. is a product solely of social and cultural environments, and has no basis in biology
    C. involves unique characteristics, none of which are shared with others
    D. is a term used to refer to the deeper core of a person, rather than superficial aspects

44. In transactional analysis, nonverbal behaviors are often used to assess

   A. hidden and unresolved conflicts and "armoring"
   B. mixed messages
   C. ego states
   D. mistaken logic

45. A practitioner in a small rural community is considering entering a dual relationship with a client–specifically, the practitioner has a flat tire and the client owns the only tire shop in town. The practitioner should
   I. warn the client about the potential risks of adding a business association to their professional relationship
   II. accept a discounted rate for services only if it is offered by the client
   III. consult with colleagues about how to handle the dual relation ships
   IV. not enter into a dual relationship with the client under any cir cumstances

   A. I only
   B. I, II and III
   C. I and III
   D. IV only

46. According to Erving Goffman, the function of stigma is to

   A. reward those who conform
   B. diminish the importance of a behavior
   C. define a behavior as deviant
   D. punish a person for violating a norm

47. The Americans with Disabilities Act addresses each of the following, EXCEPT

   A. access of disabled persons to public and private facilities
   B. disability benefits
   C. hiring
   D. accommodation of disabled persons on the job

48. A clinician is working with a client from an ethnic group that is different from her own, and is unsure about how to address the client or even what term to use to describe his community. The best practice for working with this person would be to

   A. tentatively offer the best guess and see how it is received
   B. ask him what titles or labels are most comfortable for him
   C. adopt the terminology that is most widely used throughout the agency
   D. check the prevailing literature beforehand

49. The knowledge base of direct social work practice in health care settings is typically informed by one or more of the following models, EXCEPT the _____ model.

   A. psychiatric
   B. wellness prevention and promotion
   C. developmental
   D. behavioral

50. Generally speaking, the standard age of consent for psychotherapy is _____ years.

   A. 14
   B. 16
   C. 18
   D. 21

51. Ideologies provide
   I. practical guide for decision-making
   II. a rationale for action
   III. a way to interpret events
   IV. facts'

   A. I and II
   B. I, II and III
   C. II and III
   D. I, II, III and IV

52. The phase in case management during which the case manager must draw upon advanced clinical skills to assist the client in making use of services is known as

   A. service implementation and coordination
   B. monitoring service delivery
   C. assessment and diagnosis
   D. advocacy

53. During an assessment interview, a practitioner asks a client: "Is there anything going on with you physically—the way you eat, smoke, or sleep, for example—that affects or leads to this problem?" The practitioner is trying to identify _____ antecedents to the client's problem.

   A. behavioral
   B. affective
   C. somatic
   D. contextual

54. Ethically, a clinician should

   A. inform a client that a diagnosis can become a permanent part of a file and have ramifications in terms of insurance costs and employment
   B. inform clients that their records are the property of the clinician or the agency
   C. be willing to alter case notes if they will prove damaging to a client's case in court
   D. be available to vulnerable clients 24 hours a day

55. Because of the social stigma attached to mental illness by many Asian Americans, it is important that services be

   A. delivered by traditional helpers within the community
   B. educational and matter-of-fact
   C. presented in language that refers to the spiritual or religious
   D. disguised as social gatherings

56. Clinical social workers so NOT typically consult with   56.____

    A. administrators
    B. other professionals in different fields who are working with the same clients
    C. other mental health professionals about legal issues
    D. other mental health professionals about clinical decisions

57. In clinical practice, "obsessions" refer to   57.____

    A. psychosis
    B. behaviors
    C. ritualistic patterns
    D. thoughts

58. When a client tries to resist compliance with a suggestion or treatment by manipulating the image of the person making the recommendation (the clinician), the client is engaging in   58.____

    A. identity management
    B. altercasting
    C. negotiation
    D. non-negotiation

59. Strategic planning within a human services organization   59.____

    A. must be tailored to the organization's planning culture
    B. by its nature, affects volunteers but does not involve them in the process
    C. is an undertaking limited to top management
    D. generally requires more time than money

60. In Maslow's model, high levels of a fear of success are correlated with high   60.____

    A. affective habituation
    B. fear of failure
    C. extrinsic motivation
    D. self-esteem

61. A popular assessment tool for determining the degree of a person's intent to harm him/herself divide indicators into Level 1 through Level 4, with Level 4 being the most urgent and probably requiring hospitalization. Which of the following would be considered a Level 4 indicator?   61.____

    A. Occasional suicidal ideation, but without behavioral indicators of intent
    B. An acute episode of mental health illness requiring new medication
    C. A moderate impairment in social and occupational functioning
    D. An inability to control of the stability of one's behavior, with or without a supportive social environment

62. Because social workers are increasingly called upon to coordinate services on behalf of clients, human service organizations are encouraged to develop   62.____

    A. case management services
    B. horizontal affiliations

C. systems-of-care models
D. vertical integration

63. In Gestalt therapy, _____ occurs when a client attributes a characteristic to the outside world that truly belongs to himself.

    A. confluence
    B. retroflection
    C. projection
    D. deflection

64. When working with a client who is encountering serious economic need, the most valuable task a practitioner can perform is to

    A. help the client find a paying job
    B. verify that the client is deserving of benefits
    C. give accurate information about benefits and ensure entitlement
    D. advocate and obtain benefits for the client

65. Which of the following is NOT a component of the therapeutic relationship?

    A. Teaching/instructing
    B. Transference/countertransference
    C. Therapeutic alliance
    D. Collaboration

66. The ethical principle of _____ refers to a practitioner's acceptance of the responsibility to promote what is good for others.

    A. nonmaleficence
    B. justice
    C. beneficence
    D. autonomy

67. According to Kohlberg's theory of moral development, a child who is greatly concerned about pleasing his parents and teachers is at the _____ level of development.

    A. conventional
    B. pre-moral
    C. pre-conventional
    D. post-moral

68. The "Socratic method" is proposed by some as a technique for social work supervision. Which of the following is NOT an element of the Socratic method?

    A. Systematic questioning
    B. Inductive reasoning
    C. Utilitarian ethics
    D. Universal definitions

69. Which of the following is NOT one of the basic concepts of psychosocial therapy?

    A. Recognition of the unconscious
    B. Recognition of the nature of pathology

C. A skeptical perception of the human potential
D. Focusing on everyday living

70. A client has been released from an inpatient program for the mentally ill, but must be maintained with medication and talk therapy. Most likely, the client will make use of

   A. the local mental health center
   B. the hospital emergency room
   C. a private clinician
   D. a psychiatric nurse practitioner

71. Research suggests that homosexuality is best understood in terms of

   A. intrapsychic disposition
   B. identity formation
   C. specific genetic factors
   D. childhood sexual experience

72. The increased demand for social workers to do formal diagnosis of mental disorders has been influenced by several factors. Which of the following is NOT one of these factors?

   A. Nearly half of all Americans will have a significant mental illness in their lifetimes.
   B. Nonmedical professionals are increasingly required to serve the mentally ill as mental health services are decreased.
   C. Payers for services require a diagnosis before authorizing or reimbursing for mental health services.
   D. Generally, knowledge of the *DSM-IV* is limited to clinical professionals.

73. Which of the following is NOT an advantage associated with private practice social work?

   A. Greater consumer choice among service providers
   B. More manageable paperwork and meeting requirements
   C. Fewer incidences of conflict-of-interest situations
   D. Fewer organizational constraints

74. The Bowen family systems theory centers on the counterbalancing life forces of

   A. togetherness and individuality
   B. nature and nurturance
   C. cohesiveness and adaptability
   D. conflict and harmony

75. A clinician is working with a family in conflict. To the mother, the conflict is about the quality of interactions within the family and managing interpersonal tension and hostility. In other words, the mother sees it as a(n) _____ conflict.

   A. pseudo-
   B. ego
   C. expressive
   D. instrumental

KEY (CORRECT ANSWERS)

1. A	16. C	31. C	46. C	61. D
2. A	17. B	32. A	47. B	62. B
3. A	18. A	33. D	48. B	63. C
4. B	19. A	34. B	49. D	64. C
5. D	20. A	35. A	50. C	65. A
6. D	21. B	36. C	51. C	66. C
7. D	22. D	37. B	52. A	67. A
8. A	23. D	38. B	53. C	68. C
9. B	24. C	39. D	54. A	69. C
10. C	25. C	40. A	55. B	70. A
11. B	26. A	41. A	56. C	71. B
12. B	27. A	42. A	57. D	72. D
13. B	28. D	43. A	58. A	73. C
14. C	29. C	44. C	59. A	74. A
15. B	30. D	45. C	60. D	75. C

EXAMINATION SECTION
TEST 1

DIRECTIONS: Each question or incomplete statement is followed by several suggested answers or completions. Select the one the BEST answers the question or completes the statement. *PRINT THE LETTER OF THE CORRECT ANSWER IN THE SPACE AT THE RIGHT.*

1. At the outset of treatment, a client tells the social worker that she must promise never to involuntarily hospitalize her, no matter how depressed or suicidal she may seem. In formulating a response to this request, the social worker should use the underlying ethical principle of

    A. the need to do whatever is necessary to maintain a therapeutic relationship with a client
    B. never making a promise that is in conflict with legal and ethical requirements
    C. the client"s right to self-determination
    D. the understanding that the client has legitimate, defensible reasons for making this request

1.____

2. For a Gestalt therapist, a primary goal of treatment is to help the client

    A. integrate the present with his/her past and future
    B. develop a "success identity"
    C. integrate the functioning of his/her mind and body
    D. incorporate the external into the internal

2.____

3. What is the term for a social system that is part of a larger system and made up of several smaller systems?

    A. Focal system
    B. Schema
    C. Holon
    D. Gemeinschaft

3.____

4. The most commonly occurring psychological disorders are _____ disorders.

    A. Dissociative
    B. Psychosexual
    C. Mood
    D. Somatoform

4.____

5. In the early stages of problem-solving communication training with a family, the practitioner should FIRST assess

    A. family cognitions about communication/arguments
    B. the history of the problem
    C. family assets
    D. specific skill deficits

5.____

6. An intern at an agency for the chronically mentally ill meets with a 24-year-old client who has been referred by his family doctor. The primary basis for this referral is the client's isolation from peers and general lack of social skills. In many ways, the client reminds the intern of the quiet, studious friends she made in graduate school, who had very little time to socialize because of studies and part-time jobs. The client tells the intern he doesn't think he belongs in this place, and she silently agrees, though her supervisor and more experienced workers seem to believe that this is the right place for him. In her assessment of this client's situation, the intern has relied on the _____ heuristic.

   A. theoretical
   B. schematic
   C. availability
   D. representativeness

7. Which of the following types of feminism proposes that men and women have different values due to the structure of sex and gender roles in society?

   A. socialist
   B. reactionary
   C. radical
   D. liberal

8. The most significant problem with establishing "comparable worth" at an agency is that

   A. males and females may use different strategies to reach the same decision or solution
   B. the job evaluation techniques themselves may be gender-biased
   C. job evaluation techniques are not as useful for very complex jobs
   D. it is difficult to compare achievement across different domains

9. A social worker decides that solution-focused therapy is the most appropriate approach for a family that has come to see her about financial problems. The social worker's FIRST intervention would be to

   A. discuss time constraints and make sure the family knows the intervention will be brief
   B. get a clear picture of how the system functions
   C. get a history of the origins of the symptoms
   D. discuss how things would be for the family if the problem was already solved

10. Social service agencies, in attempting to make a certain program more efficient and useful, may sometimes get lost in pursuing a prescribed means of service delivery at the expense of accomplishing program goals. This is known as

    A. output loss
    B. goal displacement
    C. bounded rationality
    D. organizational shaping

11. According to Elkind, the most significant descriptor of adolescent thought is

    A. concrete
    B. irrational

C. egocentric
D. moralistic

12. In a program evaluation, which type of data is concerned primarily with whether or not the program goals are being met?   12._____

    A. throughput
    B. process
    C. product
    D. input

13. Which of the following problems or disorders is LEAST likely to be changed through psychotherapy?   13._____

    A. Anorexia nervosa
    B. Conduct disorder
    C. Antisocial personality disorder
    D. Compulsive behavior

14. The record-keeping requirements at a typical social services agency require the completion of a review treatment plan at an interval no longer than   14._____

    A. after every client contact
    B. weekly
    C. every 30 days
    D. every 90 days

15. For social workers, it is usually most appropriate to view a woman's separation from an abusive husband as   15._____

    A. a series of losses which initiates a mourning process
    B. a solution that must be accomplished as quickly as possible
    C. a partial process at best if children are involved
    D. the best of all possible solutions to the problem of domestic abuse

16. Formative policy research at social services agencies   16._____

    A. is usually conducted in response to legislative mandates
    B. focuses on policy development rather than on its impact on clients and agencies
    C. identifies social policy as the independent variable
    D. is based entirely on output goals

17. Abusive families are most often characterized by   17._____

    A. openness and affection
    B. rigid boundaries and clear roles
    C. a strong parental subsystem
    D. denial and enmeshed boundaries

18. The principal assessment tool for clinicians working from the intergenerational perspective on the family is the   18._____

    A. life cycle matrix
    B. social history

C. genogram
D. ecomap

19. The "output goals" of a social service program are MOST likely to include

    A. specified ratings of services by clients on a standardized scale
    B. observable effects on a given community or clientele
    C. the number of units of service provided
    D. the number of clients served

20. A 35-year-old client, a high school teacher, reports to a practitioner at an outpatient clinic and reports the following incident: he, a high school teacher, was in the middle of a lesson during a class period that had been particularly difficult for him over the past several months, because the class was large and often noisy. During the middle of today's lesson, the client suddenly began to sweat profusely and his heart started to race. He continued with the lesson but soon felt dizzy and fearful that he was about to die. The feeling was so overwhelming that he had to leave the class unattended and retreat to the teacher's lounge, where he was found sitting alone and trembling. The client's physician has found no evidence of medical problems. The most likely DSM-IV diagnosis for this client would be

    A. panic disorder
    B. posttraumatic stress disorder
    C. dissociative disorder
    D. social phobia

21. Which of the following statements reveals a client with a formal-operational emotional orientation?

    A. I'm so sad right now that my stomach hurts. I haven't eaten all day.
    B. I suppose there are two different ways of looking at this. On one hand, these arguments are really painful, but I know I have to set limits for my son and it's part of my role as a parent. I know he needs to find his own space, but his decisions are sometimes questionable.
    C. I feel great about the new relationship I'm in. I think I've met the perfect man.
    D. As I think about it, I feel bad because it seems as if we've been arguing a lot lately. It's almost a ritual--every time I get ready to leave the house, an argument starts.

22. The purpose of the mental status examination in psychotherapy is

    A. personality testing
    B. to make a diagnosis
    C. reality testing
    D. to determine the severity of psychotic symptoms

23. Which of the following interviewing skills is most useful for discovering the deeply held thoughts and feelings underlying the client's experience?

    A. Confrontation
    B. Open-ended questioning
    C. Focusing
    D. Reflection of meaning

24. A client who has a history of hypomanic and major depressive episodes would have a diagnosis of

   A. Hypomanic disorder
   B. Cyclothymic disorder
   C. Bipolar I disorder
   D. Bipolar II disorder

25. Which of the following theoretical frameworks establishes equity and distributive justice as its ideal ends of development

   A. Behavioral/social exchange
   B. Ego psychology
   C. Symbolic interactionism
   D. Structural functionalism

26. A "Theory X" manager in an organization is likely to

   A. adopt a team approach to problem-solving
   B. use tangible rewards and sanctions to shape employee behavior
   C. work to set up and maintain a work environment that promotes growth and creativity
   D. assume that subordinates want to work toward organization goal attainment

27. Which of the following is generally NOT recommended as part of an intervention with a Native American client who follows older traditions?

   A. Serving food
   B. Emphasizing the past
   C. Giving gifts
   D. Including friends and family

28. The process of transforming a piece of legislation into a specific program or policy, by means of identifying specific guidelines and operating procedures to be used in administering the program, is known as

   A. rationalization
   B. promulgation
   C. consignment
   D. confederation

29. Which of the following is NOT an ego-defense mechanism?

   A. Regression
   B. Reality testing
   C. Displacement
   D. Sublimation

30. Which of the following is probably the MOST appropriate candidate for an intensive, heterogeneous outpatient therapy group?

   A. A paranoid person
   B. A person with bipolar II disorder

C. An alcoholic or drug addict
D. A person with brain damage

31. In removing intracultural barriers to achievement for clients of color, interventions should be aimed at

    A. active encouragement of family involvement
    B. recognition and affirmation of client system strengths
    C. changes in institutional policies, practices, and administration
    D. improved educational/vocational opportunities through greater teacher/employer awareness of diversity, history and customs

32. Which of the following is a means-tested program?

    A. Medicare
    B. Social Security
    C. Public education
    D. Police protection

33. One of the greatest risks associated with too little self-disclosure in the group therapy process is

    A. severely limited reality testing
    B. low group cohesiveness
    C. yielding an inappropriate amount of member control
    D. severe dependence

34. In behavioral therapy, the systematic desensitization process, usually performed by dis-associating a neutral stimulus from a situation that has created fear or anxiety, is also known as

    A. extinction
    B. aversion therapy
    C. overcorrection
    D. counterconditioning

35. The primary function of reflecting feelings during a client interview is to

    A. help the client sort out mixed or ambivalent feelings
    B. grounding the worker and client in concrete experience
    C. bring out additional details of the client's emotional world
    D. make implicit, sometimes hidden emotions clear to the client

36. Which of the following is NOT a privileged relationship during the prosecution of child abuse?

    A. Priest-confessor
    B. Lawyer-client
    C. Psychotherapist-patient
    D. Physician-patient

37. According to ego psychology, the ego

A. mediates between erotic energies and superego constraints
B. is a drive for pleasure
C. imposes a set of rules to control unbridled pleasure-seeking
D. offers ideals for the individual to strive for

38. Which of the following statements reveals a discrepancy that is external to the speaker?

    A. I don't mind talking about that at all.
    B. I wanted to go to business school, but my grades weren't good enough.
    C. My mother is a saint, but she doesn't respect me.
    D. This is a nice office. It's too bad it's in this neighborhood.

39. During an intake interview for a woman who has committed a violent crime, the clinician notes that whenever the woman talks of the act she does so without any emotion—anger, shame, guilt, or sadness—whatsoever. From the psychoanalytic perspective, the woman is using the defense mechanism of

    A. isolation
    B. fantasy formation
    C. repression
    D. rationalization

40. A humanist, looking at an individual's misbehavior, would conclude that a person who acts badly is

    A. suffering from a kind of illness
    B. experiencing a detachment from her moral compass
    C. willfully disregarding the norms which characterize her community
    D. reacting to the deprivation of her basic needs

41. Clinicians in private practice are generally paid for
    I. direct services to clients
    II. number of hours on the job
    III. indirect services

    A. I only
    B. I and II
    C. II only
    D. I, II and III

42. A clinician is meeting with a transactional group for the first time and works intensely at studying the members and their transactions. In the early stages of work with this group, the clinician's greatest challenge is likely to be

    A. defusing conflict between members
    B. identifying the self-talk or cognitions that lie behind a transaction
    C. heading off the tendency toward subgroupings
    D. determining which ego state a transaction comes from

43. A social worker has been seeing a client for several months and has developed a good working relationship. The client loses her job and cannot afford to pay for therapy. Under the social worker's professional code and value system, the BEST option in this case would be to

A. refer the client to low-cost therapy from another provider
B. allow the client to divert payments until she gets another job
C. provide the therapy free of charge until the client can find employment
D. reduce the fee for this client and/or offer her shorter sessions

44. "Acceptance" in the therapeutic relationship mean that the practitioner
   I. separates the client from her behavior
   II. indicates approval of the client's behavior
   III. expresses sympathy for the client
   IV. demonstrates tolerance for client's behavior

   A. I only
   B. I and II
   C. II, III and IV
   D. I, II, III and IV

45. According to Papernow, most people first enter a stepfamily with
   A. a clear awareness of the reality of their situation
   B. a growing sense of realistic intimacy with new family members
   C. the fantasy that they will rescue the new partner and any children from the deficiencies of a previous marriage
   D. a feeling of resentment toward new family members who place new demands on their time, money, and other resources

46. An ideal therapeutic relationship in social work is one that
   A. connects the client with the proper support services
   B. allows and helps the client's capacity to work out his own issues
   C. is an ongoing source of support
   D. the client can rely upon as a problem-solving tool

47. Which of the following is NOT characteristic of a clinician who is conducting reality therapy with a client?
   A. Viewing mental illness labels as destructive
   B. Focusing on behavior rather than feelings
   C. Discouraging value judgements
   D. Not offering sympathy

48. In general, a DSM-IV diagnosis of a specific disorder includes a criterion of
   A. no medical involvement
   B. a clinically significant impairment or distress in a social or occupational area
   C. an identifiable etiology
   D. distress that has exceeded a period of 8 weeks

49. A client interview is interrupted by a long silence that makes the social worker uncomfortable. The FIRST thing the social worker should do is
   A. inform the client that of his/her (the worker's) discomfort and observe the client's reaction
   B. restate the last words spoken by the client

C. say, "I wonder why you're so quiet"
D. study the client to see if he/she appears comfortable with the silence

50. A social worker is seeing a Latino family that immigrated to the United States several years ago. The social worker is not Latino. The family often arrive late for their sessions, causing some scheduling problems—and mild annoyance—for the social worker. The best way for the social worker to handle this would be to

   A. be aware that time may be perceived differently in their culture and invite them to discuss what being late means to them
   B. understand that being late is probably an expression of cultural resistance to disclosing family issues
   C. be aware that time may be perceived differently in their culture, and take a more flexible approach to beginning scheduled sessions
   D. consider referring the family to a Hispanic therapist

51. The foundation of clinical supervisory techniques—and the focus of supervision—is/are typically

   A. case material
   B. educational assessment
   C. long-term practitioner development goals
   D. practitioner attitudes and values

52. A practitioner grew up as the oldest child of alcoholic parents, and was often placed in the role of parent to his three younger siblings. In order to establish solid therapeutic relationships with his clients, the most important challenge this practitioner will probably face is

   A. being able to trust that clients have the capacity to work through their problems
   B. being able to see clearly the problems faced by alcoholic clients
   C. the risk that he will impose an undue level of responsibility on clients early in the intervention process
   D. a lack of faith in his ability to help clients change

53. A married couple and their two teenage sons see a clinician for the first time for help with what they view as an unhealthy spirit of competition between the two boys. The clinician observes the family's interactions and characterizes them as high-functioning and relatively flexible. Which of the following models of intervention is probably MOST appropriate for this family?

   A. Structural-functional
   B. Strategic
   C. Experiential
   D. Solution-focused

54. According to the lifespan perspective of human development and behavior, development is NOT

   A. contextual
   B. historically embedded
   C. unidirectional
   D. lifelong

55. The sole motivation for a client's feigning illness in factitious disorder is to

    A. obtain prescription drugs
    B. draw attention away from his/her psychological problems
    C. assume a sick role.
    D. escape material and everyday responsibilities

56. In school, an 8-year-old boy has considerably impaired social interactions with other children, along with severely impaired language skills. The boy also pulls at his hair constantly, sometimes leaving ragged bald patches, and often bites himself, leaving wounds and scars that his parents have made the primary concern for treatment. Appropriate diagnoses for this boy include
    I. Asperger's disorder
    II. Stereotypic movement disorder
    III. Autism
    IV. Mental retardation

    A. I and II
    B. II and III
    C. III only
    D. IV only

57. In order to ensure a margin of error no greater than 5%, what is the size of the sample required to represent a population of 10,000?

    A. 108
    B. 370
    C. 1235
    D. 9,500

58. Social learning theory recognizes each of the following as a key factor in human development, EXCEPT

    A. cognition
    B. heredity
    C. behavior
    D. environment

59. According to Annon, clients in sex therapy need interventions at very specific levels. The first of these levels is

    A. specific suggestions
    B. intensive therapy
    C. limited information
    D. permission

60. Which of the following is named as the etiological agent for adjustment disorder?

    A. Depressed mood
    B. Stress
    C. Sudden trauma
    D. Organic chemistry imbalance

61. Social workers generally observe several distinct characteristics in the life cycle of poor African-American families. Which of the following is NOT one of these?

    A. Households that are frequently female-headed and isolated from the community
    B. A scarceness of resources that compels a reliance on government institutions
    C. A truncated life cycle with less time to resolve developmental tasks
    D. A life cycle punctuated by numerous unpredictable life events

62. A 50-year-old client has been significantly depressed for more than a year. For the past two months, the client has been convinced that he has developed lung cancer. The most appropriate DSM-IV diagnosis for the client would be

    A. conversion disorder
    B. major depressive episode
    C. somatoform disorder, not otherwise specified
    D. hypochondriasis

63. Persuasive arguments for flexible-rate fee schedules include
    I. Services more accessible to disadvantaged clients
    II. Endorsements of insurers and other third-party organizations
    III. No means testing
    IV. Consistency with consumer protection laws

    A. I only
    B. I and III
    C. I, II and IV
    D. I, II, III and IV

64. The psychoanalytical perspective views _____ as the most powerful and pervasive defense mechanism.

    A. projection
    B. rationalization
    C. repression
    D. denial

65. Which of the following approaches to client interviewing is MOST likely to make use of interpretation or refraining?

    A. Psychodynamic
    B. Solution-focused
    C. Client-centered
    D. Behavioral

66. When a clinician is on a provider panel for a managed health care company, he or she:

    A. is guaranteed a certain number of referrals from this company per year.
    B. has met the qualifications for company, and has no guarantee of referrals.
    C. agree to see any referral within your specialty.
    D. will receive a full fee from the company when he/she sees a client

67. When a therapeutic relationship is functioning on the cognitive level, the therapist will probably engage in each of the following processes, EXCEPT

A. highlighting inconsistencies
B. reassuring
C. refraining
D. asking key questions

68. Several days after losing her job, a woman becomes so depressed that she is unable to get out of bed until well into the afternoon, and rarely leaves her home. By the time she reports to a practitioner for treatment, she has been depressed and had trouble sleeping for about 4 months. The most appropriate DSM-IV diagnosis for this client is

    A. major depressive episode
    B. dysthmic disorder
    C. adjustment disorder with depressed mood
    D. depressive disorder, not otherwise specified

69. The NASW code's prohibition of dual relationships is most likely to be challenged by social workers who

    A. are part of an interdisciplinary team
    B. live and work in rural areas
    C. are involved in direct practice
    D. perform supervisory functions

70. Many practitioners make use of informal assessment instruments such as self-reporting questionnaires, indexes, and profiles. The main risk associated with these instruments as assessment tools is that they

    A. often put the client on the defensive
    B. may place too much emphasis on relatively unimportant details
    C. suggest that the practitioner may be lazy or incompetent
    D. often provoke client dissembling

71. The term "active listening" mostly refers to a person's ability to

    A. indicate with numerous physical cues that he/she is listening
    B. take an active role in determining which information is provided by the client
    C. concentrate on what is being said
    D. both listen to the client and accomplish other meaningful tasks at the same time

72. Which of the following is a latent function of the family unit?

    A. Economic production
    B. Socialization of children
    C. Provision of emotional support to members
    D. Contribution to institutional arrangements

73. Current knowledge of post-traumatic stress disorder (PTSD) indicates that if the initial stage of anxiety and obsession with the trauma persist for longer than _____, the patient then enters stage 2, or acute PTSD.

    A. 5-10 days
    B. 4-6 weeks
    C. 8-12 weeks
    D. 3-6 months

74. After making contact with a person in crisis and establishing a relationship, a clinician faces the task of examining the dimensions of the problem, in order to define it. Which of the following is NOT typically a task of this phase of crisis intervention?

    A. Exploring alternatives
    B. Assessing the dangerousness or lethality of the situation
    C. Identifying the precipitating event that led to the crisis
    D. Detailing a client's previous coping methods

75. In general, administrative evaluation at a social services agency differs from practice evaluation in that administrative evaluation is

    A. external to the supervisory relationship
    B. continuous
    C. basically self-contained
    D. specific

KEY (CORRECT ANSWERS)

1. B	16. B	31. A	46. B	61. A
2. C	17. D	32. A	47. C	62. B
3. C	18. C	33. A	48. B	63. A
4. C	19. C	34. D	49. D	64. C
5. D	20. A	35. D	50. A	65. A
6. D	21. D	36. D	51. A	66. B
7. A	22. C	37. A	52. A	67. B
8. B	23. D	38. B	53. D	68. C
9. D	24. D	39. A	54. C	69. B
10. B	25. A	40. D	55. C	70. B
11. C	26. B	41. A	56. B	71. C
12. C	27. B	42. D	57. B	72. D
13. C	28. B	43. D	58. B	73. B
14. D	29. B	44. A	59. D	74. A
15. A	30. B	45. C	60. B	75. A

TEST 2

DIRECTIONS: Each question or incomplete statement is followed by several suggested answers or completions. Select the one the BEST answers the question or completes the statement. *PRINT THE LETTER OF THE CORRECT ANSWER IN THE SPACE AT THE RIGHT.*

1. An 18-year-old girl is brought into a hospital emergency room by her family, who reported that she experienced sudden blindness. She had been arguing with her mother about why her mother was so much stricter with her than her father, when her mother suddenly blurted out that she and the father were seeking a divorce. The girl continued to argue for several minutes but then suddenly stopped and announced that she couldn't see anything. An examination reveals no neurological deficits. The client should most likely receive a diagnosis of   1.____

    A. conversion disorder
    B. somatoform disorder, not otherwise specified
    C. dissociative disorder
    D. hypochondriasis

2. An important difference between brief psychotherapy and crisis intervention is that   2.____

    A. brief therapy focuses on pathology
    B. crisis intervention focuses on specific issues
    C. brief therapy focuses on specific issues
    D. crisis intervention focuses on pathology

3. During an evaluation session in which the supervisor and practitioner are discussing the progress of the practitioner's current caseload, the practitioner admits to being unhappy with the overall progress of his clients, but attributes it to problems he has been experiencing because of excessive pressure placed on him by the supervisor. At this point in the evaluation, the supervisor should   3.____

    A. reassure the practitioner that whatever pressures have been placed on him have been for the benefit of his professional development
    B. apologize and suggest that the practitioner think of ways in which the supervisory relationship can be made more comfortable
    C. try to steer the focus of the discussion toward client progress
    D. remind the practitioner that he is the one ultimately responsible for handling the pressures that come with social work practice

4. In the time series design of program evaluation, the primary threat to internal validity is   4.____

    A. history
    B. selection
    C. testing
    D. regression to the mean

5. A client tells her clinician that members of an international espionage ring are after her to torture her and find out what she knows. She suspects that there are higher forces at work behind her persecution, but she can't tell the clinician what these forces are. Her beliefs have interfered with her work and social life for more than a year. The most appropriate diagnosis for this client is   5.____

A. psychotic disorder, not otherwise specified
B. schizophrenia, paranoid type
C. delusional disorder
D. schizoaffective disorder

6. Which of the following factors is NOT typically associated with ethnicity?

   A. Language
   B. Physical type
   C. Economic status
   D. Culture

7. A 19-year-old male client's father calls the social worker and requests information about his son's treatment. In this situation, the social worker should

   A. confirm that the son is in treatment but give no other information
   B. tell the father about his son's progress but not reveal any specifics
   C. set up a conjoint therapy session
   D. refuse to reveal any information

8. In an approach-avoidance conflict, as the person nears the goal,

   A. attraction and aversion both increase
   B. attraction and aversion both decrease
   C. attraction increases and aversion decreases
   D. atraction decreases and aversion increases

9. According the Herzberg's model of employee motivation, which of the following is a "hygiene" factor?

   A. Potential for growth
   B. Interesting, challenging work
   C. Freedom
   D. Salary

10. A disturbance of consciousness accompanied by some changes in cognition is the distinguishing feature of

    A. schizophrenia
    B. dementia
    C. delusion
    D. delirium

11. Public and private social service agencies generally differ in each of the following ways, EXCEPT

    A. practitioner certification requirements
    B. philosophy of service
    C. service eligibility requirements
    D. scope of services

12. Consistently, an employee is observed to be extremely friendly toward his boss, whom he really despises. From a Freudian perspective, the employee is exhibiting

A. reaction formation
B. isolation of affect
C. projection
D. sublimation

13. The purpose of an explanatory design for practice evaluation is to

    A. determine the causes of specific client behaviors
    B. examine and reflect on the intervention being used
    C. examine the impact of the intervention on the target behavior
    D. monitor client progress

14. Which of the following neurotransmitters or neuropeptides is generally deficient in clients with anorexia nervosa?

    A. Serotonin
    B. Cholecystokinin
    C. Dopamine
    D. Neuropeptide Y

15. Services that are provided to clients without a means test are described as

    A. pro-rated
    B. contributory
    C. eclectic
    D. universal

16. In a family intervention formed in the strategic model, a clinician who uses a "restraining strategy" will begin the intervention by

    A. warning the family of the danger of continuing its symptomatic behavior
    B. directing the family to stop its symptomatic behavior
    C. warning the family of the negative consequences of behavioral change
    D. instructing the family to engage in only nonsymptomatic behavior

17. The primary disadvantage associated with purchase-of-service agreements in social services is

    A. higher agency costs
    B. further fragmentation of the social service system
    C. decreased innovation in problem-solving
    D. diminished scope of services

18. Roles in the alcoholic family system have been labeled by Wegscheider and others. Typically, the youngest child in an alcoholic family occupies the role of

    A. mascot
    B. lost child
    C. hero
    D. scapegoat

19. The primary purpose for using confrontation in a client interview is to

A. teach mediation and conflict resolution skills
B. activate the client's potential for change
C. identify mixed messages in behaviors and thoughts or feelings
D. identify the processes the client uses to make changes

20. A clinician at a mental health clinic decides to work from the perspective of Rogers client-centered therapy. If the counselor goes against the policy of the clinic and decides to reject the use of diagnosis, it will be because from the person-centered perspective,

    A. the validity of diagnostic labels has not been empirically demonstrated
    B. diagnosis forces the therapist, rather than the client, to assume the expert role
    C. labeling results in an incongruence between self and experience
    D. labeling discourages the process of in-depth interpretation of the client's behavior

21. Which of the following interventions is one of the most frequently used therapies in the treatment of phobias?

    A. Exposure therapy
    B. Object relations
    C. Extinction
    D. Social skills training

22. Which of the following statements about therapeutic group composition is generally FALSE?

    A. Task groups that are homogeneous are less productive and cohesive than heterogeneous groups.
    B. Homogeneous groups of task-oriented, high-structure, impersonal people function as effective, change-producing human relations groups.
    C. Heterogeneous encounter groups are more effective in producing greater self-actualization of members.
    D. Homogeneous groups of person-oriented, low-structure people do not generally function as effective human relations groups.

23. When behaviors are known and categorized prior to an observation, and the intention is to collect quantitative data, the method of choice is

    A. structured observation
    B. the Likert scale
    C. participant observation
    D. structured interview

24. A client who was abused as a child, whenever speaking of her parents, tends to cast the father in the most negative light possible, describing his as evil and every encounter with him as a disaster. Of her mother, however, she has only the most glowing praise, often referring to her as a saint. From a psychodynamic perspective, the client is using the defense mechanism known as

    A. reaction formation
    B. primitive idealization
    C. projection
    D. splitting

25. In the transactional analysis model of social intercourse, the safest type of interaction is   25.____

    A. a game
    B. intimate
    C. ritualistic
    D. a pastime

26. Dissociative amnesia is usually   26.____
    I. related to the inability to recall important personal information
    II. retrograde
    III. selective
    IV. accompanied by apraxia

    A. I and II
    B. II and III
    C. I, II and III
    D. II, III and IV

27. People often have difficulty receiving information because of an impairment or other barrier. Which of these will probably NOT help such a person to better understand a message?   27.____

    A. Repeating the message
    B. Changing the sequence of the message
    C. Changing the form in which the message is transmitted
    D. Using an interpreter

28. A social worker is working with an autistic child who is mute. The major goal of intervention is the development of language. The social worker begins by rewarding the child with food whenever he vocalizes. The social worker then begins to reward the child only when his vocalizations occur within ten seconds of the social worker's vocalization, then only if the child's vocalizations resemble the social worker's, and so on, until the child's vocalizations are identical to those of the social worker. The technique is used until the child is eventually using words and sentences. This technique is known as: 28.____

    A. counterconditioning
    B. chaining
    C. shaping
    D. prompting

29. Potential limitations on confidentiality should be discussed with a client   29.____

    A. when the social worker determines it to be appropriate
    B. at the onset of the professional relationship
    C. at the onset of the professional relationship and thereafter as needed
    D. and documented in writing as soon as possible

30. Other than describing a client's problem in a way that imposes meaning on a large amount of information, the primary cognitive task of assessment is to   30.____

    A. establish client comfort with the therapeutic plan
    B. selectively focus on the information that will be most useful to the treatment planning process

C. infer whether a specific groups of facts or observations belongs to a larger known category of problems
D. identify the client's feelings of concern

31. The status of the practitioner/client therapeutic relationship is seen as an important aspect of therapy in each of the following models, EXCEPT

   A. ecosystems
   B. psychoanalysis
   C. client-centered
   D. behavioral

32. Among the skills important to effective communication with clients, the most sophisticated and complex is/are

   A. encouraging, paraphrasing, and summarization
   B. confrontation
   C. influencing skills
   D. open and closed questions

33. The _____ approach to human behavior attempts to describe behaviors in ways that allow for generalization across cultures.

   A. etic
   B. holistic
   C. emic
   D. pluralist

34. The most widely-used bivariate statistical measure in social work is

   A. regression analysis
   B. cross-tabulation
   C. slope/drift
   D. correlation

35. Which of the following statements is most abstract?

   A. Last night my mother told me I was a disappointment.
   B. I cry all day long. I can't eat.
   C. My daughter just sent me a letter.
   D. My family is very close.

36. Each of the following is viewed by clinicians as an important element of the therapeutic relationship, EXCEPT

   A. confidentiality
   B. dependability
   C. sympathy
   D. confidence

37. The _____ theory of human development holds that human behavior is strongly influenced by biology, is tied to evolution, and is characterized by critical and sensitive periods.

A. Biosocial
B. Ecological
C. Social learning
D. Ethological

38. The residual model of social welfare
    I. is developed piecemeal as a reaction to the development of social problems, rather than in anticipation of them
    II. views government as the last line of defense for people experiencing problems
    III. views family and work as the first line of defense
    IV. expects individuals to have trouble meeting the needs of modern living

    A. I only
    B. I and II
    C. I, II, and III
    D. I, II, III and IV

39. One of the helping models for multiproblem families is the Multiple-Impact Family-Therapy (MIFT) model, which includes each of the following elements, EXCEPT

    A. a long-term, client-centered approach
    B. an extended session format
    C. use of a team of professionals who work directly with the family
    D. immediate response to a request for service

40. Which of the following has NOT been a factor in the recent growth of the for-profit sector of social services in the United States?

    A. The ability of for-profit agencies to offer more stable financial sources of income than other investments
    B. The historical ability of private-sector solutions to solve problems that the government has failed to solve
    C. The growing complexity and number of problems experienced by the disadvantaged
    D. The existence of for-profit opportunities outside of public health insurance benefits

41. Which of the following is NOT typically a factor used by private clinicians to determine fees for clients?

    A. The amount charged by local psychiatrists of equal experience
    B. What the worker thinks will be the most attractive rate to the clientele she hopes to attract
    C. What third-party financing organizations identify as reasonable and customary charges
    D. How much other helping professionals charge for such services

42. Erikson's final stage of psychosocial development, experienced during late adulthood, is

    A. industry vs. inferiority
    B. generativity vs. stagnation
    C. intimacy vs. isolation
    D. integrity vs. despair

43. Which of the following approaches to social services policymaking assess the process of moving from the identification of a social problem to implementing a policy and assessing the impact the policy has on the original problem?

    A. Prescriptive
    B. Investment
    C. Cause and consequences
    D. Formative

44. Research suggests that negative emotional effects from divorce are LEAST likely to impact

    A. women who do not remarry
    B. women who remarry
    C. men who do not remarry
    D. men who remarry

45. Closed questions typically do NOT begin with the word

    A. how
    B. is
    C. do
    D. are

46. In order to receive a diagnosis of acute stress disorder that conforms to DSM-IV standards, a client's symptoms must occur within _____ of a traumatic event.

    A. 5 days
    B. 4 weeks
    C. 3 months
    D. 6 months

47. Which of the following types of programs is typically administered exclusively at the county level?

    A. Food stamps
    B. AFDC
    C. Medical assistance
    D. General assistance

48. In the clinical supervision of a social work practitioner, a good general policy is to

    A. begin with technical skill learning and then move to theoretical and perspective learning
    B. begin with perspective learning and then move to technical skill learning
    C. teach a supervisee technical skills and theory simultaneously
    D. avoid both technical skills and theory and instead focus on smaller, concrete problems faced by the practitioner

49. Approximately what percentage of child maltreatment/abuse cases involve sexual abuse?

    A. 5   B. 10   C. 30   D. 50

50. In the United States, most social policy is formulated

    A. by individual agency boards
    B. in a de facto manner by the direct practice of social workers
    C. through legislation
    D. by state boards

51. Which of the following terms is used to describe memory loss that has a purely psychological cause?

    A. Anterograde
    B. Organic
    C. Retrograde
    D. Inorganic

52. Which of the following statements reveals a client with a sensorimotor emotional orientation?

    A. A lot of us are angry. I know my boss is busy, but his forgetting to sign the payroll is going to cost some of us our weekend plans.
    B. I'm feeling lost I start to tremble when I go out in public.
    C. It seems that every time my wife is late meeting me somewhere, I get really angry with her. My time is valuable.
    D. I feel really angry because my best friend borrowed my car without asking.

53. In order to receive a diagnosis of adjustment disorder that conforms to DSM-IV standards, a client's symptoms must occur within _____ of a traumatic event

    A. 5 days
    B. 4 weeks
    C. 3 months
    D. 6 months

54. In the static-group comparison design of program evaluation, the primary threat to external validity is

    A. maturation-treatment interaction
    B. selection-treatment interaction
    C. reactive effects
    D. history-treatment interaction

55. According to Ainsworth, a "Type B" baby

    A. exhibits insecurity by avoiding the mother
    B. exhibits insecurity by resisting the mother
    C. exhibits insecurity by clinging to the mother
    D. uses the mother as a secure base from which to explore the environment

56. Which of the following is a primary social work setting?

A. Community center
B. Child protective services agency
C. Hospital
D. Nursing home

57. A client is a 40-year-old man who works as a night custodian at a local bank building. He keeps to himself and seems to have no interests outside his job, his stamp collection, and his two cats. He lives alone in a small apartment, has no close friends, and appears to have to interest in making friends. If this client is to receive a DSM-IV diagnosis, what would it be?

    A. Avoidant personality disorder
    B. Schizoid personality disorder
    C. Antisocial personality disorder
    D. No diagnosis—the man's isolation is not a disorder

58. A social or financial service that requires an applicant to prove financial need in order to receive the service is described as

    A. means-tested
    B. prescriptive
    C. residual
    D. eclectic

59. The initial aim in treating a client with conversion disorder is

    A. removal of the symptom
    B. determining predisposing factors
    C. forming a description of interpersonal relationships
    D. discovering precipitating stressors

60. Which of the following is NOT a preexperimental design for program evaluation?

    A. One-group pretest/posttest
    B. Client satisfaction surveys
    C. Static-group comparison
    D. Solomon four-group approach

61. In their definition of "family," many Asian Americans, especially Chinese Americans, are likely to include
    I. members of the nuclear family
    II. members of the extended family
    III. the informal network of community relations
    IV. all their ancestors and descendants

    A. I and II
    B. I, II and III
    C. I, II and IV
    D. I, II, III and IV

11 (#2)

62. Within the context of the therapeutic relationship, practitioners and clients deal either explicitly or implicitly with
    I. past experiences that have affected abilities to relate to others
    II. the present physical, emotional, and perceptual state of the transaction
    III. each person's expectations of the process

    A. I only
    B. I and II
    C. II and III
    D. I, II and II

63. Assertiveness and social skills training are interventions MOST likely to be useful to clients with

    A. panic disorder with agoraphobia
    B. avoidant personality disorder
    C. narcissistic personality disorder
    D. schizoid personality disorder

64. A client reports to a practitioner at an outpatient care clinic in clear psychological distress, exhibiting paranoia and severe anxiety. The clinician is certain that the client has some form of anxiety disorder. The patient has severe liver disease, but the clinician can't determine whether this is a factor; it's possible that the problem is related to other factors such as the client's persistent substance abuse. The most likely DSM-IV diagnosis would be Anxiety Disorder,

    A. provisional
    B. not otherwise specified
    C. with generalized anxiety
    D. undifferentiated

65. Which of the following is NOT generally a guideline for supervisors to follow regarding case presentation?

    A. The presentation should be organized around questions to be answered.
    B. The supervisor should present a case first.
    C. The presentation should progress from practitioner dynamics to client dynamics.
    D. The presentation should be based on written or audiovisual material.

66. A thirty-five-year-old client was referred by a friend because of her sadness and talk of suicide, which were brought on by the death of her lover several years ago but never fully subsided. A practitioner working from the existential viewpoint would view the goal of assessment with this client as

    A. an in-depth understanding of her subjective experience
    B. identifying the support resources already available to her
    C. the identification of situations and stimuli that reinforce her depressive responses
    D. achieving transference

67. Which of the following processes typically occurs LATEST in the therapeutic relationship?

    A. Individuation
    B. Idealization

C. Individualization
D. Identification

68. A social worker has been seeing a client who whose wife left him and moved out of state with the children. During a session, the client says he wishes he could find out where she lives, so he could make her pay for what she's done. The social worker should

    A. call domestic violence experts and document the statement
    B. call domestic violence experts and get legal advice
    C. call the police
    D. try to find the ex-wife and warn her

69. Some Marxist-oriented behavioral theorists believe that when individuals meet in face-to-face encounters, they make several different adaptations. For example, when individuals of different classes meet, the interaction tends to be very narrow and role-prescribed. This is an example of _____ generalization.

    A. means-end
    B. feelings
    C. control-purposiveness
    D. detachment

70. A practitioner using rational-emotive therapy to help a child who is depressed has gathered information from the child's parents and teachers, and has collected formal assessment instruments that were completed by the parents and the child. The practitioner then meets with the parents and the child together, and asks the parents a series of questions about their child's symptoms and their history of attempts to deal with the problem. The practitioner's NEXT step should be to

    A. question both the parents and the child about treatment goals
    B. assess the parents and the child for secondary disturbance
    C. ask for the child's opinion of her parents' statements
    D. assess the practical and/or emotional problems presented

71. The record-keeping requirements at a typical social services agency require the completion of progress notes at an interval no longer than

    A. after every client contact
    B. weekly
    C. every 30 days
    D. every 90 days

72. NASW policy regarding foster care and transracial adoption states that placement decisions should reflect a child's need for

    A. basic material comforts
    B. continuity
    C. ethnic/racial integrity
    D. a stimulating, challenging environment

73. Which of the following statements about the behavioral approach to treatment is FALSE?

A. Behavioral interventions are intended to modify only certain, limited aspects of human behavior
B. Under certain conditions, behaviorists are concerned with affect and cognitions
C. Behaviorists prefer observation over introspection
D. Behaviorists believe that a client's symptoms are merely observable behaviors that have been labeled as problematic

74. Within the family life-cycle perspective, divorces are sometimes referred to as   74.____

    A. derailments
    B. dislocations
    C. non-normative crises
    D. ruptures

75. Which of the following statements is TRUE regarding summative program evaluations?   75.____

    A. Interpretive approaches using qualitative data are particularly useful.
    B. They make no attempt to determine causality.
    C. Validity is a central concern.
    D. Evaluations provide detail about a program's strengths and weaknesses.

KEY (CORRECT ANSWERS)

1. A	16. C	31. D	46. B	61. C
2. A	17. B	32. C	47. D	62. D
3. C	18. A	33. A	48. A	63. B
4. A	19. B	34. B	49. B	64. B
5. B	20. B	35. D	50. C	65. C
6. C	21. A	36. C	51. A	66. A
7. D	22. A	37. D	52. B	67. A
8. A	23. A	38. C	53. C	68. B
9. D	24. D	39. A	54. B	69. A
10. D	25. C	40. C	55. D	70. C
11. A	26. C	41. A	56. B	71. C
12. A	27. B	42. D	57. B	72. B
13. C	28. C	43. C	58. A	73. A
14. C	29. C	44. A	59. A	74. B
15. D	30. C	45. A	60. D	75. C

EXAMINATION SECTION
TEST 1

DIRECTIONS: Each question or incomplete statement is followed by several suggested answers or completions. Select the one the BEST answers the question or completes the statement. *PRINT THE LETTER OF THE CORRECT ANSWER IN THE SPACE AT THE RIGHT.*

1. Which of the following statements about working with elderly clients in therapy is TRUE? 1.____

   A. Cognitive approaches are usually contraindicated because of the cognitive demands placed on the client.
   B. Elderly clients often become over-dependent on the therapist due to their relative isolation and loneliness.
   C. The therapeutic relationship may be more difficult to form than it would with younger clients
   D. Insight-oriented therapies are usually contraindicated because of the cognitive impairments that typically accompany aging.

2. A 45-year-old client reports to a clinician for an initial consultation upon the advice of her physician. The client complains of headaches, neck pain, stomach and lower back pain, and dizziness. After an initial examination, the client's physician has failed to find any physiological cause for his problems. Which of the following conditions would justify a diagnosis of malingering by the clinician? 2.____

   A. The client demonstrates a psychological need to maintain the "sick role"
   B. Further medical examination confirms the impression that the client's symptoms have no physiological basis
   C. The client feigns symptoms in order to gain an external reward
   D. A clinical presentation characterized by laziness and an "inadequate personality"

3. According to Paul Baltes, individual development across the life span can be described in each of the following ways, EXCEPT 3.____

   A. multidirectional
   B. reversible
   C. nonsequential
   D. intermittent

4. A social worker has been seeing a mother and daughter for several sessions because of the daughter's repeated defiance of the mother. The mother's responses during most of the sessions have been very child-like. If the social worker were to use transactional analysis with this mother and daughter, he might 4.____

   A. confront the child's fearful behaviors
   B. explore mother's feelings toward the child
   C. ask the mother and daughter to perform a role reversal
   D. encourage the mother to talk to the child as "parent to child"

5. A clinician decides to use rational-emotive therapy to help a child who is depressed. The FIRST thing the clinician should do to begin the process is 5.____

119

- A. administer the Reynolds Child Depression Scale
- B. interview the child
- C. assess the parents and the child for secondary disturbance
- D. interview the child's parents and teachers

6. According to the ecological theory of human development and behavior, a "macrosystem" consists of

    - A. relations between microsystems or connections between contexts
    - B. the patterning of environmental events and transitions over the life course
    - C. the attitudes and ideologies of the culture
    - D. family, school, peers, and church groups

7. During a client interview, the social worker tends to phrase his questions so that the client gives "yes" or "no" answers. The overall effect on the communication process will be that

    - A. the social worker will be able to develop a clear chronological picture of the presenting problem
    - B. the client's attitudes and beliefs will eventually be revealed
    - C. very little useful information will be elicited
    - D. the client will likely become wary and defensive

8. A client has been forced by the court to attend therapy with a social worker. From a clinical standpoint, it will be MOST important for the social worker to address

    - A. the client's ability to form a relationship with the social worker
    - B. the client's ambivalence about treatment
    - C. the nature of the client's offense
    - D. the latent factors in the client's legal problems

9. Which of the following does NOT typically characterize a therapy group in its early stages?

    - A. Relatively stereotyped and restricted content and communication style
    - B. A concern for closeness and intimacy
    - C. Giving and seeking advice
    - D. Hesitancy and dependence

10. A 42-year-old client has complained of intermittent abdominal pains, periodic nausea and vomiting, irregular menstrual periods, and periodic weakness in her limbs. Physical examinations have been normal for the last 3 years. What diagnosis should the woman receive?

    - A. Somatization disorder
    - B. Undifferentiated somatoform disorder
    - C. Hypochondriasis
    - D. Pain disorder associated with psychological factors

11. If the head of a counseling agency hires a consultant to help counselors deal with some particularly difficult cases at the agency, the agency is practicing _____ consultation.

A. consultee-centered case
B. consultee-centered administrative
C. program-centered administrative
D. client-centered case

12. In conducting case presentations, it is usually recommended that

    A. discussion be limited to the case at hand rather than additional problems
    B. the practitioner present several cases in one session
    C. practitioner dynamics be discussed before case dynamics
    D. the practitioner present a specific problem rather than the entire case in context

13. Interventions with Native American clients should generally be focused on

    A. building on client strengths to solve a particular problem
    B. removing environmental obstacles to client success
    C. teaching concrete skills to help clients become self-sufficient
    D. restoring a balance between physical well-being and spiritual harmony

14. Service eligibility requirements for social service clients are typically _____ in nature.
    I. Personal
    II. Demographic
    III. Social
    IV. Financial

    A. I and IV
    B. I, III and IV
    C. III and IV
    D. I, II, III and IV

15. Client-centered therapy asserts that each of the following therapist attitudes is necessary to effect positive changes in clients, EXCEPT

    A. genuineness
    B. positive regard
    C. empathy
    D. insightfulness

16. When communicating with the hearing-impaired, a social worker should try to do each of the following, EXCEPT

    A. speak slowly and clearly
    B. reduce background noise
    C. face the patient
    D. gradually increase the volume of his/her voice

17. Which of the following should generally be done the LATEST in a crisis intervention with a client who is a battered woman?

    A. Asking the client to describe briefly what has just happened
    B. Identifying the client's feelings as asking for a perception check
    C. Making sure the client is now safe and protected
    D. Asking the client if she is taking any medication

18. The area of difference between therapist and client that is likely to be MOST influential in a therapeutic relationship is

    A. gender
    B. socioeconomic status
    C. philosophical orientation
    D. culture

19. After a series of traumatic events at a hospital involving a mother and her young daughter, who has been experiencing hypoglycemic seizures throughout the night, the mother, who has been fiercely devoted to her daughter and has remained at her bedside for more than 24 hours, is inadvertently caught by a nurse in the act of preparing an insulin injection for the girl. The mother later admitted to giving the insulin to her daughter. The mother could be said to be suffering from

    A. factitious disorder
    B. dissociative disorder
    C. conversion disorder
    D. somatoform disorder

20. Which of the following, if used during the first 3 months of pregnancy, may cause a cleft palate or other congenital malformation?

    A. Alcohol
    B. Tranquilizers
    C. Cocaine
    D. Nicotine

21. Purposes of the Adult Abuse Protocol, an assessment and intervention guide for the abused adult, include
    I. documenting the violent incident for legal purposes
    II. alerting the involved hospital staff to provide appropriate clinical care
    III. provide a formal support network for the client in recovery

    A. I only
    B. I and II
    C. II and III
    D. I, II, and III

22. Which of the following listening skills is LEAST likely to be used in a client interview that conforms to the behavioral approach?

    A. Open questions
    B. Closed questions
    C. Feedback
    D. Reflection of meaning

23. The most dangerous side effect associated with phenothiazines is

    A. Parkinson-like symptoms
    B. nausea
    C. epileptic seizures
    D. delusional behavior

24. People who are experiencing anomie are said to adapt in one of five ways. Which of the following is NOT one of these?

    A. Martyrdom
    B. Innovation
    C. Rebellion
    D. Ritualism

25. Erikson's second stage of psychosocial development, which occurs in late infancy and toddlerhood (1-3 years), is

    A. initiative vs. guilt
    B. trust vs. mistrust
    C. identity vs. identity confusion
    D. autonomy vs. shame and doubt

26. Questionnaires can be used in preference over other data collection techniques when
    I. anonymity is important
    II. budgets are limited
    III. respondents are literate
    IV. a high response rate is important

    A. I only
    B. I and II
    C. I, II and III
    D. I, II, III and IV

27. Unlike traditional approaches to psychotherapy, cultural approaches try to understand mental illness from the inside—they attempt to clarify the individual or group's experience of the illness within the cultural context. In this way, cultural approaches adopt an _____ perspective.

    A. etiological
    B. endogenous
    C. emic
    D. etic

28. When a person's moral reasoning is controlled by external rewards and punishment, it is said to be

    A. role-focused
    B. preconventional
    C. circular
    D. preoperational

29. Which of the following individuals if probably the most inappropriate candidate for a long-term interactional therapy group?

    A. A secretive anorexic-bulimic client
    B. A man with a history of sexual promiscuity
    C. A client with inadequate ego strength
    D. A person who has been convicted of child molestation

30. It is probably most appropriate for a clinician to view professional and formal assessment instruments, such as the Stanford-Binet, Wecshler, and Q-sort as

    A. providing a full picture of client functions
    B. getting in the way of establishing a healthy client/worker relationship
    C. ways of confirming impressions
    D. uninstrusive means of identifying specific deficits

31. Private-practice clinicians who work full-time calculate that about _____ percent of their gross income goes for operating and overhead expenses if they maintain a full caseload.

    A. 5-15
    B. 20-30
    C. 35-45
    D. 50-70

32. Which of the following is the BEST example of a secondary prevention program?

    A. a community education program
    B. Head Start
    C. Crisis intervention
    D. a rehabilitation program

33. Most definitions of "family" tend to focus on the two most significant manifest functions of the family, which are

    A. production and consumption
    B. procreation and the socialization of children
    C. production and provision of emotional support
    D. procreation and provision of emotional support

34. Within a social services organization, the type of plan that is probably most frequently misunderstood is a(n)

    A. mission
    B. policy
    C. rule
    D. budget

35. In the psychodynamic perspective, a "love" that is based on self-doubt will play itself out as _____ love.

    A. revengeful
    B. sadistic
    C. compulsive
    D. critical

36. In order to help clients generate additional information about their situations, each of the following is an important skill in interviewing, EXCEPT

    A. influencing skills
    B. confrontation
    C. reflection
    D. focusing

37. Which of the following questions is MOST "open" in nature? 37.____

    A. What important things have happened during the week?
    B. Where does your daughter live?
    C. Could you tell me a little about your family?
    D. Do you get along with your mother?

38. Generally, the most strongest predictor of social service utilization by Asian American clients is 38.____

    A. degree of isolation
    B. severity of condition
    C. acculturation
    D. financial focus of service need

39. The impact of a therapeutic relationship depends on how well a practitioner uses herself or her sensitivity to guide clients in understanding themselves. Which of the following is NOT an important means of doing this? 39.____

    A. Exploring thoughts and feelings
    B. Listing alternatives
    C. Reflecting attitude
    D. Modeling behavior

40. For what reason is it sometimes difficult for clinicians to identify depression in young children? 40.____

    A. Depression is often manifested in a variety of symptoms which do not appear to be typical of depression
    B. Depression does not exist as a clinical syndrome at that early age
    C. Young children do not have sufficient language to describe how they feel
    D. Young children do not have the capacity for self-observation

41. Which of the following tasks of remarriage is typically performed FIRST? 41.____

    A. Community remarriage: establishing relationships outside the marriage
    B. Parental remarriage: establishing bonds with the children of a partner
    C. Legal remarriage: settling financial and other responsibilities toward children and former partners
    D. Economic remarriage: becoming interdependent in terms of financial needs and responsibilities

42. Which of the following approaches to social services policymaking tends to recommend a policy based on previous information about the impact of a policy of existing policies, with a projection of continuing future effectiveness? 42.____

    A. Secondary
    B. Rational
    C. Prescriptive
    D. Vertical

43. Most practitioners view _____ as the most important element in bringing about change in clients' lives. 43.____

A. effective service linkage
B. a strong support network
C. client skill development
D. the therapeutic relationship

44. Individuals with a diagnosis of _____ have a 6-month history of recurrent, intense, sexually arousing fantasies, urges, or behaviors involving touching and rubbing against a nonconsenting person.

    A. voyeurism
    B. exhibitionism
    C. frotteurism
    D. fetishism

45. A pregnant 14-year-old reports to a social worker complaining about her boyfriend, whom she fights with often because he won't look for work to support her and her child. The girls says she uses cocaine once a week. The social worker should:

    A. maintain confidentiality and continue therapy
    B. consult child protective services, because the girl is a minor and needs protection
    C. consult child protective services, because the girl is abusing the fetus
    D. call the girl's parents for permission to treat her

46. Of those who participate in AA, those most likely to benefit are generally

    A. members of a lower socioeconomic group
    B. women
    C. older drinkers
    D. heavy drinkers

47. Which of the following forms of elder maltreatment is LEAST commonly reported?

    A. Physical abuse
    B. Psychological abuse
    C. Financial abuse
    D. Physical neglect

48. Which of the following is a secondary social work setting?

    A. Child welfare agency
    B. Homeless shelter
    C. Alcohol and drug treatment center
    D. Family service agency

49. In a client interview, a worker may sometimes reflect the client's feelings in a way that is helpful. Which of the following statements about this technique is FALSE?

    A. Reflections in the past tense tend to be more useful than those in the present.
    B. The emotion being reflected should be clearly labeled with a word.
    C. It is often useful to add a contextual word (because, when) to broaden the reflection.
    D. It's important to refer directly to the client in the reflection.

50. The ideal of human development envisioned by ego psychology is

A. consensus and shared values
B. individual development across the life course
C. equality and the absence of alienation and exploitation
D. mutual self-respect and the absence of labeling

51. Probably the most frustrating problem encountered by clients in need of services who apply to a public social services agency is the

    A. stigma attached to those who seek services
    B. means-testing process
    C. inability to consider cases individually
    D. size and complexity of the agency's bureaucratic structure

52. Sample size is social work research has its most direct affect on

    A. internal validity
    B. the ability to infer a causal relationship between variables.
    C. experimental control
    D. generalizability

53. According to Piaget, assimilation occurs when individuals

    A. incorporate new information into their existing knowledge
    B. coordinate sensory experiences with physical actions
    C. adjust to new information
    D. represent the world in words, images and drawings

54. Typically, the relationship between a social worker and a small group differs from that of a social worker and an individual. Which of the following statements is FALSE regarding the relationship between a worker and a small group?

    A. There is greater formality than in a worker/individual relationship.
    B. There is an inherent lack of confidentiality.
    C. A greater feeling of identification usually exists among clients than in a worker/individual relationship.
    D. Acceptance of others is not mandated to other group members.

55. After the review of a case, an HMO decides to deny further payment for sessions for a social worker's client. The worker believes the client would benefit from additional therapy. The BEST approach by the worker would be to

    A. file a complaint against the HMO
    B. consult with the client about his options in this situation
    C. comply with the HMO's request, but only if the limits of treatment were discussed with the client at the beginning of therapy
    D. continue to provide therapy to the client without compensation if necessary until other arrangements can be made

56. The key personality trait in clients who suffer from avoidant personality disorder is

    A. an indifference to human contact
    B. a distaste for other people
    C. a sense of entitlement and lack of empathy
    D. a fear of rejection

57. A clinical supervisor who maintains an "open-door" policy with supervisees is MOST likely to encourage the development of

    A. unstructured supervision that operates on a crisis basis
    B. solution-focused supervision that is focused on client dynamics
    C. a proactive style of interaction that locates and attempts to solve problems early
    D. a warm peer relationship with practitioners who view the supervisor as an equal

58. In a troubled family it sometimes happens that members project their internal conflicts onto others outside them. These projections are known as

    A. triangulations
    B. stable coalitions
    C. detouring coalitions
    D. disengagements

59. The driving force behind a social service agency's resource allocation decisions should be

    A. the distribution between current vs. long-term debt
    B. the available liquid cash resources to cover current debt
    C. assets available for collateral for additional debt
    D. the mission of the organization

60. The easiest measure of data variability to calculate and understand is

    A. mean
    B. standard deviation
    C. range
    D. slope

61. The use of "systems" thinking in social work generally involves each of the following advantages, EXCEPT

    A. it can easily be adapted for the implementation of partial solutions
    B. it ensures that a worker will search for more than one way to look at a situation
    C. it helps the worker to see the world through the eyes of another
    D. it shows that behavior must be understood in the context of a number of factors

62. Sometimes, experiences in another social setting-in which the individual does not have an active role influence what the individual experiences in an immediate context. This other social setting is described as a(n)

    A. mesosystem
    B. exosystem
    C. milieu
    D. macrosystem

63. A 30-year old man visits a hospital emergency room complaining of extreme nervousness. When told that he'll have to wait for physician, he becomes irritated and argues with the receptionist, and then paces around the waiting room. An initial physical examination reveals a heart rate of 111 and a blood pressure of 170/110. The man says he's felt extremely nervous, off and on, for several days now. Based on this information only, a practitioner should FIRST investigate the possibility that the man

A. is intoxicated with a substance
B. suffers from posttraumatic stress disorder
C. suffers from acute stress disorder
D. has developed generalized anxiety disorder

64. In the stage of a client interview during which the worker and client explore alternatives and confront client incongruities, an important goal is to

    A. work toward resolution of the client's problem
    B. facilitate changes in thoughts, feelings and behaviors in daily life
    C. build a working alliance with the client
    D. discover the client's ideal world

65. A clinician decides to use Beck's cognitive approach to treat a client with panic disorder. The FIRST goal of intervention would be to for the client to

    A. see how he misinterprets the meaning of his symptoms
    B. identify the antecedents and consequences that are controlling his symptoms
    C. understand how the symptoms are controlling different aspects of his life
    D. identify the underlying causes of his symptoms

66. Problems associated with labeling in client assessment include
    I. masking clients' subjective experience and coping mechanisms
    II. a perceived loss of control by the practitioner
    III. the constraint and trivialization of clients
    IV. an emphasis on what is wrong, rather than what is right

    A. I and III
    B. I, III and IV
    C. II and IV
    D. I, II, III and IV

67. The efficiency and effectiveness factors relating to the delivery of social services are evaluated broadly in terms of

    A. influence
    B. summation
    C. accountability
    D. transactional analysis

68. The functions of an organizational advisory board typically do NOT include

    A. publicizing agency activities
    B. procuring the funds needed to operate the organization
    C. evaluating agency services and recommending improvements
    D. assisting in determining consumer needs

69. Culturally, the most significantly observed life-cycle transition among African American families is

    A. birth
    B. passing into adulthood
    C. marriage
    D. death

70. Which of the following is NOT an example of an output goal?

    A. Reduce the number of alcohol-related incidents of domestic violence by one-third (by 250 incidents)
    B. Increase the number of Alcoholics Anonymous and Al-Anon groups in the county by 40% (from 10 to 14) during the coming year.
    C. Provide inpatient treatment services to 235 persons with alcohol dependency problems, supplemented with services to their families.
    D. Develop a special unit for female alcoholics, increasing service from 40 clients a year to 80 a year.

71. Which of the following interviewing skills generally exerts the greatest amount of influence over client talk?

    A. Interpretation
    B. Open questions
    C. Focusing
    D. Paraphrasing

72. A family reports to a private practitioner out of concern for their young son, who repeatedly urinates in his bed at night and in his clothes during the day. The parents' attempts to shape the boy's behavior have failed. In order to assign the boy a diagnosis of enuresis consistent with DSM-IV standards, the practitioner must establish that

    A. the boy is at least 5 years old
    B. the problem occurs at least once a week
    C. the problem has persisted for at least 6 months
    D. the problem is not related to some external stressor

73. Which of the following processes typically occurs EARLIEST in the therapeutic relationship?

    A. Idealization
    B. Individualization
    C. Identification
    D. Individuation

74. Most developmental psychologists prefer longitudinal research designs to cross-sectional research designs, primarily for the reason that longitudinal designs

    A. use the subjects as their own experimental controls
    B. are much less likely to be influenced by cultural changes that occur over time
    C. offer the advantage of between-subjects comparisons
    D. usually yield results more quickly

75. Most social work professionals agree that paternalism may be justifiable if clients
    I. are not mentally competent
    II. might harm themselves seriously
    III. have repeatedly proven incapable of caring for themselves
    IV. do not voluntarily consent to a social worker's intervention plan

    A. I and II
    B. III only
    C. I, II, III and IV
    D. None of the above

KEY (CORRECT ANSWERS)

1. C	16. D	31. B	46. C	61. A
2. C	17. A	32. C	47. A	62. B
3. D	18. D	33. B	48. C	63. A
4. D	19. A	34. B	49. A	64. A
5. D	20. B	35. C	50. B	65. A
6. C	21. B	36. C	51. D	66. B
7. C	22. D	37. C	52. D	67. C
8. B	23. A	38. C	53. C	68. B
9. B	24. A	39. B	54. A	69. D
10. B	25. D	40. A	55. B	70. A
11. D	26. C	41. A	56. D	71. A
12. A	27. C	42. C	57. A	72. A
13. D	28. B	43. D	58. C	73. B
14. B	29. A	44. C	59. D	74. A
15. D	30. C	45. A	60. C	75. A

TEST 2

DIRECTIONS: Each question or incomplete statement is followed by several suggested answers or completions. Select the one the BEST answers the question or completes the statement PRINT THE LETTER OF THE CORRECT ANSWER IN THE SPACE AT THE RIGHT.

1. The primary purpose of assessment in clinical social work is to

    A. help set appropriate goals and objectives for treatment
    B. provide a means of measuring treatment progress and outcome
    C. identify an appropriate DSM-IV diagnosis
    D. help establish meaningful communication with other providers and insurers

2. An adolescent client, while discussing the murder of her mother by her father, relates the events in a detached, matter-of-fact manner. When emotional blunting of this type occurs in conjunction with _____ , a strong likelihood exists that the client is psychotic and in need of psychiatric evaluation.

    A. alcohol and/or drug abuse
    B. thought disorder
    C. unipolar disorder
    D. poor self-concept

3. A social worker in private practice receives a phone call from a prospective client who says that she wants to get to know the worker, free of charge, before beginning treatment. The worker should:

    A. outline his fee policy for the client
    B. see the client
    C. tell the client there will be no charge for the session if the worker decides he cannot work with her
    D. inform the client that this isn't possible

4. A clinician in family treatment is dealing with an "undifferentiated ego mass." Which of the following would be an element of the intervention?

    A. Forming and join an "emotionally triangle" in the family system in order to reduce anxiety from within
    B. Working individually with the most differentiated family member, because he/she is most capable of breaking habitual pathological patterns
    C. Unbalancing the family's homeostasis by promoting confrontations among family members
    D. Working individually with the least differentiated family member in order to bring him/her up to the level of the more differentiated family members

5. A client with a long history of depression visits a clinician for the first time. While the client is hopeful that the clinician can help with his problem, he says he cannot sign a "non-suicide" contract, and he insists on the additional condition that the clinician not involuntarily hospitalize him for extreme suicidal thoughts. The clinician should

A. inform the client that she cannot make this promise under any circumstances
B. take a medical and social history before deciding to treat this client
C. try to persuade the client to seek hospitalization for treatment
D. start a course of antidepressants and check with the client in a few weeks to see if he's changed his mind

6. Generally, the thinking today regarding phenotype and genotype is that

   A. phenotype reveals certain aspects of genotype
   B. phenotype and genotype have a bidirectional influence on each other
   C. phenotype and genotype have no relation to each other
   D. phenotype does not indicate anything about genotype

7. Within the context of employee evaluation at a social services agency, the practice of "banding"

   A. is not considered useful because it increases the likelihood that a selection technique will have an adverse impact
   B. may not reduce adverse impact unless it is combined with a minority preference component
   C. is considered useful for tracking the success rates of employees who have been hired using a particular selection technique
   D. is preferable to other techniques because it is more likely to eliminate problems related to adverse impact

8. To make acceptance clear to the client in the early stages of building the therapeutic relationship, it's important for the practitioner to
   I. maintain eye contact with the client
   II. maintain facial expressions that are consistent with the client's emotions
   III. keep an appropriate distance away from the client more than arm's length
   IV. avoid crossing his/her arms while listening

   A. I only
   B. I and II
   C. I, II and IV
   D. I, II, III and IV

9. Which of the following clinician roles will generally be LEAST important for a social worker's crisis intervention practice in an emergency room setting?

   A. Educator
   B. Activist
   C. Coordinator
   D. Broker

10. According to Dane and Simon, one of the predictable problems faced by social workers in secondary practices settings is the "marginality of token status." This means that

    A. in a given secondary setting, social workers are few and their visibility is high
    B. social work is devalued as "women's work" in settings that are predominantly male in composition
    C. there is a discrepancy between the values of the social work profession and the dominant profession of the organization

D. a worker who is responsible for developing a helping relationship with the client in an effort to solve problems must also perform in a role that reinforces the norms of the organizational setting

11. Which of the following listening skills is MOST likely to be used in a client interview that conforms to the client-centered approach? 11.____

   A. Open questions
   B. Paraphrasing
   C. Closed questions
   D. Interpretation/refraining

12. Most practitioners, when they begin their careers and begin a relationship with their supervisors, desire help in each of the following areas, EXCEPT 12.____

   A. developing skills
   B. finding a specialized niche
   C. fostering self-awareness
   D. applying theory

13. According to Lewis, the primary difference between a "healthy" and a "faltering" family appears to be in the relationship between 13.____

   A. the children
   B. the married couple
   C. the mother and the child/children
   D. the father and the child/children

14. Which of the following tasks is NOT generally appropriate for paraprofessionals in a social service agency? 14.____

   A. Arranging client transportation
   B. Referring clients to appropriate helping professionals
   C. Completing forms requesting services from other agencies
   D. Conducting intake histories

15. Which of the following term denotes the "pitch" of the voice? 15.____

   A. Tone
   B. Resonance
   C. Inflection
   D. Volume

16. The "constructivist" model of social work holds that clients' conceptions of reality are a product of 16.____

   A. experience
   B. deeds
   C. ideals
   D. language

17. Which of the following is an argument commonly given by social work practitioners AGAINST the use of worker-client contracting in the therapeutic relationship? 17.____

A. Expanded malpractice risks
B. Greater likelihood of misunderstandings about expectations
C. Increased likelihood of premature termination
D. Forces a legal requirement onto the client that damages the status of the "helping" relationship

18. The symptoms of people with somatization disorder must include the following:
    I. Four pain symptoms in different sites
    II. Two gastrointestinal symptoms without pain
    III. One sexual symptom without pain
    IV. One pseudoneurological symptom without pain

    A. I only
    B. I or II
    C. II, III and IV
    D. I, II, III and IV

19. During a family intervention session, the teen-age daughter is sitting silently in a corner of the room with her arms folded across her chest. To engage the daughter in the process, clinician using the structural model would

    A. sit next to her and tell her what she's doing is okay and makes perfect sense
    B. direct her to be participate in the agreed-upon intervention
    C. reward and praise her when and if she does speak
    D. ignore her and wait for her to speak when she's ready

20. It is common for Native American or Latino families to ascribe family status to close friends. These friends are said to take on the status of

    A. modified extended members
    B. referents
    C. fictive relatives
    D. de facto kin

21. Advantages to a shared partnership in private social work practice include
    I. Cost savings in office space
    II. Minimal problems in coverage and consultation
    III. Increased income- and client-building opportunities
    IV. Enhanced credibility with other professional groups

    A. I only
    B. I and II
    C. I, III and IV
    D. I, II, III and IV

22. A social worker is interviewing a client who is a recent immigrant from China. In general, the social worker should avoid

    A. attentive body language
    B. sustained eye contact
    C. open-ended questions
    D. verbal tracking

23. Which of the following is NOT a theory of psychoanalysis?

    A. The therapist should relate as a real, genuine person.
    B. Mental illness is not an accepted concept.
    C. Insight into problems is insufficient for producing change.
    D. Clients are not responsible for their deviant behaviors.

24. The NASW code states explicitly that a social worker has an ethical duty to provide voluntary public service that benefits society as a whole. Probably the most appropriate way to do this is to

    A. join and participate in professional organizations or associations
    B. engage in individual advocacy
    C. engage in class advocacy
    D. run for public office

25. Sherman and Wenocur propose six ways for social services workers to resolve their feelings of alienation from the agency. Of these, the most productive is

    A. withdrawal
    B. functional non-capitulation
    C. niche-finding
    D. capitulation

26. In the psychodynamic perspective, "falling in love" is best described as

    A. the unrealistic search for the perfect partner
    B. a sign that inner needs are finally being met
    C. an idealization of the sexual drive
    D. an irrational process

27. Which of the following relationships is an example of a purchase of service agreement?

    A. A child protective services agency contracts with a family services agency to provide counseling to children who have suffered abuse or neglect.
    B. A psychotherapist refers a client to a general assistance agency for help with financial management.
    C. A family services agency hires the legal advisors of the local hospital to help with a malpractice suit.
    D. A general assistance client applies for and is given food stamps to supplement his income

28. According to Freud, which of the following defense mechanisms is ALWAYS involved in neurotic behavior?

    A. sublimation
    B. regression
    C. anger
    D. repression

29. In the transactional view of human behavior,

    A. it is believed that human potential is limitless
    B. people are motivated primarily by the potential for profit

C. the primary issue is the tension between individual and collective well-being
D. people are seen as individual systems, separate from their social context

30. The client of a private practitioner complains of frequent periods of dizziness during which he experiences several unsettling feelings: he feels completely separate from his mind and body, as if he's floating and watching himself from above. The client says that during these episodes he sometimes wonders whether he's a real person or some machine that's programmed by someone else. The client is aware that the feelings are a product of his mind, but he can't control them, though he has been keeping them to himself and not telling family or friends about them. The most appropriate diagnosis for this client is

A. dementia, not otherwise specified
B. depersonalization disorder
C. delusional disorder
D. schizophreniform disorder

31. During an initial interview, a client tells the social worker that he is gay and has AIDS. For the worker and this client to have an effective long-term therapeutic relationship, it is most important for the worker to be:

A. gay
B. non-homophobic
C. ready to refer the client out
D. comfortable dealing with issues of sexuality and safe sex

32. Which of the following statements is TRUE?

A. There is no consistent correlation between ethnic, racial, or socioeconomic status and the likelihood of child abuse or neglect.
B. Mothers are more likely to be implicated in cases of abuse and neglect than fathers.
C. In general, the likelihood that a child will experience neglect decreases with age.
D. Boys are twice as likely as girls to experience abuse or neglect.

33. As a social worker leads a therapy group, a client offers constructive feedback to another client in the group, but the feedback is offered in clear irritation and agitation. The rest of the group becomes angry at the first client. The social worker should:

A. point out what the first client did well, and then offer constructive criticism
B. see the first client in an individual session to give him feedback on his performance
C. ask the group to point out what the first client has done wrong
D. focus on the needs of the client who has just received negative feedback

34. A practitioner in private practice is visited by a mother and her, an exceptionally bright 11-year-old who is not at all liked by his peers. Their dislike has become so strong that they continually tease and taunt the boy, and he has complained bitterly to his mother. Probably the most useful means of assessment in this situation would be for the practitioner to

A. arrange situations in which the boy's behavior around other children can be observed
B. begin a course of insight-oriented treatment

C. gently question the boy about what he believes might be causing the problem
D. set up a role-playing exercise in which the boy assumes the role of one of his classmates

35. In removing personal barriers to achievement for clients of color, interventions should be aimed at

   A. distributing resources through information/education
   B. actively encouraging family involvement
   C. recognizing and affirming client system strengths
   D. improving educational/vocational opportunities through greater teacher/employer awareness of diversity, history and customs

36. Which of the following is NOT a type of behavioral intervention?

   A. Systematic desensitization
   B. Assertiveness training
   C. Script analysis
   D. Contingency contracting

37. In couples therapy, it is most important for the social worker to

   A. establish rapport with each partner
   B. maintain confidentiality
   C. cut through the denial
   D. teach communication skills

38. A clinician collects different kinds of data—for example, interviews and observations—which may include both qualitative and quantitative data, for the purpose of studying the same research question. This is an example of

   A. triangulation
   B. cross-classification
   C. rival hypotheses
   D. validation

39. Ivan Nye and his associates, applying the social exchange theory to family life, concluded that behavioral choices made by family members follow a specific, rank-order pattern, beginning with choices from alternatives

   A. from which they anticipate the fewest costs
   B. that provide better immediate outcomes
   C. from which they expect the most profit
   D. that promise better long-term outcomes

40. Of the types of adolescents listed below, psychodynamic interventions will probably be MOST useful for those

   A. who are addicted and in denial
   B. with oppositional/conduct disorder
   C. who are clinically depressed
   D. with ADHD

41. A family has been seeing a social worker for almost one year, after receiving a court referraltheir 15-year-old son was found guilty of sexually molesting their 7-year-old daughter. The son has been in foster care for the last year and has been receiving individual and group therapy. In one month, he is due to begin visitations at home. The social worker should

   A. reiterate to the family what they've learned about the "cycle of incest"
   B. include the son in a family therapy session during his first visitation
   C. contact the son's individual and group therapists for copies of their opinions as to his readiness for family therapy, and coordinate treatment with them
   D. review the family's plans for what will take place in terms of the son's interactions with his sister during initial visitations

41.____

42. Which of the following question stems is particularly useful to social workers in client interviews, because it is simultaneously open and closed?

   A. What
   B. Could
   C. Is
   D. How

42.____

43. Which of the following statements is NOT characteristic of ego psychology?

   A. The social environment shapes the personality
   B. Problems are almost exclusively the function of deficits in coping capacity
   C. The ego mediates between the individual and the environment
   D. The ego is the part of the personality that allows for successful adaptation to the environment.

43.____

44. Questioning is one of the most important means for supervisors to help practitioners reflect on their own work. Which of the following is a guideline to for a supervisor to use in questioning an practitioner?

   A. When the supervisor wonders whether the practitioner has adequate knowledge of the case or diagnosis, to make treatment decision, the supervisor should move from specific to general questions.
   B. Beginning questions should be specific in nature and answered specifically.
   C. When general supervisory questions result in answers that reveal thorough knowledge of the case, the supervisor can move to questions related to treatment and intervention strategies.
   D. Questions related to treatment strategies and techniques should be more specific than questions related to diagnostic understanding.

44.____

45. In applying the ethical concept of client self-determination, a social worker upholds:

   A. the importance of helping clients make healthy choices and decisions
   B. the right and need of clients to make their own choices and decisions
   C. the importance of helping clients achieve their fullest potential
   D. the right of clients to seek help in making choices and decisions

45.____

46. According to Bowen, families deal with anxiety and tension in one of four ways. Which of the following is NOT one of these?

46.____

A. Increased emotional distance between spouses
B. Increased emotional distance between siblings
C. Physical or emotional dysfunction in a spouse
D. Impairment in a child

47. Which of the following offers the BEST example of a double-bind paradox? 47.____

    A. A father who masks hostility with a too-loving attitude
    B. An authoritarian mother
    C. A passive mother and a hostile son
    D. An aggressive mother and a timid son

48. Which of the following is a phenotypical definition of gender? 48.____

    A. Genital gender
    B. Hormonal gender
    C. Organal gender
    D. Chromosomal gender

49. Which of the following approaches to social services policymaking is designed to meet a long-term need, such as education? 49.____

    A. Formative
    B. Residual
    C. External
    D. Investment

50. In the early stages of a therapeutic relationship, the practitioner brings the focus of discussions onto the client herself, and affirming her willingness and ability to bring about necessary change. Probably the next stage for this relationship will be to 50.____

    A. connect various elements of current client problems to patterns of their life experience
    B. client internalization of appropriate goals, attitudes and behaviors
    C. creating structures and patterns of learning and awareness
    D. recognizing and admiring client abilities to grow independent and create something valuable

51. Which of the following ethnic groups are generally LEAST likely to the placement of older relations into a nursing home? 51.____

    A. Latino
    B. Chinese-American
    C. African-American
    D. Jewish-American

52. The general consensus among clinical social workers and psychologists is that a person in crisis is characterized by each of the following, EXCEPT 52.____

    A. appearing unable to modify or lessen the impact of stressful events with traditional coping methods
    B. experiencing a serious loss of function
    C. experiencing increased fear, tension and/or confusion
    D. exhibiting a high level of subjective discomfort

53. Within a social services organization, zero-based budgeting
    I. requires that a program start from scratch
    II. requires that a program justify each dollar requested
    III. is calculated annually
    IV. rolls unused funds into the next program

    A. I only
    B. I and II
    C. I, II and III
    D. I, II, III and IV

54. In the theoretical construct of self psychology, drives are seen as more _____ than in the Freudian approach.

    A. social
    B. libidmal
    C. aggressive
    D. instinctual

55. Among social work clinicians, one of the major problems with the concept of acceptance in a therapeutic relationship is that

    A. clinicians often become overinvolved and make the client's needs into their own
    B. the duration of such relationships usually doesn't allow for acceptance
    C. clinicians often confuse it with liking the person or approving of client behaviors
    D. clients often don't care whether they are accepted or not as long as their problem is solved

56. During the assessment phase of treatment for the family of a child with conduct disorder, the practitioner should focus attention on each of the following, EXCEPT

    A. information about cognitive/emotional reactions to the presenting problem
    B. solutions already attempted by the family
    C. the reasons why people react to the presenting problem in the ways that they do
    D. family myths

57. Which of the following is NOT a recent professional trend that has supported the need for clinical supervision of practitioners?

    A. Changes in professional standards
    B. Resurgence of clinical practice
    C. Complex external controls on practice structure
    D. Decreasing role of social work in mental illness treatment

58. During an initial interview session with a family, the social worker observes that family therapist notices that whenever the mother talks, the father and son contradict what she says and criticize her. The father and son's behavior is best described as:

    A. triangulation
    B. scapegoating
    C. a coalition
    D. positive feedback

59. In making her assessment of the occurrence of depression in a community, a practitioner begins to worry that the problem is not as serious as has been suggested by several recent well-publicized events. The practitioner should

    A. rely on clients' definitions of their individual problems
    B. put her theories and preconceptions on hold until she has gathered more information
    C. engage in self-exploration to heighten sensitivity to misplaced assumptions and expectations
    D. check statistical data and data on non-occurrence

60. In order to be accurate, a paraphrase of a client's statements must contain certain elements. Which of the following is NOT necessarily one of these?

    A. A succinct summary of what the client said, in the same order it was said
    B. A brief signal at the end of the paraphrase that asks whether it is accurate
    C. A sentence stem using some aspect of the client's mode of receiving information
    D. The key words and constructs used by the client to describe the situation or person.

61. Which of the following approaches to social services policymaking focuses on a specific need, such as food stamps?

    A. Institutional
    B. Consumption
    C. Coalition
    D. Prescriptive

62. By far, the most readily available data in assessment are the anecdotal data provided in interviews with the client. This type of information carries the risk of

    A. masking the client's perceptions of his own experience
    B. a focus on client deficits
    C. "pigeon-holing" the client in the worker's eyes into a neat category of presenting problem
    D. worker counter-transference

63. The Rational Decision-Making Model is used by some social service administrators in program evaluation and design. In the first stage of the model, problem formulation, administrators
    I. identify stakeholders in the evaluation
    II. specify the relationship between the evaluation and the program
    III. specify types of data to be collected
    IV. clarify the objectives of the evaluation

    A. I and II
    B. I and IV
    C. II, III and IV
    D. I, II, III and IV

64. In the conduct of life span research, effects that are due to a subject's time of birth, but which are unrelated to age, are known as

A. age-graded influences
B. chronosystems
C. normative life events
D. cohort effects

65. A practitioner incrementally adds specific treatment components to a client's treatment package, in order to monitor their collective impact. This type of intervention is known as a _____ treatment strategy.

    A. dismantling
    B. dichotomous
    C. constructive
    D. parametric

66. One of the clinician's tasks in crisis intervention is to restore a client's cognitive functioning. In developing cognitive mastery, the client must FIRST

    A. restructure, rebuild, and replace irrational beliefs with new, realistic cognitions
    B. obtain a realistic understanding of what happened and what led to the crisis
    C. explore feelings and emotions surrounding the incident
    D. understand the specific meaning the event has for him or her

67. Which of the following is NOT a type of "in-kind" social service program?

    A. Food stamps
    B. Public housing
    C. General assistance
    D. Medical assistance

68. Which of the following statements about child abuse/maltreatment is FALSE?

    A. It occurs in nearly half of all families.
    B. It is usually mild to moderate in severity.
    C. It is a diverse condition.
    D. It is only partially caused by parental personality characteristics.

69. In social work practice, the corrective experience that allows clients to experience themselves differently, and thereafter make changes, begins as a function of

    A. the client's willingness to change
    B. how much the client is able to trust the practitioner to help him make the right decisions about how to change
    C. the degree to which the practitioner can establish an empathic understanding of the client and his situation
    D. the degree to which the practitioner can establish a sense of urgency for change

70. During an initial interview with a divorced 37-year-old man, the client reports that he suspects his ex-wife, who is the custodial parent of their daughter, of abusing her. The MOST appropriate response for the worker would be to

    A. ask the client whether he has reported the abuse
    B. explore the factors that have led the client to believe this
    C. begin therapy cautiously, mindful of the possibility that the client may be using this allegation to obtain custody of his daughter

D. report child abuse in accord with a social worker's legal mandate to make
E. a suspected child abuse report whenever he or she hears about possible child abuse

71. Studies comparing the personalities of lesbian and heterosexual females have found that

   A. lesbian women are less defensive than heterosexual women
   B. lesbian women are higher in neuroticism than heterosexual women
   C. lesbian women and heterosexual women are about equally well-adjusted
   D. lesbian women are less confident than heterosexual women

72. Which of the following is a significant benefit associated with the psychoanalytical model of intervention?

   A. easily operationalized concepts
   B. attention to personality development across the entire human life span
   C. clear recognition of the subconscious in psychological functioning
   D. pan-cultural theoretical base

73. Which of the following investigative strategies is designed to achieve a precise determination of a behavior's causes?

   A. Random assignment
   B. Correlational
   C. Longitudinal
   D. Experimental

74. As part of an evaluation program, a social worker records the number of times a child replies to a specific parental request The observational method used here is

   A. time sampling
   B. recording latency
   C. counting discriminated operants
   D. frequency count

75. Which of the following questions or statements is MOST likely to be used during a client interview by a social worker using the Rogerian model?

   A. On the other hand; you see your ideal self as someone who can excel at managing both a career and a family.
   B. You say you often act awkwardly in social situations, and you'd like to develop some social skills?
   C. I think you've described your short-term and long-term goals pretty clearly.
   D. I'm beginning to see the difference here between your present situation and your desired outcome.

KEY (CORRECT ANSWERS)

1. A	16. D	31. B	46. B	61. B
2. B	17. D	32. B	47. A	62. D
3. A	18. D	33. A	48. A	63. B
4. C	19. A	34. A	49. D	64. D
5. A	20. C	35. C	50. C	65. C
6. D	21. D	36. C	51. B	66. B
7. B	22. B	37. D	52. B	67. C
8. C	23. D	38. A	53. B	68. A
9. B	24. C	39. C	54. A	69. C
10. A	25. B	40. C	55. C	70. B
11. B	26. D	41. C	56. C	71. C
12. B	27. A	42. B	57. D	72. C
13. B	28. D	43. B	58. C	73. D
14. B	29. C	44. C	59. D	74. C
15. C	30. B	45. B	60. A	75. A

EXAMINATION SECTION
TEST 1

DIRECTIONS: Each question or incomplete statement is followed by several suggested answers or completions. Select the one the BEST answers the question or completes the statement. *PRINT THE LETTER OF THE CORRECT ANSWER IN THE SPACE AT THE RIGHT.*

1. An adult client is seeking treatment at a community mental health clinic. For over a year, she has been overwhelmed with a sense of helplessness and feelings of intense fear, and has had difficulty in performing at work. During the intake interview, the client reports she was sexually abused as a child. According to the DSM-IV, the client would MOST likely be diagnosed as having which disorder?

    A. Major depressive
    B. Dysthymic
    C. Depersonalization
    D. Posttraumatic stress

2. A woman whose child was recently diagnosed with a terminal illness is referred to a hospital social worker. The woman tells the social worker that her child is not ill and will not need to see the doctor again. Which of the following defense mechanisms is represented by the mother's response?

    A. Rationalization
    B. Denial
    C. Displacement
    D. Intellectualization

3. A client who has received services for several years in a dialysis unit appears for a routine visit. The nurse notices that the client's affect is markedly different from the last visit. After ruling out compliance concerns, the nurse refers the client to the unit social worker. When seeing the social worker, the client seems detached, self-absorbed, and tearful. The social worker should FIRST:

    A. assess changes in the client's life situation
    B. schedule a family conference
    C. explore the client's concerns about dying
    D. discuss the client's feelings about dialysis

4. During the first appointment at a family agency, a mother is encouraged by the social worker to express her feelings about the recent placement of her child in a residential facility for the developmentally disabled. The client talks at length instead about her physical health problems. The social worker should FIRST:

    A. take a full developmental history on the child
    B. redirect the mother to the reasons for the child's placement
    C. evaluate the mother's focus on her own needs
    D. listen attentively to the mother as a way of building rapport

5. A social worker at a community mental health center is working with a 21-year-old client who has been experiencing a great deal of rejection from family and friends. The rejections followed an admission by the client that she is a lesbian. During the third session the client begins to cry and says *maybe my mom is right. She says all I need to do is find the right man.* After reflecting the client's unhappy feelings, the social worker should NEXT:

    A. use universalization to provide reassurance to the client about the behavior of others in these circumstances
    B. explore the client's psychosocial history to determine the origins of her sexual orientation
    C. encourage the client to spend some time rethinking her sexual orientation before continuing with the *coming out* process
    D. arrange for a family session to assist the client's family in understanding how to best support a gay family member

6. A social worker is asked to assist an elderly client in making alternative living arrangements. In the initial interview, the client repeatedly attempts to discuss past experiences. What is the social worker's MOST appropriate response to the client?

    A. Ignore the references to the past
    B. Facilitate discussion of the recollections
    C. Evaluate the client for dementia
    D. Redirect the focus to the living arrangements

7. A hospital social worker interviews a couple whose infant has recently been hospitalized for cystic fibrosis. The social worker notices that the parents are reluctant to touch the child. Based on this observation, the social worker's FIRST intervention should be to:

    A. have the parents talk about their reactions to the child's illness
    B. refer the couple to an appropriate support group
    C. evaluate the situation for out-of-home placement for the child
    D. provide the couple with information about cystic fibrosis

8. A client, diagnosed as borderline personality disorder, is verbalizing destructive thoughts directed at herself. While she does admit to depression, she denies any intention to act on the thoughts. The social worker should FIRST:

    A. seek in-patient hospitalization of the client
    B. explore with the client the basis of the depression
    C. complete a suicide risk assessment
    D. refer the client to a psychiatrist for medication

9. As part of the social work process, assessment is BEST described as a:

    A. discrete task to be completed before effective intervention can begin
    B. continuing process throughout the course of intervention
    C. way to measure the effectiveness of the intervention process
    D. method of setting the goals of the intervention process

10. Random error is assessed by:

    A. instrument reliability
    B. instrument validity
    C. external validity
    D. correlation

11. An 50-year-old client diagnosed with chronic alcoholism is at greatest risk for which of the following disorders?

    A. Parkinson's disease
    B. Alzheimer's disease
    C. Korsikoff's disease
    D. Senile dementia

12. A hospital social worker meets with three adult children of an elderly woman. The woman's physician has recommended discharge to a long-term care facility because she is unable to care for herself. The woman refuses this recommendation, and the children cannot agree on a plan. The social worker should FIRST:

    A. define the problem with the children
    B. develop a contract with the woman
    C. gather a social history from the children
    D. provide referrals to home care agencies

13. An adult client who is HIV positive and addicted to drugs and alcohol is receiving social work services from a local AIDS service organization. The client has responsibility for a young grandchild whose mother died of AIDS. The social worker suspects the child is the target of verbal abuse and possible neglect. Which assessment tool can BEST be used by the social worker to gain a better understanding of the situation?

    A. Genogram
    B. Sociogram
    C. Social network map
    D. Ecomap

14. A social worker employed with a public school system makes an initial home visit with a 15-year-old female client at the request of the client's probation officer. Before the social worker begins the assessment of the client and home situation, the client says *I don't have to tell you anything, and I won't tell you anything*. To facilitate the client's participation, the social worker's BEST response would be to tell her that:

    A. there are potential legal consequences for noncompliance
    B. she does indeed control whether she will cooperate
    C. her probation officer has requested the assessment
    D. the assessment is necessary in order to provide services

15. A social worker is interviewing the parents of an adolescent who has recently begun resisting their authority. The parents are angry and confused about how to handle the situation. When the social worker asks questions about other family members, the father says *You're not getting it; it is our son who is the problem*. The social worker should FIRST:

    A. recommend an individual assessment of the adolescent
    B. obtain a developmental history of the adolescent
    C. discuss the importance of understanding everyone's perspective
    D. redirect questions toward the adolescent's behavior

16. During the first interview in the home with a pregnant, unmarried 15-year-old and her mother, the teenager states firmly to the social worker that she wants to keep her baby. The mother asks the social worker to tell the daughter about how difficult it will be to care for the baby. The teenager states, *I don't want to be talked out of keeping my child*. The social worker's FIRST response should be to:

    A. provide the teenager with the positives and negatives of caring for an infant
    B. explore the mother's feelings about her daughter's pregnancy
    C. discuss the teenager's feelings about being forced into a decision
    D. facilitate communication between the mother and daughter

17. Which situation is an example of role reversal in a parent-child relationship?

    A. A seven-year-old girl repeatedly comforting and reassuring her distressed mother following a marital separation
    B. A nine-year-old girl sharing her mother's concerns about household bills
    C. A single mother expecting her 10-year-old son to stay at home unsupervised
    D. An 11-year-old boy demanding of his mother that his meals be on the table at a certain time and that his laundry be done

18. A client is concluding treatment at a family counseling agency. The client feels very appreciative of the social worker's services. At the end of the interview, the client offers a substantial monetary gift to the social worker in addition to paying the fee to the agency. The social worker should:

    A. accept the gift, acknowledging the client's contribution to treatment
    B. refuse the gift, basing the action on ethical standards of practice
    C. accept the money but with the understanding that it will be donated to a local charity
    D. refuse the personal gift and suggest that the client make a donation to the agency instead

19. During group therapy sessions, one of the members continuously blames others in the group for the depression and hopelessness the member experiences. In an effort to address the client's concerns, the social worker should FIRST:

    A. tell the client that these feelings stem from fears
    B. encourage the client to talk about feelings within the group
    C. reiterate the guidelines for the group process
    D. encourage the group to be more sensitive to the client's feelings

20. A child welfare worker is interviewing a parent who admits brutally abusing a child during a rage. On hearing the details, the social worker becomes very angry. To appropriately deal with the anger, the social worker should:

    A. acknowledge the anger to the parent and continue the interview
    B. ignore the anger and proceed with the interview
    C. recognize the anger and discuss it later with the supervisor
    D. request the case be transferred to another social worker

21. A false, fixed belief that is inconsistent with the intelligence and cultural background of the person holding the belief and held despite rational explanation and evidence to the contrary is BEST defined as a(n):

    A. denial
    B. illusion
    C. hallucination
    D. delusion

21.____

22. A social worker learns that a father becomes angry when his two-year-old son soils or wets his pants. The father's usual response to this behavior is to yell at the child to *grow up*. The father's behavior MOST likely reflects:

    A. dysfunctional relationship with the child
    B. a distorted perception of child development
    C. a need for developing new ways to cope with stress
    D. displacement of anger toward the other parent

22.____

23. In which instance is identifying information from an individual client's case record NOT appropriate for use?

    A. When the social worker is going on vacation, leaving another social worker in charge of the case
    B. When consulting with a professional to gain insight into the client's condition
    C. When agency data is being used for supporting grant proposals
    D. When the social worker is participating in clinical supervision

23.____

24. A woman in treatment with a social worker comments that whenever her adolescent son becomes angry, she feels as though she is a failure as a parent. The social worker comments that all adolescents become angry at times. The social worker's technique is known as:

    A. clarifying
    B. interpreting
    C. confronting
    D. normalizing

24.____

25. A new supervisor recently promoted from another part of the agency supervises a social worker who conducts group therapy with adolescent clients. In the new position, the supervisor often *drops in* on group sessions and interacts with clients. What is the FIRST step the social worker should take in dealing with this situation?

    A. Integrate the supervisor into group activities with the clients
    B. Talk with the supervisor about the impact of dropping in on groups
    C. Arrange a meeting with the agency director to clarify the supervisor's role
    D. Respect the supervisor's position and allow the supervisor to judge the situation

25.____

KEY (CORRECT ANSWERS)

1.	D	11.	C
2.	B	12.	A
3.	A	13.	D
4.	D	14.	B
5.	A	15.	C
6.	B	16.	C
7.	A	17.	A
8.	C	18.	B
9.	B	19.	B
10.	A	20.	C

21.	D
22.	B
23.	C
24.	D
25.	B

TEST 2

DIRECTIONS: Each question or incomplete statement is followed by several suggested answers or completions. Select the one the BEST answers the question or completes the statement. *PRINT THE LETTER OF THE CORRECT ANSWER IN THE SPACE AT THE RIGHT.*

1. A client who has completed treatment and resolved the targeted problem is making excessive telephone calls to the social worker. The social worker should:

    A. inform the client that the therapeutic relationship is finished
    B. refer the client to another social worker in the agency
    C. limit the number of calls the social worker will accept
    D. schedule a session to determine any current problems

2. In preparing a discharge summary, a social worker writes a case history describing the events leading up to the client's recent hospitalization. The history describes the assessment that was made and the exact symptoms that supported the assessment. The discharge summary was then placed in the client's record. The social worker's supervisor would consider this summary to be:

    A. incomplete because it did not describe what happened in treatment
    B. accurate in giving a complete account supporting admission
    C. satisfactory as a summary for use upon the client's readmission
    D. inappropriate because it contains the assessment

3. A client states to a social worker that the social worker reminds him of his former fiancee and that he very much appreciates the social worker's caring for him. This is an example of:

    A. reaction formation
    B. idealization
    C. transference
    D. unconditional positive regard

4. A client who is in therapy with a social worker has made significant progress over a period of three months. The client misses a scheduled appointment and does not return the social worker's calls. This behavior is MOST likely an indication of the client's:

    A. misunderstanding of the treatment contract
    B. negative transference in the therapeutic process
    C. establishment of satisfying relationships
    D. readiness for termination of treatment

5. In an enmeshed family the children are LEAST likely to exhibit:

    A. role ambiguity
    B. respect for authority
    C. unclear boundaries
    D. difficulty in focusing

6. A t-test is used to determine:

   A. causality
   B. standard deviation
   C. significance of differences between sample means
   D. significance at the .05 level of probability

7. A budgeting approach which categorizes expenditures and resources according to the agency's service areas is:

   A. zero-based
   B. program-based
   C. cost benefit
   D. line item

8. A married couple bring their six-year-old son in to see a social worker in private practice. The parents indicate the child recently began bedwetting after being toilet trained for three years. Upon questioning, the parents reveal the bedwetting began shortly after the parents brought their new baby home from the hospital. The six-year-old is MOST likely using the defense mechanism of:

   A. repression
   B. regression
   C. reaction formation
   D. displacement

9. A social worker may limit a client's right to self-determination when:

   A. agency policy requires the social worker to develop treatment plans that minimize liability for the agency
   B. in the social worker's professional opinion the client has made poor choices regarding treatment options
   C. there is pending legal action which would curtail the rights of the client to make decisions
   D. the client's actions or potential actions pose a serious and imminent risk to self or others

10. A social worker wants to develop insight into the ways the social worker's own attitudes and feelings affect relationships with clients. This understanding can be MOST effectively facilitated by a supervisor who promotes the use of:

    A. reflection
    B. analysis
    C. peer review
    D. problem assessment

11. At times a social worker may choose to use closed-ended questions to:

    A. permit the client to be in control
    B. provide needed structure and direction
    C. check out the client's ability to take the initiative
    D. challenge the client's point of view

12. A social worker who has mental health difficulties which interfere with professional judgment and performance should:

    A. continue to practice and engage in all regular activities but safeguard clients
    B. make a self-report on the situation to the state social work licensing board
    C. seek consultation and remedial action, which may include obtaining therapy and adjusting workloads
    D. continue to practice and use appropriate self-disclosure to assist clients to understand similar issues

13. To enhance a client's capacity to make decisions, the social worker should:

    A. analyze the situation for the client
    B. give the client written materials on decision making
    C. ask the client to make a decision independent of the social worker
    D. teach the client how to examine alternate solutions

14. A husband and wife both express to a social worker that their needs are not being met by the other. This situation described by the couple is BEST characterized by the absence of:

    A. boundaries
    B. homeostasis
    C. complementarity
    D. entropy

15. A mother, father, and 16-year-old daughter come to a social worker because the daughter is breaking curfew, running away from home, and failing in school. The mother states at the initial session that she does not know what to do and that they need help. After acknowledging the family's distress, the social worker should:

    A. establish the number of sessions the family is allowed with the social worker
    B. formulate goals for the family members
    C. clarify the parents' expectations of the social work intervention
    D. contract with the adolescent on specific behavior goals

16. A social worker is allowed to violate confidentiality if a client:

    A. initiates a lawsuit against the social worker
    B. is under the age of eighteen
    C. resides in a nursing home
    D. resists recommended social work intervention

17. A social worker faced with a practice situation that may pose an ethical dilemma should FIRST consult the:

    A. current supervisor
    B. social work licensing board'
    C. professional code of ethics
    D. most experienced colleague

18. Crisis intervention is a strategy which generally involves:

    A. having clients face their problems directly and come to terms with them
    B. acting on behalf of clients who cannot act for their own safety
    C. using chaining and sloping to change behaviors
    D. encouraging a high level of intensive activity by the client

19. When faced by a hostile client in an agency setting, it is BEST for the social worker to:

    A. suggest that the client's attitude is making the situation worse
    B. accept the client's hostility and redirect toward nonthreatening topics
    C. set limitations and structure for the interview session
    D. acknowledge the client's feelings and encourage discussion of them

20. If a client has a mood disorder that can be addressed within a limited time frame, the treatment approach of choice is:

    A. cognitive behavioral therapy
    B. crisis intervention
    C. insight-oriented psychotherapy
    D. client-centered therapy

21. A social worker is using a task-centered approach to provide services to a client. After completing an assessment on the client, the social worker's NEXT step should be to:

    A. develop a set of goals with the client
    B. redefine the relationship with the client
    C. outline tasks for the client
    D. monitor the client's progress in goal accomplishment

22. In therapy, a client describes herself as a failure because of repeated publisher rejections of her work. Although the client has a well-paying job and satisfying interpersonal relationships, she defines her identity in terms of her writing. In response to the woman's self-description, the social worker should FIRST:

    A. help the client be more realistic about her abilities
    B. determine if she uses writing to avoid other areas of her life
    C. encourage the client to find other outside interests
    D. further explore the client's feelings about being published

23. During an initial session with a social worker at a community mental health center, a self-referred adult client states, *I just need to let you know, I don't much like social workers*. The client adds that social workers *don't ever seem to be able to help anyone*. In order to facilitate the therapeutic process in this situation, the social worker should:

    A. point out to the client the discrepancy between the desire for services and the dislike of social workers
    B. reassure the client that it is safe to discuss any and all issues, problems, and concerns
    C. acknowledge that the client may have had bad experiences with social workers in the past
    D. encourage the client to explain how the stated view of social workers developed

24. A social worker conducts a home visit to a 45-year-old Latino client whose young son was killed in a recent automobile accident. The social worker observes that a large altar has been made, which contains many candles as well as pictures of the boy and other deceased relatives. The client sobs throughout the interview and tells the social worker that the boy has been communicating to the client nightly through angels. In order to most effectively work with the client, the social worker should FIRST:

   A. refer the client for a medical evaluation
   B. assess the client for psychotic symptoms
   C. explore mourning rituals of the client's family
   D. evaluate the potential of self-harm

25. A social worker is conducting an initial interview with a father and three teenage children. The mother died recently after a lengthy illness. Exploration indicates that the family members were not able to appropriately mourn the mother's death. To help them cope with the unresolved grief, the social worker should FIRST:

   A. encourage the family to discuss their loss
   B. obtain information about the mother's illness
   C. refer the family to a grief support group
   D. engage the family in structural family therapy

KEY (CORRECT ANSWERS)

1.	D	11.	B
2.	A	12.	C
3.	C	13.	D
4.	D	14.	C
5.	B	15.	C
6.	C	16.	A
7.	B	17.	C
8.	B	18.	B
9.	D	19.	D
10.	A	20.	A

21. A
22. D
23. D
24. C
25. A

EXAMINATION SECTION
TEST 1

DIRECTIONS: Each question or incomplete statement is followed by several suggested answers or completions. Select the one that BEST answers the question or completes the statement. *PRINT THE LETTER OF THE CORRECT ANSWER IN THE SPACE AT THE RIGHT.*

1. An engaged couple is seeing a social worker for premarital counseling. The woman reports that her fiance's family doesn't accept her because of her religion, and she doesn't want to convert. Her fiance agrees that this is a problem and that he is "torn" between his parents and his wife-to-be. The social worker should **FIRST**:

    A. discuss ways the couple can help his parents accept their relationship
    B. explore the impact of this issue on their relationship
    C. focus on how they plan to handle their religious differences when they are married
    D. recommend individual sessions for each to deal with their feelings

2. A single parent of two small children is being seen for an intake interview at a family service agency. She begins to cry when describing her pressures and stresses, and the decisions she is facing since the sudden death of her husband three months ago. She apologizes to the worker for "acting like a baby" and says she knows that her problems could be worse. The social worker should **FIRST**:

    A. suggest that the client prioritize her problems
    B. help the client identify her coping mechanisms
    C. suggest a referral to a bereavement group
    D. acknowledge the difficulty of dealing with numerous problems

3. Which of the following factors is **NOT** used in establishing a diagnosis using the DSM-IV?

    A. Physical functioning
    B. Psychosocial stressors
    C. Clinical syndromes
    D. Medical conditions

4. A couple in their mid-thirties seek marital counseling from a social worker because they have been experiencing conflict over their sexual relationship. The wife reports that she feels emotionally detached from her husband. They decided early in their marriage not to have children, and both are involved and committed to their careers. The social worker should focus on the couple's:

    A. career objectives
    B. parenting decision
    C. sexual relationship
    D. relationship issues

5. A couple comes to a family service agency requesting help in communicating better with each other. The social worker should **FIRST**:

A. engage the couple in a discussion of male/female communication patterns
B. facilitate role-playing of effective and dysfunctional communication techniques
C. explore what the couple means by better communication
D. gather psychosocial background information on each client, including marital history

6. Which of the following statements is **NOT** true when a social work agency employs a consultant?

   A. The consultant's role need not be sanctioned by the agency's administration.
   B. The consultant's role rests primarily on specialized knowledge and skill.
   C. Consultation is an indirect means of influencing skills of agency staff.
   D. The ultimate beneficiary of consultation is the agency clientele.

7. When a client's behavior is particularly resistant to extinction, the behavior is likely to have been maintained in the past by:

   A. consistent reinforcement
   B. consistent punishment
   C. intermittent reinforcement
   D. intermittent punishment

8. According to the DSM-IV, which of the following symptoms is **NOT** associated with a diagnosis of schizophrenia?

   A. Delusions
   B. Flight of ideas
   C. Affectional flattening
   D. Disorganized speech

9. A six-year-old exhibits repetitive whole-body movements, gross deficits in language development, and a lack of emotional responsiveness. The social worker suspects a diagnosis of:

   A. post-traumatic stress disorder
   B. organic brain syndrome
   C. attention-deficit/hyperactivity disorder
   D. autistic disorder

10. To attempt to extinguish a child's talking to himself in class, a social worker using a behavior modification approach will **FIRST**:

    A. determine how frequently the child talks to himself in class
    B. meet with the child individually and ask to whom he is talking
    C. include the child in a group for children with delayed social skills
    D. remove the child from the class each time he begins talking to himself

11. A client is being seen for symptoms of depression and anxiety, but has been resistant to efforts to refer her for a medication evaluation. The client states that medication is a "crutch" and she should be able to solve her problems without it. During a session following a very upsetting weekend, the client cries and says that she will see "a shrink for pills that will solve her problems." In facilitating the client's referral to the psychiatrist, the social worker should **FIRST**:

A. give the client a list of recommended psychiatrists
B. phone for a psychiatric appointment while the client is still in the office
C. discuss the client's expectation of the consultation
D. suggest the client review her insurance coverage

12. A mother has been referred to a family service agency after learning that her 14-year-old son is diabetic, because of the son's denial of the illness by "forgetting" to test his blood sugar and take insulin as directed. When she asks him how he is feeling, he tells her either to leave him alone or "chill out." The mother bursts into tears, saying she is a "nervous wreck," and worries about her son constantly. The social worker should **FIRST**:

    A. reassure the mother that her son's reactions are typical adolescent responses
    B. explore family and community resources available to the mother
    C. acknowledge the mother's feelings of fear and apprehension
    D. suggest that a joint interview with mother and son be scheduled

13. The **MOST** difficult aspect of conducting a cost-benefit analysis is:

    A. determining the units of services
    B. enumerating interventions
    C. establishing a control group
    D. operationally defining outcomes

14. Which of the following statistical tests is a nonparametric test of significance?

    A. Analysis of variance
    B. T-test
    C. Pearson's r
    D. Chi-square

15. A social work manager in a hospital setting decides to establish an interdisciplinary collaborative team to review advanced directive procedures. The **FIRST** step in this process is to:

    A. identify the areas of expertise needed on the team
    B. identify the persons to be assigned to the team
    C. select the leader of the proposed team
    D. develop a rationale for the inclusion of a social worker

16. The desire for control and perfection is characteristic of which of the following personality disorders?

    A. Borderline
    B. Narcissistic
    C. Obsessive-compulsive
    D. Antisocial

17. After four months of treatment, a client informs his social worker that he has received a job transfer to another city and will move the following week. The social worker should **FIRST**:

A. review with the client progress made and treatment goals not yet achieved
B. discuss with the client his reasons for not informing the social worker of his plans to move sooner
C. ask the client to sign a release of information form in case he wants to enter treatment at a later time
D. advise the client to become involved in treatment as soon as possible in the new city

18. A social work staff is experiencing an increasing number of clients who fail to keep their appointments. All of the following administrative interventions are appropriate **EXCEPT**:

    A. scheduling a meeting with the staff members to assess their views of the problem
    B. sending a questionnaire to all of the clients who have failed to keep their appointments over the last month
    C. informing clients that they will be charged for not canceling appointments they are unable to keep
    D. terminating clients who do not keep their appointments

19. A five-year-old is scheduled for open heart surgery. Part of the procedure for the operation involves catheterization and an incision in the child's groin. The procedure has been explained to him. He responded to the idea of heart surgery with little or no anxiety but has extreme concern about the catheterization. From a psychodynamic point of view, his anxiety stems from fear of:

    A. mutilation
    B. separation
    C. annihilation
    D. pain

20. A man was referred by his attorney to a social worker after he was charged with sexually molesting a minor. The case is scheduled for trial. The goal of the social worker in treating this client should be to:

    A. gather information in order to prepare a report for the court
    B. determine whether the charge against the client is valid
    C. assist the client in examining his involvement in the charges against him
    D. assist the attorney in preparing the client for his trial

21. A new client has an argument with the agency receptionist before her initial meeting with the social worker. Upon entering the office, the client says to the social worker, in an angry tone, "Why are you looking at me like that?" This remark is an example of which of the following defense mechanisms?

    A. Displacement
    B. Projection
    C. Reaction formation
    D. Sublimation

22. An adult client, arrested for exposing himself, reports that he was urinating after excessive drinking. This is his third arrest for the same offense. He is depressed, anxious, and markedly distressed by his behavior. This client is **BEST** described by which of the following DSM-IV diagnostic categories?

- A. Narcissistic personality disorder
- B. Gender identity disorder
- C. Exhibitionism
- D. Alcohol dependence

23. A woman is referred to a hospital social worker by the emergency room physician, who states that the woman must be admitted to the hospital immediately. The woman tells the social worker that she moved to the community only last month and does not have family or friends who can care for her two preschool children during her hospitalization. The social worker's primary responsibility in this situation is to:

    - A. secure emergency financial assistance for the woman so that she can pay for the necessary child care
    - B. ask the physician to delay the hospitalization until appropriate child care arrangements are made
    - C. find a close relative of the children to care for them as soon as possible
    - D. assist the client in arranging a temporary placement for the children

24. A social worker tells his supervisor that he is very uncomfortable and anxious when seeing a client described as "intimidating" and "bullying" to others. The social worker expresses feelings of frustration, saying that nothing he says or does seems to work for the client. Initially, the supervisor's **MOST** helpful approach would be to:

    - A. observe the next interview through a two-way mirror
    - B. recommend that the next session with the client be taped
    - C. role-play the situation with the social worker
    - D. suggest appropriate reading materials

25. A manic episode includes all of the following characteristics **EXCEPT**:

    - A. distractibility
    - B. depersonalization
    - C. change in sleep pattern
    - D. increased involvement in pleasurable activities

KEY (CORRECT ANSWERS)

1. B
2. D
3. A
4. D
5. C

6. A
7. C
8. B
9. D
10. A

11. C
12. C
13. D
14. D
15. A

16. C
17. A
18. D
19. A
20. C

21. B
22. C
23. D
24. C
25. B

TEST 2

DIRECTIONS: Each question or incomplete statement is followed by several suggested answers or completions. Select the one that BEST answers the question or completes the statement. *PRINT THE LETTER OF THE CORRECT ANSWER IN THE SPACE AT THE RIGHT.*

1. The Draw-a-Person test provides diagnostic information about the client's:

    A. personality structure
    B. eye-motor coordination
    C. thought processes
    D. self-image

2. According to psychoanalytic theory, which of the following is associated with the development of neurosis?

    A. Interpersonal struggle
    B. Emotion
    C. Impulsivity
    D. Individuation

3. In working with an African-American family, it is **MOST** important for the social worker to:

    A. acknowledge possible differences in ethnic background early in the relationship
    B. provide directions and instructions to effect a change in the family's negotiation with social institutions
    C. encourage contact with the extended family as a source of material and emotional support
    D. establish contact with members of the family's church to assure them a social support system

4. A social worker has seen a family for four months, with the initial focus on the youngest child's school attendance problems. During the last two months, the child has been absent from school only once. In the last session of the planned termination, the mother reported that she was to be admitted to the hospital for surgery the following week. The social worker's **BEST** course of action is to:

    A. refer the family to a hospital social worker when the mother is admitted
    B. reevaluate with the family the decision to terminate
    C. discontinue treatment, arranging a session when the mother is again able to attend
    D. proceed with plans for the termination of family treatment

5. During an initial session with a social worker, the client describes herself as a very "private person" who doesn't like to talk about herself. She expresses deep concern and anxiety about confidentially and asks the social worker whether "everything I tell you will remain private, and just between us?" The social worker should **FIRST**:

    A. explore the basis of the client's anxiety about confidentiality
    B. discuss the difference between self-disclosure and confidentiality
    C. comment on the client's focus on the confidentiality issue
    D. discuss with the client the limits on confidentiality

6. A social worker in a regional social advocacy organization is requested by citizens in an economically depressed rural area to help improve the area's social and economic condition. Recent growth in a nearby urban area has begun to stir citizens' excitement over new employment opportunities as well as fear over unwanted encroachment. The **MOST** appropriate initial strategy for the social worker to employ with the citizen group is to:

    A. educate group members regarding political strategies for gaining power
    B. assess and document the range of services and needs in the community
    C. orient the citizen group to ways they can collect and analyze community data
    D. facilitate problem-solving and communication skills within the community

7. A couple seeks conjoint therapy from a social worker. After an initial assessment, the social worker's **MOST** appropriate intervention is to:

    A. arrange separate sessions for each client to openly express feelings about the other
    B. foster direct communication with the couple in joint sessions
    C. complete a social and developmental history for each partner
    D. encourage both partners to confront the other with areas of marital dissatisfaction

8. In an initial session, which of the following approaches is **LEAST** effective in reducing a client's hesitation to engage in the social worker-client relationship?

    A. Acknowledging the difficulty the client may have in sharing information
    B. Asking directly whether the client is willing to cooperate
    C. Providing the client with information about the number of sessions, their length, and the costs involved
    D. Developing a written contract with the client based on specific outcomes

9. A 14-year-old who has been in treatment with a social worker for the past year has a history of impulsive acting-out behavior. The adolescent is becoming increasingly depressed and is talking about suicide. The social worker should **FIRST**:

    A. request that the family monitor the client's acting-out behaviors
    B. refer the client to a physician for antidepressant medication
    C. intensify the exploration of origin and nature of the depression
    D. assess the client's potential for self-harm

10. In providing feedback to social workers, the supervisor should include all of the following comments about performance **EXCEPT**:

    A. noting how the social worker's performance mirrors the supervisor's expectation
    B. commending the social worker on a specific action
    C. publicly remarking on the positive performance of a social worker
    D. pointing out inappropriate work performance when it occurs

11. A 16-year-old who has been hospitalized frequently for control of diabetes was referred to the hospital social worker. Information about the youth's family indicates that the father is an alcoholic, and the parents experience a great deal of marital discord, arguing frequently in front of the youth. The social worker should **FIRST**:

    A. work with the family concerning the father's alcoholism
    B. refer the parents for marital therapy
    C. explore the youth's experiences in living with a chronic illness

D. discuss the youth's feelings about separation from the family during hospitalizations

12. During a first interview, a client informs a social worker that she engaged in sexual activity with her previous social worker. The sexual involvement began a year after the client began treatment and ended when she decided to terminate treatment against the social worker's advice. Which of the following actions should the social worker take?

    A. Contact the previous social worker, confronting him with the client's information
    B. Consult the state social work regulatory law regarding reporting requirements
    C. Investigate whether the client's allegations about the former social worker are true
    D. Take no action since the sexual involvement took place outside the therapy sessions

13. A client with a history of impulsive, aggressive behaviors, has been seeing a social worker for three months. During a session, he becomes angry with the social worker and storms out. He cancels his next appointment and sends a letter demanding that his records be released to him immediately, or he will take legal action. He adds that he is seeing a new therapist and has no plans to return to see the social worker. The social worker believes that releasing the record to the client will cause him serious harm. According to professional ethics, the social worker should **FIRST**:

    A. document in the file both the client's request for the record and the rationale for withholding it
    B. seek legal consultation regarding the threat to sue
    C. send the record to the client as requested
    D. alert the social worker's malpractice carrier that a suit might be filed

14. Viewing an organization as a system, which subsystem encompasses staff development functions?

    A. Support
    B. Operations
    C. Policy
    D. Service

15. A client who has been referred by his physician to a social worker reports that he has come because of "nerves." He says that for the past six months he has been feeling a lot of muscle tension, and is so "keyed up" and "irritable" that he can't concentrate and focus at work. He also has trouble sleeping and can't control his state of worry at home or on the job. According to the DSM-IV, the **MOST** likely diagnosis would be:

    A. Posttraumatic Stress Disorder
    B. Generalized Anxiety Disorder
    C. Dysthymic Disorder
    D. Major Depressive Disorder

16. A social worker observes a parent reaching out to embrace her four-year-old child. When the child approaches, the parent hugs the child, and then with an admonishing tone states, "You should never be so trusting!" In communication theory, this type of interaction observed by the social worker is referred to as:

A. conditional regard
B. double bind
C. emotional blocking
D. cognitive interference

17. A client is seeing a social worker for relationship problems with her boyfriend. She tearfully describes a recent incident in which he was verbally abusive to her. She reports he blames her for his frequent angry outbursts because she does things he considers stupid. Although her friends and family tell her to end the relationship, she says she loves him, but doesn't like the way he treats her. The social worker should **FIRST**:

    A. encourage the client to face the reality of the boyfriend's behavior
    B. explore the client's relationship with family and friends
    C. suggest reading material on abusive relationships
    D. acknowledge the client's ambivalent feelings

18. A woman who recently separated from her husband is seeing a social worker with her children, ages 10 and 16, in family therapy. The initial complaint is that the 10-year-old refuses to attend school. Using a structural family therapy approach, the social worker should **FIRST**:

    A. see the child and mother separately to explore their reactions to the separation
    B. help the mother take charge by encouraging her to insist that the child attend school
    C. arrange for homebound instruction for the child until he returns to school
    D. discuss with the mother her feelings about the recent separation

19. A woman comes to a family agency for help with her marriage. During the first interview with the social worker, she talks rapidly and intensely about her own history of physical illnesses and hospitalizations, her child's problems at school, and her husband's drinking. The **BEST** course of action for the social worker is to:

    A. listen to the client without comment, summarizing at the end of the interview
    B. wait until a pause and ask the client to specify why she came for help
    C. ask the client to elaborate on her husband's drinking and its effect on the family
    D. acknowledge that the client has many troubles and ask which she wants help with

20. In working with reluctant involuntary clients, which of the following areas is the **MOST** important for the social worker to address?

    A. The client's anger at the treatment referral source
    B. The availability of help for the client
    C. The client's ambivalence toward treatment
    D. The social worker's view of the problem for treatment

21. A social work researcher in a mental health clinic wants to measure the effectiveness of group psychotherapy in the social adjustment of recently divorced women. The researcher develops an instrument to measure social adjustment and administers it to 40 divorced women, half of whom are randomly assigned to eight sessions of group psychotherapy. The remaining 20, placed on a waiting list, receive no group psychotherapy. At the end of the eight group sessions the instrument will be re-administered to the 20 group participants and the 20 women on the waiting list. The design being utilized by the researcher is a:

A. static group comparison
B. pretest/posttest control group
C. quasi-experimental
D. one-group pretest/posttest

22. A client has been referred by an Employee Assistance Program (EAP) to a social worker for a maximum of six sessions. The costs for any additional sessions would be the client's responsibility. During the first session, the client describes longstanding personal and relationship problems that she has never resolved, and notes that she is looking forward to finally having the chance to "solve" her problems. Before developing a treatment plan, the social worker should **FIRST**:

    A. support the client's perception that treatment can reduce stress and tension
    B. advocate with the EAP for additional sessions
    C. explore the client's understanding of the referral and the coverage provided
    D. assess the client's capacity and motivation for longterm treatment

23. A cost-benefit analysis in a human service organization is primarily concerned with:

    A. program costs in human and material resources
    B. economic benefits of program goals to the community
    C. the relationship between proposed and actual costs
    D. comparison of alternative means of reaching goals

24. A social worker chairing a task group can **MOST** effectively organize its work by:

    A. rotating the facilitator role among group members
    B. providing relevant written materials to participants prior to the meeting
    C. agreeing to a consensus form of decision-making
    D. specifying the group's objectives

25. In developing a brochure for distribution to prospective clients, a social worker can include all of the following **EXCEPT**:

    A. assurances that treatment will be effective
    B. level of professional credential
    C. highest relevant academic degree
    D. policy on accepting third party payments

KEY (CORRECT ANSWERS)

1.	D	11.	C
2.	A	12.	B
3.	A	13.	A
4.	B	14.	A
5.	D	15.	B
6.	D	16.	B
7.	B	17.	D
8.	B	18.	B
9.	D	19.	D
10.	A	20.	C

21. B
22. C
23. D
24. D
25. A

EXAMINATION SECTION
TEST 1

DIRECTIONS: Each question or incomplete statement is followed by several suggested answers or completions. Select the one that BEST answers the question or completes the statement. *PRINT THE LETTER OF THE CORRECT ANSWER IN THE SPACE AT THE RIGHT.*

1. A breach of ethical conduct may exist when a social worker:
    A. discusses sports scores with a client during a session
    B. uses the client's first name
    C. exchanges books to be read for pleasure with a client
    D. exchanges social work sessions for babysitting services by the client

2. A seven-year-old child frequently expresses worry about his parents' whereabouts, is afraid of the dark, cries easily, and complains of frequent stomachaches. The child is MOST likely exhibiting:
    A. symptoms of abuse and neglect
    B. separation anxiety disorder
    C. conduct disorder
    D. panic disorder

3. Using behavior therapy for treatment of depression reflects the view that depression is the result of:
    A. role confusion
    B. negative cognition
    C. poor interpersonal skills
    D. absence of positive reinforcement

4. A client, referred by his wife, walked into the social worker's office, talking in a loud and threatening manner. He stated that there is no problem except his wife and it is she who should be in therapy. The social worker should FIRST:
    A. assure the client that he will have the opportunity to discuss his situation
    B. suggest to the client that his behavior indicates that he has a problem
    C. instruct the client to leave the office until he is better composed
    D. ask the client why he believes his wife needs treatment

5. Which of the following characteristics is usually NOT found in families in which incestuous relationships have occurred?
    A. Enmeshment of family members
    B. Distorted patterns of communication
    C. Symbiotic mother-child relationships
    D. Moralistic attitude toward extramarital affairs

6. Following the resignation of a colleague and the freezing of the colleague's position, social work employees of a non-profit agency confronted the social work administrator. They said they were worried about the financial health of the agency and their job security. In addition they complained about the financial disadvantage they experienced in working for the agency. The administrator agreed to a special meeting designed to address employee issues. When planning how to present budgetary issues in a way that would ensure client care, the administrator should focus on:

A. acknowledging the legitimacy of employees' concerns
B. explaining the fiscal environment of non-profit organizations
C. charging a committee to develop an alternative budget
D. eliciting input about programs needing priority resource allocation

7. A 28-year-old client with a long-standing history of drug use was referred by a concerned relative to a social worker. In the assessment interview, the client tells the social worker about frequent cocaine use. The social worker should FIRST:

    A. conduct a family interview to gather a comprehensive biopsychosocial history
    B. begin psychotherapy focusing on the reason for drug abuse
    C. refer the client for substance abuse treatment as a prerequisite to individual therapy
    D. evaluate the client's motivation for change

7.____

8. A family came to a social worker because of their 11-year-old daughter's behavior in the family. The daughter is an average student and has a group of good friends. Within the family, however, she barely speaks to her parents, refuses to clean her room, and rarely brings her friends home. In describing the daughter's behavior, the parents contradict each other, argue about the severity of the behavior, and disagree on methods of discipline. Using a family therapy approach, the social worker should:

    A. focus on the interpersonal communication within the family
    B. offer the parents the chance to work on the marital relationship
    C. help the daughter to function in the family
    D. involve school personnel with the family to determine the extent of the daughter's behavior

8.____

9. A social worker saw an unemployed client whose fee was paid by a concerned family member. As a result of effective treatment, the client resumed employment. Part of the benefit package included HMO coverage for behavioral health care. The client wanted to use this mental health benefit to continue with the social worker, who was already a member of the proper provider panel. To make it possible for the client to use the coverage, the social worker should FIRST:

    A. direct the client to obtain a referral from the primary physician
    B. explain the necessity of formalizing a psychiatric diagnosis
    C. seek pre-authorization for sessions before seeing the client again
    D. inform the client that a case manager controls the number of available sessions

9.____

10. A client in her late 20s tells her social worker that she "can't stand" the way she looks, saying that she is overweight and unable to use makeup well, and that she appears sloppy and unkempt, and has little fashion sense. She ends by saying "It's overwhelming to even think about how to change." The social worker should FIRST:

    A. teach the client stress reduction techniques
    B. focus on the clients strengths and skills
    C. establish specific behavioral objectives
    D. work with the client to prioritize her concerns

10.____

11. The MOST influential factor in determining the probable success of treatment by a social worker whose client is of a different racial background from that of the social worker is the:

    A. social worker's ability to identify with the client
    B. client's transference toward the social worker
    C. social worker's awareness of self
    D. client's ability to communicate openly with the social worker

12. A couple are being seen jointly for problems "with talking to each other." The husband tells the social worker that his wife was sexually abused as a child and he thinks she still has issues with that. The wife confirms the abuse, but denies that it has any relevance to their marital problems, saying she has dealt with the abuse. The husband continues to focus on this topic even after his wife repeatedly asks him to stop. When she yells at him to "just shut up," he does so and turns away from her. She becomes tense and silent. The social worker's MOST appropriate intervention is to:

    A. suggest that the wife and husband be seen individually
    B. suggest they find a topic on which they have less conflict
    C. recommend that they attend a marriage encounter weekend
    D. process with them the observed communication pattern

13. Which of the following statements is true of BOTH supervision and consultation in social work?

    A. The focus is on a continual process of resolving problems identified by the consultant or supervisor.
    B. The level of responsibility of the consultant and supervisor are the same.
    C. The final decision-making authority rests with the consultant or supervisor.
    D. The consultant or the supervisor focus on helping the social worker deal more effectively with problems or tasks.

14. A social worker asks a young child during an assessment interview, "If I asked your parents what they think about you, what would they say?" The social worker is assessing the child's:

    A. dependence on parents
    B. reality testing
    C. conscience
    D. self-concept

15. The use of silence by a social worker during a session with a client who is expressing a high degree of emotion will be MOST effective in:

    A. demonstrating empathy with the client
    B. relieving the client's tension
    C. developing better rapport with the client
    D. assuring the client that the social worker is listening

16. An adolescent boy in a coeducational inpatient group conducted by a social worker is about to be discharged. The treatment staff recommends that the boy be referred to a group home placement rather than returning home to a chaotic family situation. The group members identify with the boy's feelings of wanting to go home and become furious with the staff for its recommendation. In a group session, they become angry and verbally abuse the social worker. The social worker should FIRST:

    A. explain that the reason the boy should go to the group home is due to the family's instability
    B. explore with the group past negative experiences with group homes
    C. explain to the group that some of the material is confidential because it regards the boy's family and it should not be discussed
    D. acknowledge the group's anger and help members identify the underlying issues

17. Family therapy is contraindicated when:

    A. family members are grossly deceitful and destructive to one another
    B. there is evidence of consistent violation of generational boundaries
    C. family myths and secrets appear to be the family style
    D. the identified client is resistant and unmotivated toward change

18. In establishing a therapeutic relationship with an adult client, the social worker should focus attention on the interpersonal process during:

    A. the initial phase of treatment
    B. the establishment of goals
    C. each phase of treatment
    D. the implementation of goals

19. The major difference between process and outcome evaluation in social work practice is:

    A. outcome evaluation is limited to objective measures; process evaluation involves subjective measures
    B. process evaluation focuses on what was done to achieve results; outcome evaluation is focused on the results
    C. outcome evaluation can be conducted only during the termination stage; process evaluation begins with the assessment stage
    D. data for outcome evaluation is secured from the client; the source for process evaluation data is the social worker

20. During a utilization review phone call, a social worker is asked by the managed care representative to provide specific details of the sexual abuse incidents the client experienced. The social worker should:

    A. provide all requested information to the reviewer
    B. refuse to give specific information to protect the client's privacy
    C. review the release of information with the client prior to providing information
    D. review the managed care contract with the supervisor prior to providing information

21. After careful exploration in psychotherapy regarding mounting anxiety and fear of loss of impulse control, a client decided to seek inpatient admission on a voluntary basis. The social worker arranged for a psychiatric evaluation by a provider approved by the client's managed care insurance company. The psychiatrist refused to support admission and prescribed medication, stating the patient could be stabilized and maintained in the community with appropriate therapy. To help the client understand what happened, the social worker should:

    A. validate the client's plan and send the client for a second opinion
    B. explain the requirements of medical necessity and levels of care
    C. explore the possibility of the client paying for inpatient care
    D. mobilize family members to provide the protection needed by the client

22. In working with adult survivors of childhood sexual abuse, the MOST frequently encountered defense mechanism is:

    A. denial
    B. intellectualization
    C. suppression
    D. projection

23. A client is being seen for an initial session by a social worker in private practice. While discussing her history, the client mentions that she has been hospitalized several times for "depression." When the social worker attempts to explore the hospitalizations, the client become tense and guarded, saying it is "old history." She also declares that she won't give permission for those records to be released. The social worker should FIRST:

    A. explore with the client why this topic appears to be upsetting to her
    B. acknowledge the client's right to decide about release of her records
    C. reassure the client that the focus will be on present issues and concerns
    D. assess the client's current level of depression

24. A social worker who tends to be directive and focused on the client's presenting problem is using which of the following therapeutic models?

    A. Object relations
    B. Cognitive behavioral
    C. Psychoanalytic
    D. Existential

25. A hospital social worker is helping a family plan for the home convalescence of a nine-year-old girl injured in an automobile accident. The family reports difficulty with the school district in arranging for a home teacher. When the social worker attempts to contact the administrator responsible for home teacher assignments, the phone calls are not returned. With the child's discharge one week away, the social worker should FIRST:

    A. contact the superintendent of schools about the urgent need for action
    B. request that the primary physician contact the superintendent of schools
    C. send a registered letter to the administrator with the physician's recommendation for a home teacher
    D. arrange follow-up services with the public health nurse who will provide convalescent care

KEY (CORRECT ANSWERS)

1. D
2. B
3. D
4. A
5. C

6. D
7. C
8. A
9. A
10. D

11. C
12. D
13. D
14. D
15. B

16. D
17. A
18. C
19. B
20. C

21. B
22. A
23. B
24. B
25. C

TEST 2

DIRECTIONS: Each question or incomplete statement is followed by several suggested answers or completions. Select the one that BEST answers the question or completes the statement. *PRINT THE LETTER OF THE CORRECT ANSWER IN THE SPACE AT THE RIGHT.*

1. A client whose mother died recently following a long-term illness states to the social worker that he believes that his angry thoughts about his mother caused her death. The client's thoughts are an example of:

    A. delusions
    B. grandiosity
    C. ideas of reference
    D. magical thinking

    1.____

2. Parents of a four-year-old child are referred to a social worker after an examination reveals no physical problem preventing the child from being toilet trained. The parents reveal that the child has not been able to separate from them to attend nursery school, and often sleeps with them even though they have tried to get him to sleep in his own room. During the assessment phase, the social worker's MOST important focus is the:

    A. parents' use of rewards and punishments with the child
    B. early developmental history of each parent
    C. parents' understanding of the child's developmental processes
    D. ways in which the child affects the parents' own relationship

    2.____

3. A 24-year-old woman tells the social worker that she has felt depressed for the past two to three years. She describes herself as feeling sad, with little energy for work or social activities. She also has difficulty making decisions and concentrating on her work, and has a poor appetite. Assessment information does not reveal an apparent reason for the onset of the depressed mood. The client evidences no delusions or hallucinations. According to DSM-IV criteria, the MOST likely diagnosis for the client is:

    A. dysthymic disorder
    B. bipolar disorder, depressed
    C. cyclothymic disorder
    D. major depressive episode, recurrent

    3.____

4. An individual who believes, despite evidence to the contrary, that feelings, thoughts or actions are imposed by an external source, is suffering from:

    A. delirium
    B. delusion
    C. dissociation
    D. dysphoria

    4.____

5. Which of the following medications is used primarily for the treatment of psychosis?

    A. Haloperidol (Haldol)
    B. Alprazolam (Xanax)
    C. Bupropion (Wellbutrin)
    D. Fluoxetine hydrochloride (Prozac)

    5.____

6. A client manifests the characteristics of the early stages of Alzheimer's Disease. To help the client with the changes in her behavior, the MOST appropriate treatment approach for the social worker to use is to focus on:

    A. an understanding of the client's past behavior to enable her to project her future behavior
    B. providing her family members with a support group of other families with similar problems
    C. treatment sessions structured around whatever the client wishes to discuss
    D. observing the progression of the illness and supporting the client in accepting her losses

6.____

7. A new client tearfully reports to the social worker that her father, with whom she is very close, is terminally ill. The client's mother, described by her as "very dependent," has already been calling frequently for support and reassurance. The client says "I just don't know how to cope with dad's illness, my mother's demands and my family's needs," and begins to sob. The social worker should FIRST:

    A. acknowledge the client's feelings of being overwhelmed and sad
    B. discuss a referral for hospice care for the father
    C. identify the client's social and family support network
    D. begin exploring ways the client can set limits for her mother

7.____

8. A social worker is seeing a lesbian client who is experiencing feelings of frustration, depression, and sadness related to her inability to conceive a child after unsuccessful treatment for infertility problems. She and her partner are considering adoption, but have been rejected by a local agency because of their same gender relationship. The client feels helpless, and does not think she will be successful in fighting the agency bias against same-gender couples. In assisting the client to formulate goals for intervention, the social worker should:

    A. explore the client's motivation to pursue adoption at this time
    B. evaluate where the client is in her coming-out process
    C. help the client to confront the discriminatory policies of the agency
    D. refer the client for medication evaluation for depression

8.____

9. A client is complaining about her friend, stating that she is selfish and insensitive. The social worker asks if this is the same friend whom the client had described the week before as caring and a true friend. The client confirms that it is the same person. The social worker comments that this is a complete change in the client's way of thinking. The social worker is using the intervention of:

    A. Interpretation   B. Reality testing
    C. Confrontation   D. Clarification

9.____

10. Which of the following actions by a social worker is considered unethical?

    A. Receiving a fee for the referral of a client to another practitioner
    B. Informing the client of fees in advance of services
    C. Engaging in private practice while holding an agency employment
    D. Establishing rates for professional services not commensurate with that of other professionals

11. A social worker, many of whose clients are in crisis, carries a heavy and difficult case load. In discussing the cases with the supervisor, the social worker reports that clients "come in with a laundry list of complaints" and efforts to help them resolve their problems result in the social worker feeling angry and frustrated or distant and bored. The social worker is MOST likely dealing with the issue of:

    A. transference
    B. countertransference
    C. job-related stress
    D. depression

12. When authorization for treatment from a managed care company is requested, the PRIMARY determinant for approval is based upon:

    A. treatment goals that are explicit and measurable
    B. a diagnosis covered by the insurance plan
    C. documentation that medical necessity criteria are met
    D. a treatment plan providing the least restrictive level of care

13. After six marital therapy sessions with a social worker, a couple continued their destructive pattern of fighting. During the next session, the couple began yelling at each other in a loud and threatening manner. The social worker stopped them and stated, "Your situation is hopeless; fight as often as you wish." This technique is known as:

    A. encouragement
    B. reframing
    C. prescribing a ritual
    D. paradoxical directive

14. According to ego psychology, projective identification is a concept that describes the process of:

    A. unconsciously perceiving others' behavior as a reflection of one's own attitudes
    B. consciously imitating the characteristics of a significant other
    C. showing another person how to develop a better self-image through modeling
    D. associating characteristics from a significant person in the past with another in the present

15. The executive director in an expanding nonprofit social service agency increasingly involved the Director of Professional Services (DPS) in overall agency planning and decision-making. To participate and still perform DPS functions, this manager delegated some activities to senior professionals. According to principles of delegation, the DPS could shift:

    A. responsibility for task completion
    B. authority to perform tasks
    C. power and influence
    D. responsibility for managerial decisions

16. In interviewing a client, a social worker seeks concreteness from the client for all of the following purposes EXCEPT to:

   A. avoid emotionally charged topics
   B. elicit the client's specific feelings
   C. clarify a client message
   D. focus on the "here and now"

17. In planning to evaluate social work treatment in an agency, the MOST important consideration is:

   A. the amount of clinical staff time the evaluation will require
   B. whether the results of the evaluation can be applied to other services
   C. information the evaluation will yield for treatment decision-making
   D. involvement of clinical staff in the planning of the evaluation strategy

18. A couple in their mid-50s came to a family agency accompanied by their adult daughter who lives in their home. They describe marital difficulties which began after the husband suffered a mild stroke. The wife said that he has frequent outbursts of anger, has lost interest in his personal care, and is fearful of being left alone. The husband stated that his wife is overprotective of him, and described the daughter as "nervous when I try to do anything for myself." Using a structural family therapy approach, the social worker would focus on:

   A. obtaining a complete history of the marital and family relationships
   B. creating a situation in the interview which would place the husband in a dependent role
   C. exploring with all family members their feelings about the effects of the stroke on family relationships
   D. arranging individual treatment sessions for each family member

19. A social worker used three different techniques with a depressed client, introducing each of the treatment techniques in order over a period of time. To compare the effectiveness of each of the techniques in helping the client reach the treatment goal, which of the following designs should the social worker use?

   A. A-B design
   B. Multiple baseline across behaviors design
   C. A-B-A-B design
   D. Within-series design

20. An adult who has come to a hospital emergency room complains of visual hallucinations, confusion, and restlessness. Physical symptoms include chills, dilated pupils, and nausea. When interviewed by the social worker, the client states, "Nothing is wrong; I just need some sleep. Which of the following substances is MOST likely the cause of the client's condition?

   A. Alcohol
   B. Marijuana
   C. Cocaine
   D. Barbiturates

21. After several sessions in individual treatment with a social worker, a married woman client reveals that she has had an ongoing affair during the last five years. She says that she is unhappy in her marriage but wants to remain with her husband until her children are in college. She believes her husband does not suspect her

infidelity but is often upset that she does not spend enough time with him. The BEST plan for the social worker in this situation is to:

- A. focus the treatment on the client's feelings about the situation
- B. schedule sessions with the entire family
- C. see the couple together
- D. refer the husband to another therapist

22. A social worker has been appointed to the board of directors of a family counseling agency. All of the following are appropriate actions for the social worker as a board member EXCEPT:

    - A. determining the performance criteria for the agency director position
    - B. reviewing data about utilization of agency services by clients
    - C. acting as a paid consultant to agency staff who deliver direct services
    - D. serving as chair of a board committee on service delivery

22.____

23. For the fifth session with a social worker, a client arrived ten minutes late. Upon entering the social worker's office, the client remained standing and said in an anxious tone, "I know I'm late, but I had other things to do, I just couldn't leave work today." The social worker's BEST response would be to say:

    - A. "You seem to think more of your work than you do of coming here."
    - B. "Maybe we need to explore what it means to you to come here for our sessions."
    - C. "I know that your work is important, but my time is valuable. We will just have less time together today."
    - D. "You seem to think that I would be angry with you for being late today. Let's talk about what you anticipated I would say."

23.____

24. When reviewing a social worker's performance, the supervisor recognized that the social worker conveyed little empathy toward clients who had recently left welfare and were holding first jobs. In order to help the social worker increase the number of empathetically accurate statements made to clients, the supervisor should:

    - A. explain welfare-to-work procedures from the client's perspective
    - B. suggest that the social worker enter therapy to become a more empathic person
    - C. model empathic communication when engaging with the worker
    - D. assert clearly the agency's commitment to supporting these clients

24.____

25. Borderline personality disorder is characterized by all of the following characteristics EXCEPT:
    - A. intense long-term relationships
    - B. primitive delusional fantasies
    - C. lack of control of aggressive drives
    - D. self-destructive behavior

25.____

KEY (CORRECT ANSWERS)

1. D
2. C
3. A
4. B
5. A

6. D
7. A
8. C
9. C
10. A

11. B
12. C
13. D
14. A
15. B

16. A
17. C
18. B
19. D
20. C

21. A
22. C
23. D
24. C
25. A

———————

PREPARING WRITTEN MATERIAL

PARAGRAPH REARRANGEMENT
COMMENTARY

The sentences that follow are in scrambled order. You are to rearrange them in proper order and indicate the letter choice containing the correct answer at the space at the right.

Each group of sentences in this section is actually a paragraph presented in scrambled order. Each sentence in the group has a place in that paragraph; no sentence is to be left out. You are to read each group of sentences and decide upon the best order in which to put the sentences so as to form a well-organized paragraph.

The questions in this section measure the ability to solve a problem when all the facts relevant to its solution are not given.

More specifically, certain positions of responsibility and authority require the employee to discover connection between events sometimes, apparently, unrelated. In order to do this, the employee will find it necessary to correctly infer that unspecified events have probably occurred or are likely to occur. This ability becomes especially important when action must be taken on incomplete information.

Accordingly, these questions require competitors to choose among several suggested alternatives, each of which presents a different sequential arrangement of the events. Competitors must choose the MOST logical of the suggested sequences.

In order to do so, they may be required to draw on general knowledge to infer missing concepts or events that are essential to sequencing the given events. Competitors should be careful to infer only what is essential to the sequence. The plausibility of the wrong alternatives will always require the inclusion of unlikely events or of additional chains of events which are NOT essential to sequencing the given events.

It's very important to remember that you are looking for the best of the four possible choices, and that the best choice of all may not even be one of the answers you're given to choose from.

There is no one right way to solve these problems. Many people have found it helpful to first write out the order of the sentences, as they would have arranged them, on their scrap paper before looking at the possible answers. If their optimum answer is there, this can save them some time. If it isn't, this method can still give insight into solving the problem. Others find it most helpful to just go through each of the possible choices, contrasting each as they go along. You should use whatever method feels comfortable and works for you.

While most of these types of questions are not that difficult, we've added a higher percentage of the difficult type, just to give you more practice. Usually there are only one or two questions on this section that contain such subtle distinctions that you're unable to answer confidently. And you then may find yourself stuck deciding between two possible choices, neither of which you're sure about.

EXAMINATION SECTION

TEST 1

DIRECTIONS: The following groups of sentences need to be arranged in an order that makes sense. Select the letter preceding the sequence that represents the BEST sentence order. *PRINT THE LETTER OF THE CORRECT ANSWER IN THE SPACE AT THE RIGHT.*

1.
   I. The keyboard was purposely designed to be a little awkward to slow typists down.
   II. The arrangement of letters on the keyboard of a typewriter was not designed for the convenience of the typist.
   III. Fortunately, no one is suggesting that a new keyboard be designed right away.
   IV. If one were, we would have to learn to type all over again.
   V. The reason was that the early machines were slower than the typists and would jam easily.
   The CORRECT answer is:
   A. I, III, IV, II, V
   B. II, V, I, IV, III
   C. V, I, II, III, IV
   D. II, I, V, III, IV

   1.____

2.
   I. The majority of the new service jobs are part-time or low-paying.
   II. According to the U.S. Bureau of Labor Statistics, jobs in the service sector constitute 72% of all jobs in this country.
   III. If more and more workers receive less and less money, who will buy the goods and services needed to keep the economy going?
   IV. The service sector is by far the fastest growing part of the United States economy.
   V. Some economists look upon this trend with great concern.
   The CORRECT answer is:
   A. II, IV, I, V, III
   B. II, III, IV, I, V
   C. V, IV, II, III, I
   D. III, I, II, IV, V

   2.____

3.
   I. They can also affect one's endurance.
   II. This can stabilize blood sugar levels, and ensure that the brain is receiving a steady, constant, supply of glucose, so that one is *hitting on all cylinders* while taking the test.
   III. By food, we mean real food, not junk food or unhealthy snacks.
   IV. For this reason, it is important not to skip a meal, and to bring food with you to the exam.
   V. One's blood sugar levels can affect how clearly one is able to think and concentrate during an exam.
   The CORRECT answer is:
   A. V, IV, II, III, I
   B. V, II, I, IV, III
   C. V, I, IV, III, II
   D. V, IV, I, III, II

   3.____

4. I. Those who are the embodiment of desire are absorbed in material quests, and those who are the embodiment of feeling are warriors who value power more than possession.
    II. These qualities are in everyone, but in different degrees.
    III. But those who value understanding yearn not for goods or victory, but for knowledge.
    IV. According to Plato, human behavior flows from three main sources: desire, emotion, and knowledge.
    V. In the perfect state, the industrial forces would produce but not rule, the military would protect but not rule, and the forces of knowledge, the philosopher kings, would reign.
    The CORRECT answer is:
    A. IV, V, I, II, III
    B. V, I, II, III, IV
    C. IV, III, II, I, V
    D. IV, II, I, III, V

    4.____

5. I. Of the more than 26,000 tons of garbage produced daily in New York City, 12,000 tons arrive daily at Fresh Kills.
    II. In a month, enough garbage accumulates there to fill the Empire State Building.
    III. In 1937, the Supreme Court halted the practice of dumping the trash of New York City into the sea.
    IV. Although the garbage is compacted, in a few years the mounds of garbage at Fresh Kills will be the highest points south of Maine's Mount Desert Island on the Eastern Seaboard.
    V. Instead, tugboats now pull barges of much of the trash to Staten Island and the largest landfill in the world, Fresh Kills.
    The CORRECT answer is:
    A. III, V, IV, I, II
    B. III, V, II, IV, I
    C. III, V, I, II, IV
    D. III, II, V, IV, I

    5.____

6. I. Communists rank equality very high, but freedom very low.
    II. Unlike communists, conservatives place a high value on freedom and a very low value on equality.
    III. A recent study demonstrated that one way to classify people's political beliefs is to look at the importance placed on two words: freedom and equality.
    IV. Thus, by demonstrating how members of these groups feel about the two words, the study has proved to be useful for political analysts in several European countries.
    V. According to the study, socialists and liberals rank both freedom and equality very high, while fascists rate both very low.
    The CORRECT answer is:
    A. III, V, I, II, IV
    B. V, IV, III, I, II
    C. III, V, IV, II, I
    D. III, I, II, IV, V

    6.____

7. I. "Can there be anything more amazing than this?"
    II. If the riddle is successfully answered, his dead brothers will be brought back to life.
    III. "Even though man sees those around him dying every day," says Dharmaraj, "he still believes and acts as if he were immortal."
    IV. "What is the cause of ceaseless wonder?" asks the Lord of the Lake.
    V. In the ancient epic, The Mahabharata, a riddle is asked of one of the Pandava brothers.
    The CORRECT answer is:
    A. V, II, I, IV, III
    B. V, IV, III, I, II
    C. V, II, IV, III, I
    D. V, II, IV, I, III

8. I. On the contrary, the two main theories—the cooperative (neoclassical) theory and the radical (labor theory)—clearly rest on very different assumptions, which have very different ethical overtones.
    II. The distribution of income is the primary factor in determining the relative levels of material well-being that different groups or individuals attain.
    III. Of all issues in economics, the distribution of income is one of the most controversial.
    IV. The neoclassical theory tends to support the existing income distribution (or minor changes), while the labor theory ends to support substantial changes in the way income is distributed.
    V. The intensity of the controversy reflects the fact that different economic theories are not purely neutral, *detached* theories with no ethical or moral implications.
    The CORRECT answer is:
    A. II, I, V, IV, III
    B. III, II, V, I, IV
    C. III, V, II, I, IV
    D. III, V, IV, I, II

9. I. The pool acts as a broker and ensures that the cheapest power gets used first.
    II. Every six seconds, the pool's computer monitors all of the generating stations in the state and decides which to ask for more power and which to cut back.
    III. The buying and selling of electrical power is handled by the New York Power Pool in Guilderland, New York.
    IV. This is to the advantage of both the buying and selling utilities.
    V. The pool began operation in 1970, and consists of the state's eight electric utilities.
    The CORRECT answer is:
    A. V, I, II, III, IV
    B. IV, II, I, III, V
    C. III, V, I, IV, II
    D. V, III, IV, II, I

10. I. Modern English is much simpler grammatically than Old English.
    II. Finnish grammar is very complicated; there are some fifteen cases, for example.
    III. Chinese, a very old language, may seem to be the exception, but it is the great number of characters/words that must be mastered that makes it so difficult to learn, not its grammar.
    IV. The newest literary language—that is, written as well as spoken—is Finish, whose literary roots go back only to about the middle of the nineteenth century.
    V. Contrary to popular belief, the longer a language is been in use the simpler its grammar—not the reverse.
    The CORRECT answer is:
    A. IV, I, II, III, V
    B. V, I, IV, II, III
    C. I, II, IV, III, V
    D. IV, II, III, I, V

KEY (CORRECT ANSWERS)

1. D	6. A
2. A	7. C
3. C	8. B
4. D	9. C
5. C	10. B

TEST 2

DIRECTIONS: This type of question tests your ability to recognize accurate paraphrasing, well-constructed paragraphs, and appropriate style and tone. It is important that the answer you select contains only the facts or concepts given in the original sentences. It is also important that you be aware of incomplete sentences, inappropriate transitions, unsupported opinions, incorrect usage, and illogical sentence order. Paragraphs that do not include all the necessary facts and concepts, that distort them, or that add new ones are not considered correct.

The format for this section may vary. Sometimes, long paragraphs are given, and emphasis is placed on style and organization. Our first five questions are of this type. Other times, the paragraphs are shorter, and there is less emphasis on style and more emphasis on accurate representation of information. Our second group of five questions are of this nature.

For each of Questions 1 through 10, select the paragraph that BEST expresses the ideas contained in the sentences above it. *PRINT THE LETTER OF THE CORRECT ANSWER IN THE SPACE AT THE RIGHT.*

1.
   I. Listening skills are very important for managers.
   II. Listening skills are not usually emphasized.
   III. Whenever managers are depicted in books, manuals or the media, they are always talking, never listening.
   IV. We'd like you to read the enclosed handout on listening skills and to try to consciously apply them this week.
   V. We guarantee they will improve the quality of your interactions.

   1.____

   A. Unfortunately, listening skills are not usually emphasized for managers. Managers are always depicted as talking, never listening. We'd like you to read the enclosed handout on listening skills. Please try to apply these principles this week. If you do, we guarantee they will improve the quality of your interactions.
   B. The enclosed handout on listening skills will be important improving the quality of your interactions. We guarantee it. All you have to do is take sometime this week to read and to consciously try to apply the principles. Listening skills are very important for manages, but they are not usually emphasized. Whenever managers are depicted in books, manuals or the media, they are always talking, never listening.
   C. Listening well is one of the most important skills a manager can have, yet it's not usually given much attention. Think about any representation of managers in books, manuals, or in the media that you may have seen. They're always talking, never listening. We'd like you to read the enclosed handout on listening skills and consciously try to apply them the rest of the week. We guarantee you will see a difference in the quality of your interactions.

D. Effective listening, one very important tool in the effective manager's arsenal, is usually not emphasized enough. The usual depiction of managers in books, manuals or the media is one in which they are always talking, never listening. We'd like you to read the enclosed handout and consciously try to apply the information contained therein throughout the rest of the week. We feel sure that you will see a marked difference in the quality of your interactions.

2.
I. Chekhov wrote three dramatic masterpieces which share certain themes and formats: Uncle Vanya, The Cherry Orchard, and The Three Sisters.
II. They are primarily concerned with the passage of time and how this erodes human aspirations.
III. The plays are haunted by the ghosts of the wasted life.
IV. The characters are concerned with life's lesser problems; however, such as the inability to make decisions, loyalty to the wrong cause, and the inability to be clear.
V. This results in sweet, almost aching, type of a sadness referred to as Chekhovian.

   A. Chekhov wrote three dramatic masterpieces: Uncle Vanya, The Cherry Orchard, and The Three Sisters. These masterpieces share certain themes and formats: the passage of time, how time erodes human aspirations, and the ghosts of wasted life. Each masterpiece is characterized by a sweet, almost aching, type of sadness that has become known as Chekhovian. The sweetness of this sadness hinges on the fact that it is not the great tragedies of life which are destroying these characters, but their minor flaws: indecisiveness, misplaced loyalty, unclarity.
   B. The Cherry Orchard, Uncle Vanya, and The Three Sisters are three dramatic masterpieces written by Chekhov that use similar formats to explore a common theme. Each is primarily concerned with the way that passing time wears down human aspirations, and each is haunted by the ghosts of the wasted life. The characters are shown struggling futilely with the lesser problems of life: indecisiveness, loyalty to the wrong cause, and the inability to be clear. These struggles create a mood of sweet, almost aching, sadness that has become known as Chekhovian.
   C. Chekhov's dramatic masterpieces are, along with The Cherry Orchard, Uncle Vanya, and The Three Sisters. These plays share certain thematic and formal similarities. They are concerned most of all with the passage of time and the way in which time erodes human aspirations. Each play is haunted by the specter of the wasted life. Chekhov's characters are caught, however, by life's lesser snares: indecisiveness, loyalty to the wrong cause, and unclarity. The characteristic mood is a sweet, almost aching type of sadness that has come to be known as Chekhovian.
   D. A Chekhovian mood is characterized by sweet, almost aching, sadness. The term comes from three dramatic tragedies by Chekhov which revolve around the sadness of a wasted life. The three masterpieces (Uncle Vanya, The Three Sisters, and The Cherry Orchard) share the same

theme and format. The plays are concerned with how the passage of time erodes human aspirations. They are peopled with characters who are struggling with life's lesser problems. These are people who are indecisive, loyal to the wrong causes, or are unable to make themselves clear.

3. I. Movie previews have often helped producers decide which parts of movies they should take out or leave in.
    II. The first 1933 preview of King Kong was very helpful to the producers because many people ran screaming from the theater and would not return when four men first attacked by Kong were eaten by giant spiders.
    III. The 1950 premiere of Sunset Boulevard resulted in the filming of an entirely new beginning, and a delay of six months in the film's release.
    IV. In the original opening scene, William Holden was in a morgue talking with thirty-six other "corpses" about the ways some of them had died.
    V. When he began to tell them of his life with Gloria Swanson, the audience found this hilarious, instead of taking the scene seriously.

    A. Movie previews have often helped producers decide what parts of movies they should leave in or take out. For example, the first preview of King Kong in 1933 was very helpful. In one scene, four men were first attacked by Kong and then eaten by giant spiders. Many members of the audience ran screaming from the theater and would not return. The premiere of the 1950 film Sunset Boulevard was also very helpful. In the original opening scene, William Holden was in a morgue with thirty-six other "corpses," discussing the ways some of them had died. When he began to tell them of his life with Gloria Swanson, the audience found this hilarious. They were supposed to take the scene seriously. The result was a delay of six months in the release of the film while a new beginning was added.
    B. Movie previews have often helped producers decide whether they should change various parts of a movie. After the 1933 preview of King Kong, a scene in which four men who had been attacked by Kong were eaten by giant spiders was taken out as many people ran screaming from the theater and would not return. The 1950 premiere of Sunset Boulevard also led to some changes. In the original opening scene, William Holden was in a morgue talking with thirty-six other "corpses" about the ways some of them had died. When he began to tell them of his life with Gloria Swanson, the audience found this hilarious, instead of taking the scene seriously.
    C. What do Sunset Boulevard and King Kong have in common? Both show the value of using movie previews to test audience reaction. The first 1933 preview of King Kong showed that a scene showing four men being eaten by giant spiders after having been attacked by Kong was too frightening for many people. They ran screaming from the theater and couldn't be coaxed back. The 1950 premiere of Sunset Boulevard was also a scream, but not the kind the producers intended. The movie opens

4 (#2)

with William Holden lying in a morgue discussing the ways they had died with thirty-six other "corpses." When he began to tell them of his life with Gloria Swanson, the audience couldn't take him seriously. Their laughter caused a six-month delay while the beginning was rewritten.

D. Producers very often use movie previews to decide if changes are needed. The premiere of Sunset Boulevard in 1950 led to a new beginning and a six-month delay in film release. At the beginning, William Holden and thirty-six other "corpses" discuss the ways some of them died. Rather than taking this seriously, the audience thought it was hilarious when he began to tell them of his life with Gloria Swanson. The first 1933 preview of King Kong was very helpful for its producers because one scene so terrified the audience that many of them ran screaming from the theater and would not return. In this particular scene, four men who had first been attacked by Kong were eaten by giant spiders.

4. I. It is common for supervisors to view employees as "things" to be manipulated.   4.____
    II. This approach does not motivate employees, nor does the carrot-and-stick approach because employees often recognize these behaviors and resent them.
    III. Supervisors can change these behaviors by using self-inquiry and persistence.
    IV. The best managers genuinely respect those they work with, are supportive and helpful, and are interested in working as a team with those they supervise.
    V. They disagree with the Golden Rule that says "he or she who has the gold makes the rules."

    A. Some managers act as if they think the Golden Rule means "he or she who has the gold makes the rules." They show disrespect to employees by seeing them as "things" to be manipulated. Obviously, this approach does not motivate employees any more than the carrot-and-stick approach motivates them. The employees are smart enough to spot these behaviors and resent them. On the other hand, the managers genuinely respect those they work with, are supportive and helpful, and are interested in working as a team. Self-inquiry and persistence can change even the former type of supervisor into the latter.
    B. Many supervisors all into the trap of viewing employees as "things" to be manipulated, or try to motivate them by using a carrot-and-stick approach. These methods do not motivate employees, who often recognize the behaviors and resent them. Supervisors can change these behaviors, however, by using self-inquiry and persistence. The best managers are supportive and helpful, and have genuine respect for those with whom they work. They are interested in working as a team with those they supervise. To them, the Golden Rule is not "he or she who has the gold makes the rules."
    C. Some supervisors see employees as "things" to be used or manipulated using a carrot-and-stick technique. These methods don't work. Employees often see through them and resent them. A supervisor who

wants to change may do so. The techniques of self-inquiry and persistence can be used to turn him or her into the type of supervisor who doesn't think the Golden Rule is "he or she who has the gold makes the rules." They may become like the best managers who treat those with whom they work with respect and give them help and support. These are the manager who know how to build a team.

D. Unfortunately, many supervisors act as if their employees are objects whose movements they can position at will. This mistaken belief has the same result as another popular motivational technique—the carrot-and-stick approach. Both attitudes can lead to the same result—resentment from those employees who recognize the behaviors for what they are. Supervisors who recognize these behaviors can change through the use of persistence and the use of self-inquiry. It's important to remember that the best managers respect their employees. They readily give necessary help and support and are interested in working as a team with those they supervise. To these managers, the Golden Rule is not "he or she who has the gold makes the rules."

5. I. The first half of the nineteenth century produced a group of pessimistic poets—Byron, De Musset, Heine, Pushkin, and Leopardi.
    II. It also produced a group of pessimistic composers—Schubert, Chopin, Schumann, and even the later Beethoven.
    III. Above all, in philosophy, there was the profoundly pessimistic philosopher, Schopenhauer.
    IV. The Revolution was dead, the Bourbons were restored, the feudal barons were reclaiming their land, and progress everywhere was being suppressed, as the great age was over.
    V. "I thank God," said Goethe, "that I am not young in so thoroughly finished a world."

5._____

   A. "I thank God," said Goethe, "that I am not young in so thoroughly finished a world." The Revolution was dead, the Bourbons were restored, the feudal barons were reclaiming their land, and progress everywhere was being suppressed. The first half of the nineteenth century produced a group of pessimistic poets: Byron, De Musset, Heine, Pushkin, and Leopardi. It also produced pessimistic composers: Schubert, Chopin, Schumann. Although Beethoven came later, he fits into this group, too. Finally and above all, it also produced a profoundly pessimistic philosopher, Schopenhauer. The great age was over.
   B. The first half of the nineteenth century produced a group of pessimistic poets: Byron, De Musset, Heine, Pushkin, and Leopardi. It produced a group of pessimistic composers: Schubert, Chopin, Schumann, and even the later Beethoven. Above all, it produced a profoundly pessimistic philosopher, Schopenhauer. For each of these men, the great age was over. The Revolution was dead, and the Bourbons were restored. The feudal barons were reclaiming their land, and progress everywhere was being suppressed.

C. The great age was over. The Revolution was dead—the Bourbons were restored, and the feudal barons were reclaiming their land. Progress everywhere was being suppressed. Out of this climate came a profound pessimism. Poets, like Byron, De Musset, Heine, Pushkin, and Leopardi; composers, like Schubert, Chopin, Schumann, and even the later Beethoven; and above all, a profoundly pessimistic philosopher, Schopenauer. This pessimism which arose in the first half of the nineteenth century is illustrated by these words of Goethe, "I thank God that I am not young in so thoroughly finished a world."

D. The first half of the nineteenth century produced a group of pessimistic poets, Byron, De Musset, Heine, Pushkin, and Leopardi—and a group of pessimistic composers, Schubert, Chopin, Schumann, and the later Beethoven. Above it all, it produced a profoundly pessimistic philosopher, Schopenhauer. The great age was over. The Revolution was dead, the Bourbons were restored, the feudal barons were reclaiming their land, and progress everywhere was being suppressed. "I thank God," said Goethe, "that I am not young in so thoroughly finished a world."

6.
 I. A new manager sometimes may feel insecure about his or her competence in the new position.
 II. The new manager may then exhibit defensive or arrogant behavior towards those one supervises, or the new manager may direct overly flattering behavior toward one's new supervisor.

 A. Sometimes, a new manager may feel insecure about his or her ability to perform well in this new position. The insecurity may lead him or her to treat others differently. He or she may display arrogant or defensive behavior towards those he or she supervises, or be overly flattering to his or her new supervisor.
 B. A new manager may sometimes feel insecure about his or her ability to perform well in the new position. He or she may then become arrogant, defensive, or overly flattering towards those he or she works with.
 C. There are times when a new manager may be insecure about how well he or she can perform in the new job. The new manager may also behave defensive or act in an arrogant way towards those he or she supervises, or overly flatter his or her boss.
 D. Sometimes a new manager may feel insecure about his or her ability to perform well in the new position. He or she may then display arrogant or defensive behavior towards those they supervise, or become overly flattering towards their supervisors.

6.____

7.
 I. It is possible to eliminate unwanted behavior by bringing it under stimulus control—tying the behavior to a cue, and then never, or rarely, giving the cue.
 II. One trainer successfully used this method to keep an energetic young porpoise from coming out of her tank whenever she felt like it, which was potentially dangerous.
 III. Her trainer taught her to do it for a reward, in response to a hand signal, and then rarely gave the signal.

7.____

A. Unwanted behavior can be eliminated by tying the behavior to a cue, and then never, or rarely, giving the cue. This is called stimulus control. One trainer was able to use this method to keep an energetic young porpoise from coming out of her tank by teaching her to come out for a reward in response to a hand signal, and then rarely giving the signal.
B. Stimulus control can be used to eliminate unwanted behavior. In this method, behavior is tied to a cue, and then the cue is rarely, if ever, given. One trainer was able to successfully use stimulus control to keep an energetic young porpoise from coming out of her tank whenever she felt like it—a potentially dangerous practice. She taught the porpoise to come out for a reward when she gave a hand signal, and then rarely gave the signal.
C. It is possible to eliminate behavior that is undesirable by bringing it under stimulus control by tying behavior to a signal, and then rarely giving the signal. One trainer successfully used this method to keep an energetic porpoise from coming out of her tank, a potentially dangerous situation. Her trainer taught the porpoise to do it for a reward, in response to a hand signal, and then would rarely give the signal.
D. By using stimulus control, it is possible to eliminate unwanted behavior by tying the behavior to a cue, and then rarely or never give the cue. One trainer was able to use this method to successfully stop a young porpoise from coming out of her tank whenever she felt like it. To curb this potentially dangerous practice, the porpoise was taught by the trainer to come out of the tank for a reward, in response to a hand signal, and then rarely given the signal.

8. I. There is a great deal of concern over the safety of commercial trucks, caused by their greatly increased role in serious accidents since federal deregulation in 1981.
   II. Recently, 60 percent of trucks in New York and Connecticut and 70 percent of trucks in Maryland randomly stopped by state troopers failed safety inspections.
   III. Sixteen states in the United States require no training at all for truck drivers.

   A. Since federal deregulation in 1981, there has been a great deal of concern over the safety of commercial trucks, and their greatly increased role in serious accidents. Recently, 60 percent of trucks in New York and Connecticut, and 70 percent of trucks in Maryland failed safety inspections. Sixteen states in the United States require no training at all for truck drivers.
   B. There is a great deal of concern over the safety of commercial trucks since federal deregulation in 1981. Their role in serious accidents has greatly increased. Recently, 60 percent of trucks randomly stopped in Connecticut and New York and 70 percent in Maryland failed safety inspections conducted by state troopers. Sixteen states in the United States provide no training at all for truck drivers.
   C. Commercial trucks have a greatly increased role in serious accidents since federal deregulation in 1981. This has led to a great deal of concern.

Recently, 70 percent of trucks in Maryland and 60 percent of trucks in New York and Connecticut failed inspection of those that were randomly stopped by state troopers. Sixteen states in the United States require no training for all truck drivers.

D. Since federal deregulation in 1981, the role that commercial trucks have played in serious accidents has greatly increased, and this has led to a great deal of concern. Recently, 60 percent of trucks in New York and Connecticut, and 70 percent of trucks in Maryland randomly stopped by state troopers failed safety inspections. Sixteen states in the U.S. don't require any training for truck drivers.

9.
I. No matter how much some people have, they still feel unsatisfied and want more, or want to keep what they have forever.
II. One recent television documentary showed several people flying from New York to Paris for a one-day shopping spree to buy platinum earrings, because they were bored.
III. In Brazil, some people were ordering coffins that cost a minimum of $45,000 and are equipping them with deluxe stereos, televisions, and other graveyard necessities.

9.____

A. Some people, despite having a great deal, still feel unsatisfied and want more, or think they can keep what they have forever. One recent documentary on television showed several people enroute from Paris to New York for a one day shopping spree to buy platinum earrings, because they were bored. Some people in Brazil are even ordering coffins equipped with such graveyard necessities as deluxe stereos and televisions. The price of the coffins start at $45,000.
B. No matter how much some people have, they may feel unsatisfied. This leads them to want more, or to want to keep what they have forever. Recently, a television documentary depicting several people flying from New York to Paris for a one day shopping spree to buy platinum earrings. They were bored. Some people in Brazil are ordering coffins that cost at least $45,000 and come equipped with deluxe televisions, stereos and other necessary graveyard items.
C. Some people will be dissatisfied no matter how much they have. They may want more, or they may want to keep what they have forever. One recent television documentary showed several people, motivated by boredom, jetting from New York to Paris for a one-day shopping spree to buy platinum earrings. In Brazil, some people are ordering coffins equipped with deluxe stereos, televisions and other graveyard necessities. The minimum price for these coffins—$45,000.
D. Some people are never satisfied. No matter how much they have they still want more, or think they can keep what they have forever. One television documentary recently showed several people flying from New York to Paris for the day to buy platinum earrings because they were bored. In Brazil, some people are ordering coffins that cost $45,000 and are equipped with deluxe stereos, televisions and other graveyard necessities.

10.
I. A television signal or video signal has three parts.
II. Its parts are the black-and-white portion, the color portion, and the synchronizing (sync) pulses, which keep the picture stable.
III. Each video source, whether it's a camera or a video-cassette recorder contains its own generator of these synchronizing pulses to accompany the picture that it's sending in order to keep it steady and straight.
IV. In order to produce a clean recording, a video-cassette recorder must "lock-up" to the sync pulses that are part of the video it is trying to record, and this effort may be very noticeable if the device does not have gunlock.

  A. There are three parts to a television or video signal: the black-and-white part, the color part, and the synchronizing (sync) pulses, which keep the picture stable. Whether it's a video-cassette recorder or a camera, each video source contains its own pulse that synchronizes and generates the picture it's sending in order to keep it straight and steady. A video-cassette recorder must "lock up" to the sync pulses that are part of the video it's trying to record. If the device doesn't have gunlock, this effort must be very noticeable.
  B. A video signal or television is comprised of three parts: the black-and-white portion, the color portion, and the sync (synchronizing) pulses, which keep the picture stable. Whether it's a camera or a video-cassette recorder, each video source contains its own generator of these synchronizing pulses. These accompany the picture that it's sending in order to keep it straight and steady. A video-cassette recorder must "lock up" to the sync pulses that are part of the video it is trying to record in order to produce a clean recording. This effort may be very noticeable if the device does not have gunlock.
  C. There are three parts to a television or video signal: the color portion, the black-and-white portion, and the sync (synchronizing pulses). These keep the picture stable. Each video source, whether it's a video-cassette recorder or a camera, generates these synchronizing pulses accompanying the picture it's sending in order to keep it straight and steady. If a clean recording is to be produced, a video-cassette recorder must store the sync pulses that are part of the video it is trying to record. This effort may not be noticeable if the device does not have gunlock.
  D. A television signal or video signal has three parts: the black-and-white portion, the color portion, and the synchronizing (sync) pulses. It's the sync pulses which keep the picture stable, which accompany it and keep it steady and straight. Whether it's a camera or a video-cassette recorder, each video source contains its own generator of these synchronizing pulses. To produce a clean recording, a video-cassette recorder must "lock up" to the sync pulses that are part of the video it is trying to record. If the device does not have gunlock, this effort may be very noticeable.

KEY (CORRECT ANSWERS)

1. C
2. B
3. A
4. B
5. D
6. A
7. B
8. D
9. C
10. D

EXAMINATION SECTION
TEST 1

DIRECTIONS: The sentences that follow are in scrambled order. You are to rearrange them in proper order and indicate the letter choice containing the correct answer. *PRINT THE LETTER OF THE CORRECT ANSWER IN THE SPACE AT THE RIGHT.*

1. Below are four statements labeled W, X, Y and Z.
   W. He was a strict and fanatic drillmaster.
   X. The word is always used in a derogatory sense and generally shows resentment and anger on the part of the user.
   Y. It is from the name of this Frenchman that we derive our English word, martinet.
   Z. Jean Martinet was the Inspector-General of Infantry during the reign of King Louis XIV.
   The PROPER order in which these sentences should be placed in a paragraph is:
   A. X, Z, W, Y   B. X, Z, Y, W   C. Z, W, Y, X   D. Z, Y, W, X

1.____

2. In the following paragraph, the sentences, which are numbered, have been jumbled.
   I. Since then it has undergone changes.
   II. It was incorporated in 1955 under the laws of the State of New York.
   III. Its primary purposes, a cleaner city, has, however, remained the same.
   IV. The Citizens Committee works in cooperation with the Mayor's Inter-departmental Committee for a Clean City.
   The order in which these sentences should be arranged to form a well-organized paragraph is:
   A. II, IV, I, III   B. III, IV, I, II   C. IV, II, I, III   D. IV, III, II, I

2.____

3.____

Questions 3-5.

DIRECTIONS: The sentences listed below are part of a meaningful paragraph but they are not given in their proper order. You are to decide what would be the BEST order in which to put the sentences so as to form a well-organized paragraph. Each sentence has a place in the paragraph; there are no extra sentences. You are then to answer Questions 3 through 5 inclusive on the basis of your rearrangements of these scrambled sentences into a properly organized paragraph.

In 1887 some insurance companies organized an Inspection Department to advise their clients on all phases of fire prevention and protection. Probably this has been due to the smaller annual fire losses in Great Britain than in the United States. It tests various fire prevention devices and appliances and determines manufacturing hazards and their safeguards. Fire research began earlier in the United States and is more advanced than in Great Britain. Later they established a laboratory specializing in electrical, mechanical, hydraulic, and chemical fields.

3. When the five sentences are arranged in proper order, the paragraph starts with the sentence which begins
    A. "In 1887…"   B. "Probably this…"   C. "It tests…"
    D. "Fire research…"   E. "Later they…"

4. In the last sentence listed above, "they" refers to
    A. the insurance companies   B. the United States and Great Britain
    C. the Inspection Department   D. clients
    E. technicians

5. When the above paragraph is properly arranged, it ends with the words
    A. "…and protection."   B. "…the United States."
    C. "…their safeguards."   D. "…in Great Britain."
    E. "…chemical fields."

KEY (CORRECT ANSWERS)

1. C
2. C
3. D
4. A
5. C

TEST 2

DIRECTIONS: In each of the questions numbered I through V, several sentences are given. For each question, choose as your answer the group of number that represents the MOST logical order of these sentences if they were arranged in paragraph form. *PRINT THE LETTER OF THE CORRECT ANSWER IN THE SPACE AT THE RIGHT.*

1.
   I. It is established when one shows that the landlord has prevented the tenant's enjoyment of his interest in the property leased.
   II. Constructive eviction is the result of a breach of the covenant of quiet enjoyment implied in all leases.
   III. In some parts of the United States, it is not complete until the tenant vacates within a reasonable time.
   IV. Generally, the acts must be of such serious and permanent character as to deny the tenant the enjoyment of his possessing rights.
   V. In this event, upon abandonment of the premises, the tenant's liability for that ceases.
   The CORRECT answer is:
   A. II, I, IV, III, V
   B. V, II, III, I, IV
   C. IV, III, I, II, V
   D. I, III, V, IV, II

   1.____

2.
   I. The powerlessness before private and public authorities that is the typical experience of the slum tenant is reminiscent of the situation of blue-collar workers all through the nineteenth century.
   II. Similarly, in recent years, this chapter of history has been reopened by anti-poverty groups which have attempted to organize slum tenants to enable them to bargain collectively with their landlords about the conditions of their tenancies.
   III. It is familiar history that many of the worker remedied their condition by joining together and presenting their demands collectively.
   IV. Like the workers, tenants are forced by the conditions of modern life into substantial dependence on these who possess great political aid and economic power.
   V. What's more, the very fact of dependence coupled with an absence of education and self-confidence makes them hesitant and unable to stand up for what they need from those in power.
   The CORRECT answer is:
   A. V, IV, I, II, III
   B. II, III, I, V, IV
   C. III, I, V, IV, II
   D. I, IV, V, III, II

   2.____

3.
   I. A railroad, for example, when not acting as a common carrier may contract away responsibility for its own negligence.
   II. As to a landlord, however, no decision has been found relating to the legal effect of a clause shifting the statutory duty of repair to the tenant.
   III. The courts have not passed on the validity of clauses relieving the landlord of this duty and liability.
   IV. They have, however, upheld the validity of exculpatory clauses in other types of contracts.

   3.____

V. Housing regulations impose a duty upon the landlord to maintain leased premises in safe condition.
VI. As another example, a bailee may limit his liability except for gross negligence, willful acts, or fraud.

The CORRECT answer is:
A. II, I, VI, IV, III, V
B. I, III, IV, V, VI, II
C. III, V, I, IV, II, VI
D. V, III, IV, I, VI, II

4. I. Since there are only samples in the building, retail or consumer sales are generally eschewed by mart occupants, and in some instances, rigid controls are maintained to limit entrance to the mart only to those persons engaged in retailing.
II. Since World War I, in many larger cities, there has developed a new type of property, called the mart building.
III. It can, therefore, be used by wholesalers and jobbers for the display of sample merchandise.
IV. This type of building is most frequently a multi-storied, finished interior property which is a cross between a retail arcade and a loft building.
V. This limitation enables the mart occupants to ship the orders from another location after the retailer or dealer makes his selection from the samples.

The CORRECT answer is:
A. II, IV, III, I, V
B. IV, III, V, I, II
C. I, III, II, IV, V
D. I, IV, II, III, V

5. I. In general, staff-line friction reduces the distinctive contribution of staff personnel.
II. The conflicts, however, introduce an uncontrolled element into the managerial system.
III. On the other hand, the natural resistance of the line to staff innovations probably usefully restrains over-eager efforts to apply untested procedures on a large scale.
IV. Under such conditions, it is difficult to know when valuable ideas are being sacrificed.
V. The relatively weak position of staff, requiring accommodation to the line, tends to restrict their ability to engage in free, experimental innovation.

The CORRECT answer is:
A. IV, II, III, I, V
B. I, V, III, II, IV
C. V, III, I, II, IV
D. II, I, IV, V, III

KEY (CORRECT ANSWERS)

1. A
2. D
3. D
4. A
5. B

TEST 3

DIRECTIONS: Questions 1 through 4 consist of six sentences which can be arranged in a logical sequence. For each question, select the choice which places the numbered sentences in the MOST logical sequent. *PRINT THE LETTER OF THE CORRECT ANSWER IN THE SPACE AT THE RIGHT.*

1.   I. The burden of proof as to each issue is determined before trial and remains upon the same party throughout the trial.
     II. The jury is at liberty to believe one witness' testimony as against a number of contradictory witnesses.
     III. In a civil case, the party bearing the burden of proof is required to prove his contention by a fair preponderance of the evidence.
     IV. However, it must be noted that a fair preponderance of evidence does not necessarily mean a greater number of witnesses.
     V. The burden of proof is the burden which rests upon one of the parties to an action to persuade the trier of the facts, generally the jury, that a proposition he asserts is true.
     VI. If the evidence is equally balanced, or if it leaves the jury in such doubt as to be unable to decide the controversy either way, judgment must be given against the party upon whom the burden of proof rests.
     The CORRECT answer is:
     A. III, II, V, IV, I, VI   B. I, II, VI, V, III, IV
     C. III, IV, V, I, II, VI   D. V, I, III, VI, IV, II

1.____

2.   I. If a parent is without assets and is unemployed, he cannot be convicted of the crime of non-support of a child.
     II. The term "sufficient ability" has been held to mean sufficient financial ability.
     III. It does not matter if his unemployment is by choice or unavoidable circumstances.
     IV. If he fails to take any steps at all, he may be liable to prosecution for endangering the welfare of a child.
     V. Under the penal law, a parent is responsible for the support of his minor child only if the parent is "of sufficient ability."
     VI. An indigent parent may meet his obligation by borrowing money or by seeking aid under the provisions of the Social Welfare Law.
     The CORRECT answer is:
     A. VI, I, V, III, II, IV   B. I, III, V, II, IV, VI
     C. V, II, I, III, VI, IV   D. I, VI, IV, V, II, III

2.____

3.   I. Consider, for example, the case of a rabble rouser who urges a group of twenty people to go out and break the windows of a nearby factory.
     II. Therefore, the law fills the indicated gap with the crime of inciting to riot.
     III. A person is considered guilty of inciting to riot when he urges ten or more persons to engage in tumultuous and violent conduct of a kind likely to create public alarm.
     IV. However, if he has not obtained the cooperation of at least four people, he cannot be charged with unlawful assembly.

3.____

V. The charge of inciting to riot was added to the law to cover types of conduct which cannot be classified as either the crime of "riot" or the crime of "unlawful assembly."
VI. If he acquires the acquiescence of at least four of them, he is guilty of unlawful assembly even if the project does not materialize.

The CORRECT answer is:
A. III, V, I, VI, IV, II
B. V, I, IV, VI, II, III
C. III, IV, I, V, II, VI
D. V, I, IV, VI, III, II

4. I. If, however, the rebuttal evidence presents an issue of credibility, it is for the jury to determine whether the presumption has, in fact, been destroyed.
    II. Once sufficient evidence to the contrary is introduced, the presumption disappears from the trial.
    III. The effect of a presumption is to place the burden upon the adversary to come forward with evidence to rebut the presumption.
    IV. When a presumption is overcome and ceases to exist in the case, the fact or facts which gave rise to the presumption still remain.
    V. Whether a presumption has been overcome is ordinarily a question for the court.
    VI. Such information may furnish a basis for a logical inference.

    The CORRECT answer is:
    A. IV, VI, II, V, I, III
    B. III, II, V, I, IV, VI
    C. V, III, VI, IV, II, I
    D. V, IV, I, II, VI, III

KEY (CORRECT ANSWERS)

1. D
2. C
3. A
4. B

PREPARING WRITTEN MATERIALS

EXAMINATION SECTION
TEST 1

DIRECTIONS: Each of the two sentences in the following questions may contain errors in punctuation, capitalization, or grammar.
If there is an error in only Sentence I, mark your answer A. If there is an error in only Sentence II, mark your answer B.
If there is an error in both Sentence I and Sentence II, mark your answer C. If both Sentence I and II are correct, mark your answer D.
PRINT THE LETTER OF THE CORRECT ANSWER IN THE SPACE AT THE RIGHT.

1. I. The task of typing these reports is to be divided equally between you and me. 1.____
   II. If it was he, I would use a different method for filing these records.

2. I. The new clerk is just as capable as some of the older employees, if not more capable. 2.____
   II. Using his knowledge of arithmetic to check the calculation, the supervisor found no errors in the report.

3. I. A typist who does consistently superior work probably merits promotion. 3.____
   II. In its report on the stenographic unit, the committee pointed out that neither the stenographers nor the typists were adequately trained.

4. I. Entering the office, the desk was noticed immediately by the visitor. 4.____
   II. Arrangements have been made to give this training to whoever applies for it.

5. I. The office manager estimates that this assignment, which is to be handled by you and I, will require about two weeks for completion. 5.____
   II. One of the recommendations of the report is that these kind of forms be discarded because they are of no value.

6. I. The supervisor knew that the typist was a quiet, cooperative, efficient, employee. 6.____
   II. The duties of stenographer are to take dictation notes at conferences and transcribing them.

7. I. The stenographer has learned that she, as well as two typists, is being assigned to the new unit. 7.____
   II. We do not know who you have designated to take charge of the new program.

8. I. He asked, "When do you expect to return?" 8.____
   II. I doubt whether this system will be successful here; it is not suitable for the work of our agency.

9. I. It is a policy of this agency to encourage punctuality as a good habit for we employees to adopt.
   II. The successful completion of the task was due largely to them cooperating effectively with the supervisor.

9.____

10. I. Mr. Smith, who is a very competent executive has offered his services to our department.
    II. Every one of the stenographers who work in this office is considered trustworthy.

10.____

11. I. It is very annoying to have a pencil sharpener, which is not in proper working order.
    II. The building watchman checked the door of Charlie's office and found that the lock has been jammed.

11.____

12. I. Since he went on the New York City council a year ago, one of his primary concerns has been safety in the streets.
    II. After waiting in the doorway for about 15 minutes, a black sedan appeared.

12.____

13. I. When you are studying a good textbook is important.
    II. He said he would divide the money equally between you and me.

13.____

14. I. The question is, "How can a large number of envelopes be sealed rapidly without the use of sealing machine?"
    II. The administrator assigned two stenographers, Mary and I, to the new bureau.

14.____

15. I. A dictionary, in addition to the office management textbooks, were placed on his desk.
    II. The concensus of opinion is that none of the employees should be required to work overtime.

15.____

16. I. Mr. Granger has demonstrated that he is as courageous, if not more courageous, than Mr. Brown.
    II. The successful completion of the project depends on the manager's accepting our advisory opinion.

16.____

17. I. Mr. Ames was in favor of issuing a set of rules and regulations for all of us employees to follow.
    II. It is inconceivable that the new clerk knows how to deal with that kind of correspondence.

17.____

18. I. The revised referrence manual is to be used by all of the employees.
    II. Mr. Johnson told Miss Kent and me to accumulate all the letters that we receive.

18.____

19. I. The supervisor said, that before any changes would be made in the attendance report, there must be ample justification for them.
    II. Each of them was asked to amend their preliminary report.

19.____

20. I. Mrs. Peters conferred with Mr. Roberts before she laid the papers on his desk.
    II. As far as this report is concerned, Mr. Williams always has and will be responsible for its preparation.

20.____

KEY (CORRECT ANSWERS)

1.	B	11.	C
2.	D	12.	C
3.	D	13.	A
4.	A	14.	B
5.	C	15.	C
6.	C	16.	A
7.	B	17.	B
8.	D	18.	A
9.	C	19.	C
10.	A	20.	B

TEST 2

DIRECTIONS: Each question or incomplete statement is followed by several suggested answers or completions. Select the one that BEST answers the question or completes the statement. *PRINT THE LETTER OF THE CORRECT ANSWER IN THE SPACE AT THE RIGHT.*

Questions 1-9.

DIRECTIONS: Questions 1 through 9 consist of pairs of sentences which may or may not contain errors in grammar, capitalization, or punctuation.
If both sentences are correct, mark your answer A.
If the first sentence only is correct, mark your answer B.
If the second sentence only is correct, mark your answer C.
If both sentences are incorrect, mark your answer D.
NOTE: Consider a sentence correct if it contains no errors, although there may be other correct ways of writing the sentence.

1. I. An unusual conference will be held today at George Washington high school.
    II. The principal of the school, Dr. Pace, described the meeting as "a unique opportunity for educators to exchange ideas.
    1.____

2. I. Studio D, which they would ordinarily use, will be occupied at that time.
    II. Any other studio, which is properly equipped, may be used instead.
    2.____

3. I. D.H. Lawrence's <u>Sons and Lovers</u> were discussed on today's program.
    II. Either Eliot's or Yeats's work is to be covered next week.
    3.____

4. I. This program is on the air for three years now, and has a well-established audience.
    II. We have received many complimentary letters from listeners, and scarcely no critical ones.
    4.____

5. I. Both Mr. Owen and Mr. Mitchell have addressed the group.
    II. As has Mr. Stone, whose talks have been especially well received.
    5.____

6. I. The original program was different in several respects from the version that eventually went on the air.
    II. Each of the three announcers who Mr. Scott thought had had suitable experience was asked whether he would be willing to take on the special assignment.
    6.____

7. I. A municipal broadcasting system provides extensive coverage of local events, but also reports national and international news.
    II. A detailed account of happenings in the South may be carried by a local station hundreds of miles away.
    7.____

8. I. Jack Doe the announcer and I will be working on the program.
    II. The choice of musical selections has been left up to he and I.
    8.____

9. I. Mr. Taylor assured us that "he did not anticipate any difficulty in making arrangements for the broadcast."
   II. Although there had seemed at first to be certain problems; these had been solved.

9._____

Questions 10-14.

DIRECTIONS: Questions 10 through 14 consist of pairs of sentences which may contain errors in grammar, sentence structure, punctuation, or spelling, or both sentences may be correct. Consider a sentence correct if it contains no errors, although there may be other correct ways of writing the sentence.
If only Sentence I contains an error, mark your answer A.
If only Sentence II contains an error, mark your answer B.
If both sentences contain errors, mark your answer C.
If both sentences are correct, mark your answer D.

10. I. No employee considered to be indispensable will be assigned to the new office.
    II. The arrangement of the desks and chairs give the office a neat appearance.

10._____

11. I. The recommendation, accompanied by a report, was delivered this morning.
    II. Mr. Green thought the procedure would facilitate his work; he knows better now.

11._____

12. I. Limiting the term "property" to tangible property, in the criminal mischief setting, accords with prior case law holding that only tangible property came within the purview of the offense of malicious mischief.
    II. Thus, a person who intentionally destroys the property of another, but under an honest belief that he has title to such property, cannot be convicted of criminal mischief under the Revised Penal Law.

12._____

13. I. Very early in its history, New York enacted statutes from time to time punishing, either as a felony or as a misdemeanor, malicious injuries to various kinds of property: piers, booms, dams, bridges, etc.
    II. The application of the statute is necessarily restricted to trespassory takings with larcenous intent: namely with intent permanently or virtually permanently to "appropriate" property or "deprive" the owner of its use.

13._____

14. I. Since the former Penal Law did not define the instruments of forgery in a general fashion, its crime of forgery was held to be narrower than the common law offense in this respect and to embrace only those instruments explicitly specified in the substantive provisions.
    II. After entering the barn through an open door for the purpose of stealing, it was closed by the defendants.

14._____

Questions 15-20.

DIRECTIONS: Questions 15 through 20 consist of pairs of sentences which may or may not contain errors in grammar, capitalization, or punctuation.
If both sentences are correct, mark your answer A.
If the first sentence only is correct, mark your answer B.
If the second sentence only is correct, mark your answer C.
If both sentences are incorrect, mark your answer D.
NOTE: Consider a sentence correct if it contains no errors, although there may be other ways of writing the sentence.

15. I. The program, which is currently most popular, is a news broadcast.
    II. The engineer assured his supervisor that there was no question of his being late again.

    15.____

16. I. The announcer recommended that the program originally scheduled for that time be cancelled.
    II. Copies of the script may be given to whoever is interested.

    16.____

17. I. A few months ago it looked like we would be able to broadcast the concert live.
    II. The program manager, as well as the announcers, were enthusiastic about the plan.

    17.____

18. I. No speaker on the subject of education is more interesting than he.
    II. If he would have had the time, we would have scheduled him for a regular weekly broadcast.

    18.____

19. I. This quartet, in its increasingly complex variations on a simple theme, admirably illustrates Professor Baker's point.
    II. Listeners interested in these kind of ideas will find his recently published study of Haydn rewarding.

    19.____

20. I. The Commissioner's resignation at the end of next month marks the end of a long public service career.
    II. Outstanding among his numerous achievements were his successful implementation of several revolutionary schemes to reorganize the agency.

    20.____

KEY (CORRECT ANSWERS)

1.	C	11.	D
2.	B	12.	C
3.	C	13.	B
4.	D	14.	A
5.	B	15.	C
6.	A	16.	A
7.	A	17.	D
8.	D	18.	B
9.	D	19.	B
10.	B	20.	B

PREPARING WRITTEN MATERIAL
EXAMINATION SECTION
TEST 1

DIRECTIONS: Each question consists of a sentence which may or may not be an example of good English usage. Examine each sentence, considering grammar, punctuation, spelling, capitalization, and awkwardness. Then choose the correct statement about it from the four choices below it. If the English usage in the sentence given is better than any of the changes suggested in choices B, C, or D, pick choice A. (Do not pick a choice that will change the meaning of the sentence.) *PRINT THE LETTER OF THE CORRECT ANSWER IN THE SPACE AT THE RIGHT.*

1. We attended a staff conference on Wednesday the new safety and fire rules were discussed. 1.____
    A. This is an example of acceptable writing.
    B. The words "safety," "fire," and "rules" should begin with capital letters.
    C. There should be a comma after the word "Wednesday."
    D. There should be a period after the word "Wednesday" and the word "the" should begin with a capital letter.

2. Neither the dictionary or the telephone directory could be found in the office library. 2.____
    A. This is an example of acceptable writing.
    B. The word "or" should be changed to "nor."
    C. The word "library" should be spelled "libery."
    D. The word "neither" should be changed to "either."

3. The report would have been typed correctly if the typist could read the draft. 3.____
    A. This is an example of acceptable writing.
    B. The word "would" should be removed.
    C. The word "have" should be inserted after the word "could."
    D. The word "correctly" should be changed to "correct."

4. The supervisor brought the reports and forms to an employees desk. 4.____
    A. This is an example of acceptable writing.
    B. The word "brought" should be changed to "took."
    C. There should be a comma after the word "reports" and a comma after the word "forms."
    D. The word "employees" should be spelled "employee's."

5. It's important for all the office personnel to submit their vacation schedules on time. 5.____
    A. This is an example of acceptable writing.
    B. The word "It's" should be spelled "Its."
    C. The word "their" should be spelled "they're."
    D. The word "personnel" should be spelled "personal."

6. The report, along with the accompanying documents, were submitted for review.
   A. This is an example of acceptable writing.
   B. The words "were submitted" should be changed to "was submitted."
   C. The word "accompanying" should be spelled "accompaning."
   D. The comma after the word "report" should be taken out.

7. If others must use your files, be certain that they understand how the system works, but insist that you do all the filing and refiling.
   A. This is an example of acceptable writing.
   B. There should be a period after the word "works," and the word "but" should start a new sentence.
   C. The words "filing" and "refiling" should be spelled "fileing" and "refileing."
   D. There should be a comma after the word "but."

8. The appeal was not considered because of its late arrival.
   A. This is an example of acceptable writing.
   B. The word "its" should be changed to "it's."
   C. The word "its" should be changed to "the."
   D. The words "late arrival" should be changed to "arrival late."

9. The letter must be read carefuly to determine under which subject it should be filed.
   A. This is an example of acceptable writing.
   B. The word "under" should be changed to "at."
   C. The word "determine" should be spelled "determin."
   D. The word "carefuly" should be spelled "carefully."

10. He showed potential as an office manager, but he lacked skill in delegating work.
    A. This is an example of acceptable writing.
    B. The word "delegating" should be spelled "delagating."
    C. The word "potential" should be spelled "potencial."
    D. The words "he lacked" should be changed to "was lacking."

KEY (CORRECT ANSWERS)

1.	D	6.	B
2.	B	7.	A
3.	C	8.	A
4.	D	9.	D
5.	A	10.	A

TEST 2

DIRECTIONS: Each question consists of a sentence which may or may not be an example of good English usage. Examine each sentence, considering grammar, punctuation, spelling, capitalization, and awkwardness. Then choose the correct statement about it from the four choices below it. If the English usage in the sentence given is better than any of the changes suggested in choices B, C, or D, pick choice A. (Do not pick a choice that will change the meaning of the sentence.) *PRINT THE LETTER OF THE CORRECT ANSWER IN THE SPACE AT THE RIGHT.*

1. The supervisor wants that all staff members report to the office at 9:00 A.M.   1.____
   A. This is an example of acceptable writing.
   B. The word "that" should be removed and the word "to" should be inserted after the word "members."
   C. There should be a comma after the word "wants" and a comma after the word "office."
   D. The word "wants" should be changed to "want" and the word "shall" should be inserted after the word "members."

2. Every morning the clerk opens the office mail and distributes it.   2.____
   A. This is an example of acceptable writing.
   B. The word "opens" should be changed to "open."
   C. The word "mail" should be changed to "letters."
   D. The word "it" should be changed to "them."

3. The secretary typed more fast on a desktop computer than on a laptop computer.   3.____
   A. This is an example of acceptable writing.
   B. The words "more fast" should be changed to "faster."
   C. There should be a comma after the words "desktop computer."
   D. The word "than" should be changed to "then."

4. The new stenographer needed a desk a computer, a chair and a blotter.   4.____
   A. This is an example of acceptable writing.
   B. The word "blotter" should be spelled "blodder."
   C. The word "stenographer" should begin with a capital letter.
   D. There should be a comma after the word "desk."

5. The recruiting officer said, "There are many different goverment jobs available."   5.____
   A. This is an example of acceptable writing.
   B. The word "There" should not be capitalized.
   C. The word "government" should be spelled "government."
   D. The comma after the word "said" should be removed.

6. He can recommend a mechanic whose work is reliable.   6.____
   A. This is an example of acceptable writing.
   B. The word "reliable" should be spelled "relyable."
   C. The word "whose" should be spelled "who's."
   D. The word "mechanic should be spelled "mecanic."

215

7. She typed quickly; like someone who had not a moment to lose. 7._____
   A. This is an example of acceptable writing.
   B. The word "not" should be removed.
   C. The semicolon should be changed to a comma.
   D. The word "quickly" should be placed before instead of after the word "typed."

8. She insisted that she had to much work to do. 8._____
   A. This is an example of acceptable writing.
   B. The word "insisted" should be spelled "incisted."
   C. The word "to" used in front of "much" should be spelled "too."
   D. The word "do" should be changed to "be done."

9. He excepted praise from his supervisor for a job well done. 9._____
   A. This is an example of acceptable writing.
   B. The word "excepted" should be spelled "accepted."
   C. The order of the words "well done" should be changed to "done well."
   D. There should be a comma after the word "supervisor."

10. What appears to be intentional errors in grammar occur several times in the passage. 10._____
    A. This is an example of acceptable writing.
    B. The word "occur" should be spelled "occurr."
    C. The word "appears" should be changed to "appear."
    D. The phrase "several times" should be changed to "from time to time."

KEY (CORRECT ANSWERS)

1. B   6. A
2. A   7. C
3. B   8. C
4. D   9. B
5. C   10. C

TEST 3

DIRECTIONS: Each question consists of a sentence which may or may not be an example of good English usage. Examine each sentence, considering grammar, punctuation, spelling, capitalization, and awkwardness. Then choose the correct statement about it from the four choices below it. If the English usage in the sentence given is better than any of the changes suggested in choices B, C, or D, pick choice A. (Do not pick a choice that will change the meaning of the sentence.) *PRINT THE LETTER OF THE CORRECT ANSWER IN THE SPACE AT THE RIGHT.*

1. The clerk could have completed the assignment on time if he knows where these materials were located.
    A. This is an example of acceptable writing.
    B. The word "knows" should be replaced by "had known."
    C. The word "were" should be replaced by "had been."
    D. The words "where these materials were located" should be replaced by "the location of these materials."

2. All employees should be given safety training. Not just those who accidents.
    A. This is an example of acceptable writing.
    B. The period after the word "training" should be changed to a colon.
    C. The period after the word "training" should be changed to a semicolon, and the first letter of the word "Not" should be changed to a small "n."
    D. The period after the word "training" should be changed to a comma, and the first letter of the word "Not" should be changed to a small "n."

3. This proposal is designed to promote employee awareness of the suggestion program, to encourage employee participation in the program, and to increase the number of suggestions submitted.
    A. This is an example of acceptable writing.
    B. The word "proposal" should be spelled "proposal."
    C. The words "to increase the number of suggestions submitted" should be changed to "an increase in the number of suggestions is expected."
    D. The word "promote" should be changed to "enhance" and the word "increase" should be changed to "add to."

4. The introduction of inovative managerial techniques should be preceded by careful analysis of the specific circumstances and conditions in each department.
    A. This is an example of acceptable writing.
    B. The word "technique" should be spelled "techneques."
    C. The word "inovative" should be spelled "innovative."
    D. A comma should be placed after the word "circumstances" and after the word "conditions."

5. This occurrence indicates that such criticism embarrasses him.   5._____
   A. This is an example of acceptable writing.
   B. The word "occurrence" should be spelled "occurence."
   C. The word "criticism" should be spelled "critisism.
   D. The word "embarrasses" should be spelled "embarasses.

KEY (CORRECT ANSWERS)

1. B
2. D
3. A
4. C
5. A

PRINCIPLES AND PRACTICES, OF ADMINISTRATION, SUPERVISION AND MANAGEMENT

TABLE OF CONTENTS

	Page
GENERAL ADMINISTRATION	1
SEVEN BASIC FUNCTIONS OF THE SUPERVISOR	2
I. Planning	2
II. Organizing	3
III. Staffing	3
IV. Directing	3
V. Coordinating	3
VI. Reporting	3
VII. Budgeting	3
PLANNING TO MEET MANAGEMENT GOALS	4
I. What is Planning	4
II. Who Should Make Plans	4
III. What are the Results of Poor Planning	4
IV. Principles of Planning	4
MANAGEMENT PRINCIPLES	5
I. Management	5
II. Management Principles	5
III. Organization Structure	6
ORGANIZATION	8
I. Unity of Command	8
II. Span of Control	8
III. Uniformity of Assignment	9
IV. Assignment of Responsibility and Delegation of Authority	9
PRINCIPLES OF ORGANIZATION	9
I. Definition	9
II. Purpose of Organization	9
III. Basic Considerations in Organizational Planning	9
IV. Bases for Organization	10
V. Assignment of Functions	10
VI. Delegation of Authority and Responsibility	10
VII. Employee Relationships	11

DELEGATING		11
	I. WHAT IS DELEGATING:	11
	II. TO WHOM TO DELEGATE	11
REPORTS		12
	I. DEFINITION	12
	II. PURPOSE	12
	III. TYPES	12
	IV. FACTORS TO CONSIDER BEFORE WRITING REPORT	12
	V. PREPARATORY STEPS	12
	VI. OUTLINE FOR A RECOMMENDATION REPORT	12
MANAGEMENT CONTROLS		13
	I. Control	13
	II. Basis for Control	13
	III. Policy	13
	IV. Procedure	14
	V. Basis of Control	14
FRAMEWORK OF MANAGEMENT		14
	I. Elements	14
	II. Manager's Responsibility	15
	III. Control Techniques	16
	IV. Where Forecasts Fit	16
PROBLEM SOLVING		16
	I. Identify the Problem	16
	II. Gather Data	17
	III. List Possible Solutions	17
	IV. Test Possible Solutions	18
	V. Select the Best Solution	18
	VI. Put the Solution into Actual Practice	19
COMMUNICATION		19
	I. What is Communication?	19
	II. Why is Communication Needed?	19
	III. How is Communication Achieved?	20
	IV. Why Does Communication Fail?	21
	V. How to Improve Communication	21
	VI. How to Determine If You Are Getting Across	21
	VII. The Key Attitude	22
HOW ORDERS AND INSTRUCTIONS SHOULD BE GIVEN		22
	I. Characteristics of Good Orders and Instructions	22
FUNCTIONS OF A DEPARTMENT PERSONNEL OFFICE		23

SUPERVISION	23
I. Leadership	23
A. The Authoritarian Approach	23
B. The Laissez-Faire Approach	24
C. The Democratic Approach	24
II. Nine Points of Contrast Between Boss and Leader	25
EMPLOYEE MORALE	25
I. Some Ways to Develop and Maintain Good Employee Morale	25
II. Some Indicators of Good Morale	26
MOTIVATION	26
EMPLOYEE PARTICIPATION	27
I. WHAT IS PARTICIPATION	27
II. WHY IS IT IMPORTANT?	27
III. HOW MAY SUPERVISORS OBTAIN IT?	28
STEPS IN HANDLING A GRIEVANCE	28
DISCIPLINE	29
I. THE DISCIPLINARY INTERVIEW	29
II. PLANNING THE INTERVIEW	29
III. CONDUCTING THE INTERVIEW	30

PRINCIPLES AND PRACTICES, OF ADMINISTRATION, SUPERVISION AND MANAGEMENT

Most people are inclined to think of administration as something that only a few persons are responsible for in a large organization. Perhaps this is true if you are thinking of Administration with a capital A, but administration with a lower case a is a responsibility of supervisors at all levels each working day.

All of us feel we are pretty good supervisors and that we do a good job of administering the workings of our agency. By and large, this is true, but every so often it is good to check up on ourselves. Checklists appear from time to time in various publications which psychologists say tell whether or not a person will make a good wife, husband, doctor, lawyer, or supervisor.

The following questions are an excellent checklist to test yourself as a supervisor and administrator.

Remember, Administration gives direction and points the way but administration carries the ideas to fruition. Each is dependent on the other for its success. Remember, too, that no unit is too small for these departmental functions to be carried out. These statements apply equally as well to the Chief Librarian as to the Department Head with but one or two persons to supervise.

GENERAL ADMINISTRATION: General Responsibilities of Supervisors

1. Have I prepared written statements of functions, activities, and duties for my organizational unit?

2. Have I prepared procedural guides for operating activities?

3. Have I established clearly in writing, lines of authority and responsibility for my organizational unit?

4. Do I make recommendations for improvements in organization, policies, administrative and operating routines and procedures, including simplification of work and elimination of non-essential operations?

5. Have I designated and trained an understudy to function in my absence?

6. Do I supervise and train personnel within the unit to effectively perform their assignments?

7. Do I assign personnel and distribute work on such a basis as to carry out the organizational unit's assignment or mission in the most effective and efficient manner?

8. Have I established administrative controls by:

    a. Fixing responsibility and accountability on all supervisors under my direction for the proper performance of their functions and duties.

b. Preparations and submitting periodic work load and progress reports covering the operations of the unit to my immediate superior.

c. Analysis and evaluation of such reports received from subordinate units.

d. Submission of significant developments and problems arising within the organizational unit to my immediate superior.

e. Conducting conferences, inspections, etc., as to the status and efficiency of unit operations.

9. Do I maintain an adequate and competent working force?

10. Have I fostered good employee-department relations, seeing that established rules, regulations, and instructions are being carried out properly?

11. Do I collaborate and consult with other organizational units performing related functions to insure harmonious and efficient working relationships?

12. Do I maintain liaison through prescribed channels with city departments and other governmental agencies concerned with the activities of the unit?

13. Do I maintain contact with and keep abreast of the latest developments and techniques of administration (professional societies, groups, periodicals, etc.) as to their applicability to the activities of the unit?

14. Do I communicate with superiors and subordinates through prescribed organizational channels?

15. Do I notify superiors and subordinates in instances where bypassing is necessary as soon thereafter as practicable?

16. Do I keep my superior informed of significant developments and problems?

SEVEN BASIC FUNCTIONS OF THE SUPERVISOR

I. PLANNING
This means working out goals and means to obtain goals. <u>What</u> needs to be done, <u>who</u> will do it, <u>how</u>, <u>when</u>, and <u>where</u> it is to be done.

SEVEN STEPS IN PLANNING

A. Define job or problem clearly.
B. Consider priority of job.
C. Consider time-limit—starting and completing.
D. Consider minimum distraction to, or interference with, other activities.
E. Consider and provide for contingencies—possible emergencies.
F. Break job down into components.

G. Consider the 5 W's and H:
   - WHY..........is it necessary to do the job? (Is the purpose clearly defined?)
   - WHAT........needs to be done to accomplish the defined purpose?
     ....is needed to do the job? (Money, materials, etc.)
   - WHO..........is needed to do the job?
     ....will have responsibilities?
   - WHERE......is the work to be done?
   - WHEN........is the job to begin and end? (Schedules, etc.)
   - HOW..........is the job to bed done? (Methods, controls, records, etc.)

II. ORGANIZING

This means dividing up the work, establishing clear lines of responsibility and authority and coordinating efforts to get the job done.

III. STAFFING

The whole personnel function of bringing in and <u>training</u> staff, getting the right man and fitting him to the right job—the job to which he is best suited.

In the normal situation, the supervisor's responsibility regarding staffing normally includes providing accurate job descriptions, that is, duties of the jobs, requirements, education and experience, skills, physical, etc.; assigning the work for maximum use of skills; and proper utilization of the probationary period to weed out unsatisfactory employees.

IV. DIRECTING

Providing the necessary leadership to the group supervised. Important work gets done to the supervisor's satisfaction.

V. COORDINATING

The all-important duty of inter-relating the various parts of the work.
The supervisor is also responsible for controlling the coordinated activities. This means measuring performance according to a time schedule and setting quotas to see that the goals previously set are being reached. Reports from workers should be analyzed, evaluated, and made part of all future plans.

VI. REPORTING

This means proper and effective communication to your superiors, subordinates, and your peers (in definition of the job of the supervisor). Reports should be read and information contained therein should be used, not be filed away and forgotten. Reports should be written in such a way that the desired action recommended by the report is forthcoming.

VII. BUDGETING
This means controlling current costs and forecasting future costs. This forecast is based on past experience, future plans and programs, as well as current costs.

You will note that these seven functions can fall under three topics:

Planning) Make a plan   Staffing)   Reporting) Watch it work
Organizing)   Directing) Get things done   Budgeting)
                          Controlling)

PLANNING TO MEET MANAGEMENT GOALS

I. WHAT IS PLANNING?

   A. Thinking a job through before new work is done to determine the best way to do it
   B. A method of doing something
   C. Ways and means for achieving set goals
   D. A means of enabling a supervisor to deliver with a minimum of effort, all details involved in coordinating his work

II. WHO SHOULD MAKE PLANS?

   Everybody!
   All levels of supervision must plan work. (Top management, heads of divisions or bureaus, first line supervisors, and individual employees.) The higher the level, the more planning required.

III. WHAT ARE THE RESULTS OF POOR PLANNING?

   A. Failure to meet deadline
   B. Low employee morale
   C. Lack of job coordination
   D. Overtime is frequently necessary
   E. Excessive cost, waste of material and manhours

IV. PRINCIPLES OF PLANNING

   A. Getting a clear picture of your objectives. What exactly are you trying to accomplish?
   B. Plan the whole job, then the parts, in proper sequence.
   C. Delegate the planning of details to those responsible for executing them.
   D. Make your plan flexible.
   E. Coordinate your plan with the plans of others so that the work may be processed with a minimum of delay.
   F. Sell your plan before you execute it.
   G. Sell your plan to your superior, subordinate, in order to gain maximum participation and coordination.
   H. Your plan should take precedence. Use knowledge and skills that others have brought to a similar job.
   I. Your plan should take account of future contingencies; allow for future expansion.
   J. Plans should include minor details. Leave nothing to chance that can be anticipated.
   K. Your plan should be simple and provide standards and controls. Establish quality and quantity standards and set a standard method of doing the job. The controls will indicate whether the job is proceeding according to plan.
   L. Consider possible bottlenecks, breakdowns, or other difficulties that are likely to arise.

V. Q. WHAT ARE THE YARDSTICKS BY WHICH PLANNING SHOULD BE MEASURED?
   A. Any plan should:
   —Clearly state a definite course of action to be followed and goal to be achieved, with consideration for emergencies.
   — Be realistic and practical.
   — State what's to be done, when it's to be done, where, how, and by whom.
   — Establish the most efficient sequence of operating steps so that more is accomplished in less time, with the least effort, and with the best quality results.
   — Assure meeting deliveries without delays.
   — Establish the standard by which performance is to be judged.

   Q. WHAT KINDS OF PLANS DOES EFFECTIVE SUPERVISION REQUIRE?
   A. Plans should cover such factors as:
   — Manpower: right number of properly trained employees on the job
   — Materials: adequate supply of the right materials and supplies
   — Machines: full utilization of machines and equipment, with proper maintenance
   — Methods: most efficient handling of operations
   — Deliveries: making deliveries on time
   — Tools: sufficient well-conditioned tools
   — Layout: most effective use of space
   — Reports: maintaining proper records and reports
   — Supervision: planning work for employees and organizing supervisor's own time

MANAGEMENT PRINCIPLES

I. MANAGEMENT
    Q. What do we mean by management?
    A. Getting work done through others.

    Management could also be defined as planning, directing, and controlling the operations of a bureau or division so that all factors will function properly and all persons cooperate efficiently for a common objective.

II. MANAGEMENT PRINCIPLES

    A. There should be a hierarchy—wherein authority and responsibility run upward and downward through several levels—with a broad base at the bottom and a single head at the top.

    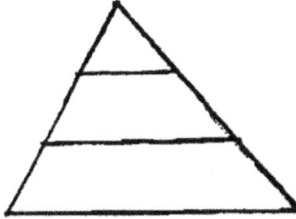

    B. Each and every unit or person in the organization should be answerable ultimately to the manager at the apex. In other words, *The buck stops here!*

C. Every necessary function involved in the bureau's objectives is assigned to a unit in that bureau.

D. Responsibilities assigned to a unit are specifically clear-cut and understood.

E. Consistent methods of organizational structure should be applied at each level of the organization.

F. Each member of the bureau from top to bottom knows: to whom he reports and who reports to him.

G. No member of one bureau reports to more than one supervisor. No dual functions.

H. Responsibility for a function is matched by authority necessary to perform that function. Weight of authority.

I. Individuals or units reporting to a supervisor do not exceed the number which can be feasibly and effectively coordinated and directed. Concept of *span of control*.

J. Channels of command (management) are not violated by staff units, although there should be staff services to facilitate and coordinate management functions.

K. Authority and responsibility should be decentralized to units and individuals who are responsible for the actual performance of operations.
Welfare – down to Welfare Centers
Hospitals – down to local hospitals

L. Management should exercise control through attention to policy problems of exceptional performance, rather than through review of routine actions of subordinates.

M. Organizations should never be permitted to grow so elaborate as to hinder work accomplishments.

III. ORGANIZATION STRUCTURE

Types of Organizations
The purest form is a leader and a few followers, such as:

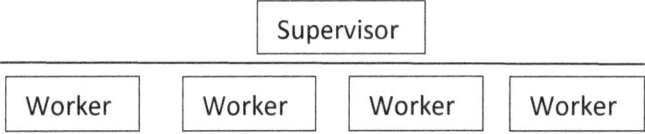

(Refer to organization chart) from supervisor to workers.

The line of authority is direct, The workers know exactly where they stand in relation to their boss, to whom they report for instructions and direction.

Unfortunately, in our present complex society, few organizations are similar to this example of a pure line organization. In this era of specialization, other people are often needed in the simplest of organizations. These specialists are known as staff. The sole purpose for their existence (staff) is to assist, advise, suggest, help or counsel line organizations. Staff has no authority to direct line people—nor do they give them direct instructions.

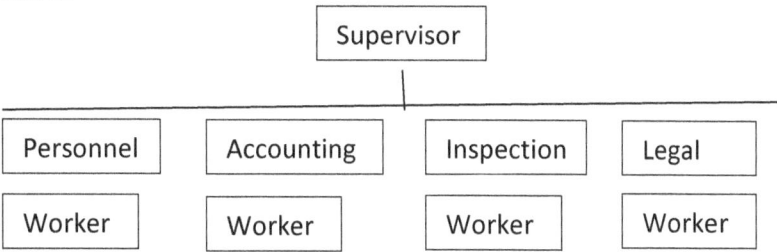

Line Functions
1. Directs
2. Orders
3. Responsibility for carrying out activities from beginning to end
4. Follows chain of command
5. Is identified with what it does
6. Decides when and how to use staff advice
7. Line executes

Staff Functions
1. Advises
2. Persuades and sells
3. Staff studies, reports, recommends but does not carry out
4. May advise across department lines
5. May find its ideas identified with others
6. Has to persuade line to want its advice
7. Staff: Conducts studies and research. Provides advice and instructions in technical matters. Serves as technical specialist to render specific services.

Types and Functions of Organization Charts
An organization chart is a picture of the arrangement and inter-relationship of the subdivisions of an organization.

A. Types of Charts:
   1. Structural: basic relationships only
   2. Functional: includes functions or duties
   3. Personnel: positions, salaries, status, etc.
   4. Process Chart: work performed
   5. Gantt Chart: actual performance against planned
   5. Flow Chart: flow and distribution of work

B. Functions of Charts:
   1. Assist in management planning and control
   2. Indicate duplication of functions
   3. Indicate incorrect stressing of functions
   4. Indicate neglect of important functions
   5. Correct unclear authority
   6. Establish proper span of control

C. Limitations of Charts:
1. Seldom maintained on current basis
2. Chart is oversimplified
3. Human factors cannot adequately be charted

D. Organization Charts should be:
1. Simple
2. Symmetrical
3. Indicate authority
4. Line and staff relationship differentiated
5. Chart should be dated and bear signature of approving officer
6. Chart should be displayed, not hidden

ORGANIZATION

There are four basic principles of organization:
1. Unity of command
2. Span of control
3. Uniformity of assignment
4. Assignment of responsibility and delegation of authority

I. UNITY OF COMMAND

Unity of command means that each person in the organization should receive orders from one, and only one, supervisor. When a person has to take orders from two or more people, (a) the orders may be in conflict and the employee is upset because he does not know which he should obey, or (b) different orders may reach him at the same time and he does not know which he should carry out first.

Equally as bad as having two bosses is the situation where the supervisor is bypassed. Let us suppose you are a supervisor whose boss bypasses you (deals directly with people reporting to you). To the worker, it is the same as having two bosses; but to you, the supervisor, it is equally serious. Bypassing on the part of your boss will undermine your authority, and the people under you will begin looking to your boss for decisions and even for routine orders.

You can prevent bypassing by telling the people you supervise that if anyone tries to give them orders, they should direct that person to you.

II. SPAN OF CONTROL

Span of control on a given level involves:
A. The number of people being supervised
B. The distance
C The time involved in supervising the people. (One supervisor cannot supervise too many workers effectively.)

Span of control means that a supervisor has the right number (not too many and not too few) of subordinates that he can supervise well.

III. UNIFORMITY OF ASSIGNMENT

In assigning work, you as the supervisor should assign to each person jobs that are similar in nature. An employee who is assigned too many different types of jobs will waste time in going from one kind of work to another. It takes time for him to get to top production in one kind of task and, before he does so, he has to start on another.
When you assign work to people, remember that:

A. Job duties should be definite. Make it clear from the beginning <u>what</u> they are to do, <u>how</u> they are to do it, and <u>why</u> they are to do it. Let them know how much they are expected to do and how well they are expected to do it.
B. Check your assignments to be certain that there are no workers with too many unrelated duties, and that no two people have been given overlapping responsibilities. Your aim should be to have every task assigned to a specific person with the work fairly distributed and with each person doing his part.

IV. ASSIGNMENT OF RESPONSIBILITY AND DELEGATION OF AUTHORITY

A supervisor cannot delegate his final responsibility for the work of his department. The experienced supervisor knows that he gets his work done through people. He can't do it all himself. So he must assign the work and the responsibility for the work to his employees. Then they must be given the authority to carry out their responsibilities.

By assigning responsibility and delegating authority to carry out the responsibility, the supervisor builds in his workers initiative, resourcefulness, enthusiasm, and interest in their work. He is treating them as responsible adults. They can find satisfaction in their work, and they will respect the supervisor and be loyal to the supervisor.

PRINCIPLES OF ORGANIZATION

I. DEFINITION

Organization is the method of dividing up the work to provide the best channels for coordinated effort to get the agency's mission accomplished.

II. PURPOSE OF ORGANIZATION

A. To enable each employee within the organization to clearly know his responsibilities and relationships to his fellow employees and to organizational units
B. To avoid conflicts of authority and overlapping of jurisdiction.
C. To ensure teamwork.

III. BASIC CONSIDERATIONS IIN ORGANIZATIONAL PLANNING

A. The basic plans and objectives of the agency should be determined, and the organizational structure should be adapted to carry out effectively such plans and objectives.
B. The organization should be built around the major functions of the agency and not individuals or groups of individuals.

C. The organization should be sufficiently flexible to meet new and changing conditions which may be brought about from within or outside the department.
D. The organizational structure should be as simple as possible and the number of organizational units kept at a minimum.
E. The number of levels of authority should be kept at a minimum. Each additional management level lengthens the chain of authority and responsibility and increases the time for instructions to be distributed to operating levels and for decisions to be obtained from higher authority.
F. The form of organization should permit each executive to exercise maximum initiative within the limits of delegated authority.

IV. BASES FOR ORGANIZATION

A. Purpose (Examples: education, police, sanitation)
B. Process (Examples: accounting, legal, purchasing)
C. Clientele (Examples: welfare, parks, veteran)
D. Geographic (Examples: borough offices, precincts, libraries)

V. ASSIGNMENTS OF FUNCTIONS

A. Every function of the agency should be assigned to a specific organizational unit. Under normal circumstances, no single function should be assigned to more than one organizational unit.
B. There should be no overlapping, duplication, or conflict between organizational elements.
C. Line functions should be separated from staff functions, and proper emphasis should be placed on staff activities.
D. Functions which are closely related or similar should normally be assigned to a single organizational unit.
E. Functions should be properly distributed to promote balance, and to avoid overemphasis of less important functions and underemphasis of more essential functions.

VI. DELEGATION OF AUTHORITY AND RESPONSIBILITY

A. Responsibilities assigned to a specific individual or organizational unit should carry corresponding authority, and all statements of authority or limitations thereof should be as specific as possible.
B. Authority and responsibility for action should be decentralized to organizational units and individuals responsible for actual performance to the greatest extent possible, without relaxing necessary control over policy or the standardization of procedures. Delegation of authority will be consistent with decentralization of responsibility but such delegation will not divest an executive in higher authority of his overall responsibility.
C. The heads of organizational units should concern themselves with important matters and should delegate to the maximum extent details and routines performed in the ordinary course of business.
D. All responsibilities, authorities, and relationships should be stated in simple language to avoid misinterpretation.
E. Each individual or organizational unit charged with a specific responsibility will be held responsible for results.

VII. EMPLOYEE RELATIONSHIPS

   A. The employees reporting to one executive should not exceed the number which can be effectively directed and coordinated. The number will depend largely upon the scope and extent of the responsibilities of the subordinates.
   B. No person should report to more than one supervisor. Every supervisor should know who reports to him, and every employee should know to whom he reports. Channels of authority and responsibility should not be violated by staff units.
   C. Relationships between organizational units within the agency and with outside organizations and associations should be clearly stated and thoroughly understood to avoid misunderstanding.

DELEGATING

I. WHAT IS DELEGATING?
Delegating is assigning a job to an employee, giving him the authority to get that job done, and giving him the responsibility for seeing to it that the job is done.

   A. What To Delegate
      1. Routine details
      2. Jobs which may be necessary and take a lot of time, but do not have to be done by the supervisor personally (preparing reports, attending meetings, etc.)
      3. Routine decision-making (making decisions which do not require the supervisor's personal attention)

   B. What Not To Delegate
      1. Job details which are *executive functions* (setting goals, organizing employees into a good team, analyzing results so as to plan for the future)
      2. Disciplinary power (handling grievances, preparing service ratings, reprimands, etc.)
      3. Decision-making which involves large numbers of employees or other bureaus and departments
      4. Final and complete responsibility for the job done by the unit being supervised

   C. Why Delegate?
      1. To strengthen the organization by developing a greater number of skilled employees
      2. To improve the employee's performance by giving him the chance to learn more about the job, handle some responsibility, and become more interested in getting the job done
      3. To improve a supervisor's performance by relieving him of routine jobs and giving him more time for *executive functions* (planning, organizing, controlling, etc.) which cannot be delegated

II. TO WHOM TO DELEGATE
People with abilities not being used. Selection should be based on ability, not on favoritism.

REPORTS

I. DEFINITION
A report is an orderly presentation of factual information directed to a specific reader for a specific purpose

II. PURPOSE
The general purpose of a report is to bring to the reader useful and factual information about a condition or a problem. Some specific purposes of a report may be:

   A. To enable the reader to appraise the efficiency or effectiveness of a person or an operation
   B. To provide a basis for establishing standards
   C. To reflect the results of expenditures of time, effort, and money
   D. To provide a basis for developing or altering programs

III. TYPES

   A. Information Report: Contains facts arranged in sequence
   B. Summary (Examination) Report: Contains facts plus an analysis or discussion of the significance of the facts. Analysis may give advantages and disadvantages or give qualitative and quantitative comparisons
   C. Recommendation Report: Contains facts, analysis, and conclusion logically drawn from the facts and analysis, plus a recommendation based upon the facts, analysis, and conclusions

IV. FACTORS TO CONSIDER BEFORE WRITING REPORT

   A. <u>Why</u> write the report?: The purpose of the report should be clearly defined.
   B. <u>Who</u> will read the report?: What level of language should be used? Will the reader understand professional or technical language?
   C. <u>What</u> should be said?: What does the reader need or want to know about the subject?
   D. <u>How</u> should it be said?: Should the subject be presented tactfully? Convincingly? In a stimulating manner?

V. PREPARATORY STEPS

   A. Assemble the facts: Find out who, why, what, where, when, and how.
   B. Organize the facts: Eliminate unnecessary information
   C. Prepare an outline: Check for orderliness, logical sequence
   D. Prepare a draft: Check for correctness, clearness, completeness, conciseness, and tone
   E. Prepare it in final form: Check for grammar, punctuation, appearance

VI. OUTLINE FOR A RECOMMENDATION REPORT

   Is the report:
   A. Correct in information, grammar, and tone?
   B. Clear?
   C. Complete?

D. Concise?
E. Timely?
F. Worth its cost?

Will the report accomplish its purpose?

MANAGEMENT CONTROLS

I. CONTROL
What is control? What is controlled? Who controls?

The essence of control is action which adjusts operations to predetermined standards, and its basis is information in the hands of managers. Control is checking to determine whether plans are being observed and suitable progress toward stated objectives is being made, and action is taken, if necessary, to correct deviations.

We have a ready-made model for this concept of control in the automatic systems which are widely used for process control in the chemical land petroleum industries. A process control system works this way. Suppose, for example, it is desired to maintain a constant rate of flow of oil through a pipe at a predetermined or set-point value. A signal, whose strength represents the rate of flow, can be produced in a measuring device and transmitted to a control mechanism. The control mechanism, when it detects any deviation of the actual from the set-point signal, will reposition the value regulating flow rate.

II. BASIS FOR CONTROL

A process control mechanism thus acts to adjust operations to predetermined standards and does so on the basis of information it receives. In a parallel way, information reaching a manager gives him the opportunity for corrective action and is his basis for control. He cannot exercise control without such information, and he cannot do a complete job of managing without controlling.

III. POLICY

What is policy?

Policy is simply a statement of an organization's intention to act in certain ways when specified types of circumstances arise. It represents a general decision, predetermined and expressed as a principle or rule, establishing a normal pattern of conduct for dealing with given types of business events—usually recurrent. A statement is therefore useful in economizing the time of managers and in assisting them to discharge their responsibilities equitably and consistently.

Policy is not a means of control, but policy does generate the need for control.

Adherence to policies is not guaranteed nor can it be taken on faith. It has to be verified. Without verification, there is no basis for control. Policy and procedures, although closely related and interdependent to a certain extent, are not synonymous. A policy may be adopted, for example, to maintain a materials inventory not to exceed one million dollars.

A procedure for inventory control could interpret that policy and convert it into methods for keeping within that limit, with consideration, too, of possible but foreseeable expedient deviation.

IV. PROCEDURE

What is procedure?

A procedure specifically prescribes:
A. What work is to be performed by the various participants
B. Who are the respective participants
C. When and where the various steps in the different processes are to be performed
D. The sequence of operations that will insure uniform handling of recurring transactions
E. The paper that is involved, its origin, transition, and disposition

Necessary appurtenances to a procedure are:
A. Detailed organizational chart
B. Flow charts
C. Exhibits of forms, all presented in close proximity to the text of the procedure

V. BASIS OF CONTROL – INFORMATION IN THE HANDS OF MANAGERS

If the basis of control is information in the hands of managers, then reporting is elevated to a level of very considerable importance.

Types of reporting may include:
A. Special reports and routine reports
B. Written, oral, and graphic reports
C. Staff meetings
D. Conferences
E. Television screens
F. Non-receipt of information, as where management is by exception
G. Any other means whereby information is transmitted to a manager as a basis for control action

FRAMEWORK OF MANAGEMENT

I. ELEMENTS

   A. Policy: It has to be verified, controlled.

   B. Organization is part of the giving of an assignment. The organizational chart gives to each individual in his title, a first approximation of the nature of his assignment and orients him as being accountable to a certain individual. Organization is not in a true sense a means of control. Control is checking to ascertain whether the assignment is executed as intended and acting on the basis of that information.

   C. Budgets perform three functions:
      1. They present the objectives, plans, and programs of the organization in financial terms.

2. They report the progress of actual performance against these predetermined objectives, plans, and programs.
3. Like organizational charts, delegations of authority, procedures, and job descriptions, they define the assignments which have flowed from the Chief Executive. Budgets are a means of control in the respect that they report progress of actual performance against the program. They provide information which enables managers to take action directed toward bringing actual results into conformity with the program.

D. Internal Check provides in practice for the principle that the same person should not have responsibility for all phases of a transaction. This makes it clearly an aspect of organization rather than of control. Internal Check is static, or built-in.

E. Plans, Programs, Objectives
People must know what they are trying to do. Objectives fulfill this need. Without them, people may work industriously and yet, working aimlessly, accomplish little. Plans and Programs complement Objectives, since they propose how and according to what time schedule the objectives are to be reached.

F. Delegations of Authority
Among the ways we have for supplementing the titles and lines of authority of an organizational chart are delegations of authority. Delegations of authority clarify the extent of authority of individuals and in that way serve to define assignments. That they are not means of control is apparent from the very fact that wherever there has been a delegation of authority, the need for control increases. This could hardly be expected to happen if delegations of authority were themselves means of control.

II. MANAGER'S RESPONSIBILITY

Control becomes necessary whenever a manager delegates authority to a subordinate because he cannot delegate and then simply sit back and forget4 about it. A manager's accountability to his own superior has not diminished one whit as a result of delegating part of his authority to a subordinate. The manager must exercise control over actions taken under the authority so delegated. That means checking serves as a basis for possible corrective action.

Objectives, plans, programs, organizational charts, and other elements of the managerial system are not fruitfully regarded as either controls or means of control. They are pre-established standards or models of performance to which operations are adjusted by the exercise of management control. These standards or models of performance are dynamic in character for they are constantly altered, modified, or revised. Policies, organizational set-up, procedures, delegations, etc. are constantly altered but, like objectives and plans, they remain in force until they are either abandoned or revised. All of the elements (or standards or models of performance), objectives, plans, and programs, policies, organization, etc. can be regarded as a *framework of management*.

III. CONTROL TECHNIQUES

Examples of control techniques:
A. Compare against established standards
B. Compare with a similar operation
C. Compare with past operations
D. Compare with predictions of accomplishment

IV. WHERE FORECASTS FIT

Control is after-the-fact while forecasts are before. Forecasts and projections are important for setting objectives and formulating plans.

Information for aiming and planning does not have to be before-the-fact. It may be an after-the-fact analysis proving that a certain policy has been impolitic in its effect on the relation of the company or department with customer, employee, taxpayer, or stockholder; or that a certain plan is no longer practical, or that a certain procedure is unworkable.

The prescription here certainly would not be in control (in these cases, control would simply bring operations into conformity with obsolete standards) but the establishment of new standards, a new policy, a new plan, and a new procedure to be controlled too.

Information is, of course, the basis for all communication in addition to furnishing evidence to management of the need for reconstructing the framework of management.

PROBLEM SOLVING

The accepted concept in modern management for problem solving is the utilization of the following steps:

A. Identify the problem
B. Gather data
C. List possible solutions
D. Test possible solutions
E. Select the best solution
F. Put the solution into actual practice

Occasions might arise where you would have to apply the second step of gathering data before completing the first step.

You might also find that it will be necessary to work on several steps at the same time.

I. IDENTIFY THE PROBLEM

Your first step is to define as precisely as possible the problem to be solved. While this may sound easy, it is often the most difficult part of the process.

It has been said of problem solving that you are halfway to the solution when you can write out a clear statement of the problem itself.

Our job now is to get below the surface manifestations of the trouble and pinpoint the problem. This is usually accomplished by a logical analysis, by going from the general to the particular; from the obvious to the not-so-obvious cause.

Let us say that production is behind schedule. WHY? Absenteeism is high. Now, is absenteeism the basic problem to be tackled, or is it merely a symptom of low morale among the workforce? Under these circumstances, you may decide that production is not the problem; the problem is *employee morale*.

In trying to define the problem, remember there is seldom one simple reason why production is lagging, or reports are late, etc.

Analysis usually leads to the discovery that an apparent problem is really made up of several subproblems which must be attacked separately.

Another way is to limit the problem, and thereby ease the task of finding a solution, and concentrate on the elements which are within the scope of your control.

When you have gone this far, write out a tentative statement of the problem to be solved.

II. GATHER DATA

In the second step, you must set out to collect all the information that might have a bearing on the problem. Do not settle for an assumption when reasonable fact and figures are available.

If you merely go through the motions of problem-solving, you will probably shortcut the information-gathering step. Therefore, do not stack the evidence by confining your research to your own preconceived ideas.

As you collect facts, organize them in some form that helps you make sense of them and spot possible relationships between them. For example, plotting cost per unit figures on a graph can be more meaningful than a long column of figures.

Evaluate each item as you go along. Is the source material absolutely, reliable, probably reliable, or not to be trusted.

One of the best methods for gathering data is to go out and look the situation over carefully. Talk to the people on the job who are most affected by this problem.

Always keep in mind that a primary source is usually better than a secondary source of information.

III. LIST POSSIBLE SOLUTIONS

This is the creative thinking step of problem solving. This is a good time to bring into play whatever techniques of group dynamics the agency or bureau might have developed for a joint attack on problems.

Now the important thing for you to do is: Keep an open mind. Let your imagination roam freely over the facts you have collected. Jot down every possible solution that occurs to you. Resist the temptation to evaluate various proposals as you go along. List seemingly absurd ideas along with more plausible ones. The more possibilities you list during this step, the less risk you will run of settling for merely a workable, rather than the best, solution.

Keep studying the data as long as there seems to be any chance of deriving additional ideas, solutions, explanations, or patterns from it.

IV. TEST POSSIBLE SOLUTIONS

Now you begin to evaluate the possible solutions. Take pains to be objective. Up to this point, you have suspended judgment but you might be tempted to select a solution you secretly favored all along and proclaim it as the best of the lot.

The secret of objectivity in this phase is to test the possible solutions separately, measuring each against a common yardstick. To make this yardstick try to enumerate as many specific criteria as you can think of. Criteria are best phrased as questions which you ask of each possible solution. They can be drawn from these general categories:

- Suitability – Will this solution do the job?
  Will it solve the problem completely or partially?
  Is it a permanent or a stopgap solution?

- Feasibility - Will this plan work in actual practice?
  Can we afford this approach?
  How much will it cost?

- Acceptability - Will the boss go along with the changes required in the plan?
  Are we trying to drive a tack with a sledge hammer?

V. SELECT THE BEST SOLUTION

This is the area of executive decision.

Occasionally, one clearly superior solution will stand out at the conclusion of the testing process. But often it is not that simple. You may find that no one solution has come through all the tests with flying colors.

You may also find that a proposal, which flunked miserably on one of the essential tests, racked up a very high score on others.

The best solution frequently will turn out to be a combination.

Try to arrange a marriage that will bring together the strong points of one possible solution with the particular virtues of another. The more skill and imagination that you apply, the greater is the likelihood that you will come out with a solution that is not merely adequate and workable, but is the best possible under the circumstances.

VI. PUT THE SOLUTION INTO ACTUAL PRACTICE

As every executive knows, a plan which works perfectly on paper may develop all sorts of bugs when put into actual practice.

Problem-solving does not stop with selecting the solution which looks best in theory. The next step is to put the chosen solution into action and watch the results. The results may point towards modifications.

If the problem disappears when you put your solution into effect, you know you have the right solution.

If it does not disappear, even after you have adjusted your plan to cover unforeseen difficulties that turned up in practice, work your way back through the problem-solving solutions.

> Would one of them have worked better?
> Did you overlook some vital piece of data which would have given you a different slant on the whole situation? Did you apply all necessary criteria in testing solutions? If no light dawns after this much rechecking, it is a pretty good bet that you defined the problem incorrectly in the first place.

You came up with the wrong solution because you tackled the wrong problem.

Thus, step six may become step one of a new problem-solving cycle.

COMMUNICATION

I. WHAT IS COMMUNICATION?

We communicate through writing, speaking, action, or inaction. In speaking to people face-to-face, there is opportunity to judge reactions and to adjust the message. This makes the supervisory chain one of the most, and in many instances the most, important channels of communication.

In an organization, communication means keeping employees informed about the organization's objectives, policies, problems, and progress. Communication is the free interchange of information, ideas, and desirable attitudes between and among employees and between employees and management.

II. WHY IS COMMUNICATION NEEDED?

A. People have certain social needs
B. Good communication is essential in meeting those social needs
C. While people have similar basic needs, at the same time they differ from each other
D. Communication must be adapted to these individual differences

An employee cannot do his best work unless he knows why he is doing it. If he has the feeling that he is being kept in the dark about what is going on, his enthusiasm and productivity suffer.

Effective communication is needed in an organization so that employees will understand what the organization is trying to accomplish; and how the work of one unit contributes to or affects the work of other units in the organization and other organizations.

III. HOW IS COMMUNICATION ACHIEVED?

Communication flows downward, upward, sideways.

A. Communication may come from top management down to employees. This is downward communication.

   Some means of downward communication are:
   1. Training (orientation, job instruction, supervision, public relations, etc.)
   2. Conferences
   3. Staff meetings
   4. Policy statements
   5. Bulletins
   6. Newsletters
   7. Memoranda
   8. Circulation of important letters

   In downward communication, it is important that employees be informed in advance of changes that will affect them.

B. Communications should also be developed so that the ideas, suggestions, and knowledge of employees will flow upward to top management.

   Some means of upward communication are:
   1. Personal discussion conferences
   2. Committees
   3. Memoranda
   4. Employees suggestion program
   5. Questionnaires to be filled in giving comments and suggestions about proposed actions that will affect field operations.

   Upward communication requires that management be willing to listen, to accept, and to make changes when good ideas are present. Upward communication succeeds when there is no fear of punishment for speaking out or lack of interest at the top. Employees will share their knowledge and ideas with management when interest is shown and recognition is given.

C. The advantages of downward communication:
   1. It enables the passing down of orders, policies, and plans necessary to the continued operation of the station.
   2. By making information available, it diminishes the fears and suspicions which result from misinformation and misunderstanding.
   3. It fosters the pride people want to have in their work when they are told of good work.
   4. It improves the morale and stature of the individual to be *in the know*.

5. It helps employees to understand, accept, and cooperate with changes when they know about them in advance.

D. The advantages of upward communication:
1. It enables the passing upward of information, attitudes, and feelings.
2. It makes it easier to find out how ready people are to receive downward communication.
3. It reveals the degree to which the downward communication is understood and accepted.
4. It helps to satisfy the basic social needs.
5. It stimulates employees to participate in the operation of their organization.
6. It encourage employees to contribute ideas for improving the efficiency and economy of operations.
7. It helps to solve problem situations before they reach the explosion point.

IV. WHY DOES COMMUNICATION FAIL?

A. The technical difficulties of conveying information clearly
B. The emotional content of communication which prevents complete transmission
C. The fact that there is a difference between what management needs to say, what it wants to day, and what it does say
D. The fact that there is a difference between what employees would like to say, what they think is profitable or safe to say, and what they do say

V. HOW TO IMPROVE COMMUNICATION

As a supervisor, you are a key figure in communication. To improve as a communicator, you should:
A. Know: Knowing your subordinates will help you to recognize and work with individual differences.
B. Like: If you like those who work for you and those for whom you work, this will foster the kind of friendly, warm, work atmosphere that will facilitate communication.
C. Trust: Showing a sincere desire to communicate will help to develop the mutual trust and confidence which are essential to the free flow of communication.
D. Tell: Tell your subordinates and superiors *what's doing*. Tell your subordinates *why* as well as *how*.
E. Listen: By listening, you help others to talk and you create good listeners. Don't forget that listening implies action.
F. Stimulate: Communication has to be stimulated and encouraged. Be receptive to ideas and suggestions and motivate your people so that each member of the team identifies himself with the job at hand.
G. Consult: The most effective way of consulting is to let your people participate, insofar as possible, in developing determinations which affect them or their work.

VI. HOW TO DETERMINE WHETHER YOU ARE GETTING ACROSS

A. Check to see that communication is received and understood
B. Judge this understanding by actions rather than words
C. Adapt or vary communication, when necessary
D. Remember that good communication cannot cure all problems

VII. THE KEY ATTITUDE

Try to see things from the other person's point of view. By doing this, you help to develop the permissive atmosphere and the shared confidence and understanding which are essential to effective two-way communication.

Communication is a two-way process:
A. The basic purpose of any communication is to get action.
B. The only way to get action is through acceptance.
C. In order to get acceptance, communication must be humanly satisfying as well as technically efficient.

HOW ORDERS AND INSTRUCTIONS SHOULD BE GIVEN

I. CHARACTERISTICS OF GOOD ORDERS AND INSTRUCTIONS

   A. Clear
      Orders should be definite as to
      —What is to be done
      —Who is to do it
      —When it is to be done
      —Where it is to be done
      —How it is to be done

   B. Concise
      Avoid wordiness. Orders should be brief and to the point.

   C. Timely
      Instructions and orders should be sent out at the proper time and not too long in advance of expected performance.

   D. Possibility of Performance
      Orders should be feasible:
      1. Investigate before giving orders
      2. Consult those who are to carry out instructions before formulating and issuing them

   E. Properly Directed
      Give the orders to the people concerned. Do not send orders to people who are not concerned. People who continually receive instructions that are not applicable to them get in the habit of neglecting instructions generally.

   F. Reviewed Before Issuance
      Orders should be reviewed before issuance:
      1. Test them by putting yourself in the position of the recipient
      2. If they involve new procedures, have the persons who are to do the work review them for suggestions.

   G. Reviewed After Issuance
      Persons who receive orders should be allowed to raise questions and to point out unforeseen consequences of orders.

H. Coordinated
Orders should be coordinated so that work runs smoothly.

I. Courteous
Make a request rather than a demand. There is no need to continually call attention to the fact that you are the boss.

J. Recognizable as an Order
Be sure that the order is recognizable as such.

K. Complete
Be sure recipient has knowledge and experience sufficient to carry out order. Give illustrations and examples.

A DEPARTMENTAL PERSONNEL OFFICE IS RESPONSIBLE FOR THE FOLLOWING FUNCTIONS

1. Policy
2. Personnel Programs
3. Recruitment and Placement
4. Position Classification
5. Salary and Wage Administration
6. Employee performance Standards and Evaluation
7. Employee Relations
8. Disciplinary Actions and Separations
9. Health and Safety
10. Staff Training and Development
11. Personnel Records, Procedures, and Reports
12. Employee Services
13. Personnel Research

SUPERVISION

I. LEADERSHIP

All leadership is based essentially on authority. This comes from two sources: It is received from higher management or it is earned by the supervisor through his methods of supervision. Although effective leadership has always depended upon the leader's using his authority in such a way as to appeal successfully to the motives of the people supervised, the conditions for making this appeal are continually changing. The key to today's problem of leadership is flexibility and resourcefulness on the part of the leader in meeting changes in conditions as they occur.

Three basic approaches to leadership are generally recognized:

A. The Authoritarian Approach
  1. The methods and techniques used in this approach emphasize the / in leadership and depend primarily on the formal authority of the leader. This authority is sometimes exercised in a hardboiled manner and sometimes in a benevolent

manner, but in either case the dominating role of the leader is reflected in the thinking, planning, and decisions of the group.
2. Group results are to a large degree dependent on close supervision by the leader. Usually, the individuals in the group will not show a high degree of initiative or acceptance of responsibility and their capacity to grow and develop probably will not be fully utilized. The group may react with resentment or submission, depending upon the manner and skill of the leader in using his authority.
3. This approach develops as a natural outgrowth of the authority that goes with the leader's job and his feeling of sole responsibility for getting the job done. It is relatively easy to use and does not require must resourcefulness.
4. The use of this approach is effective in times of emergencies, in meeting close deadline as a final resort, in settling some issues, in disciplinary matters, and with dependent individuals and groups.

B. The Laissez-Faire or Let 'em Alone Approach
1. This approach generally is characterized by an avoidance of leadership responsibility by the leader. The activities of the group depend largely on the choice of its members rather than the leader.
2. Group results probably will be poor. Generally, there will be disagreements over petty things, bickering, and confusion. Except for a few aggressive people, individuals will not show much initiative and growth and development will be retarded. There may be a tendency for informal leaders to take over leadership of the group.
3. This approach frequently results from the leader's dislike of responsibility, from his lack of confidence, from failure of other methods to work, from disappointment or criticism. It is usually the easiest of the three to use and requires both understanding and resourcefulness on the part of the leader.
4. This approach is occasionally useful and effective, particularly in forcing dependent individuals or groups to rely on themselves, to give someone a chance to save face by clearing his own difficulties, or when action should be delayed temporarily for good cause.

C. The Democratic Approach
1. The methods and techniques used in this approach emphasize the *we* in leadership and build up the responsibility of the group to attain its objectives. Reliance is placed largely on the earned authority of the leader.
2. Group results are likely to be good because most of the job motives of the people will be satisfied. Cooperation and teamwork, initiative, acceptance of responsibility, and the individual's capacity for growth probably will show a high degree of development.
3. This approach grows out of a desire or necessity of the leader to find ways to appeal effectively to the motivation of his group. It is the best approach to build up inside the person a strong desire to cooperate and apply himself to the job. It is the most difficult to develop, and requires both understanding and resourcefulness on the part of the leader.
4. The value of this approach increases over a long period where sustained efficiency and development of people are important. It may not be fully effective in all situations, however, particularly when there is not sufficient time to use it properly or where quick decisions must be made.

All three approaches are used by most leaders and have a place in supervising people. The extent of their use varies with individual leaders, with some using one approach predominantly. The leader who uses these three approaches, and varies their use with time and circumstance, is probably the most effective. Leadership which is used predominantly with a democratic approach requires more resourcefulness on the part of the leader but offers the greatest possibilities in terms of teamwork and cooperation.

The one best way of developing democratic leadership is to provide a real sense of participation on the part of the group, since this satisfies most of the chief job motives. Although there are many ways of providing participation, consulting as frequently as possible with individuals and groups on things that affect them seems to offer the most in building cooperation and responsibility. Consultation takes different forms, but it is most constructive when people feel they are actually helping in finding the answers to the problems on the job.

There are some requirements of leaders in respect to human relations which should be considered in their selection and development. Generally, the leader should be interested in working with other people, emotionally stable, self-confident, and sensitive to the reactions of others. In addition, his viewpoint should be one of getting the job done through people who work cooperatively in response to his leadership. He should have a knowledge of individual and group behavior, but, most important of all, he should work to combine all of these requirements into a definite, practical skill in leadership.

II. NINE POINTS OF CONTRAST BETWEEN *BOSS* AND *LEADER*

   A. The boss drives his men; the leader coaches them.
   B. The boss depends on authority; the leader on good will.
   C. The boss inspires fear; the leader inspires enthusiasm.
   D. The boss says I; the leader says *We*.
   E. The boss says *Get here on time*; the leader gets there ahead of time.
   F. The boss fixes the blame for the breakdown; the leader fixes the breakdown.
   G. The boss knows how it is done; the leader shows how.
   H. The boss makes work a drudgery; the leader makes work a game.
   I. The boss says *Go*; the leader says *Let's go*.

EMPLOYEE MORALE

Employee morale is the way employees feel about each other, the organization or unit in which they work, and the work they perform.

I. SOME WAYS TO DEVELOP AND MAINTAIN GOOD EMPLYEE MORALE

   A. Give adequate credit and praise when due.
   B. Recognize importance of all jobs and equalize load with proper assignments, always giving consideration to personality differences and abilities.
   C. Welcome suggestions and do not have an *all-wise* attitude. Request employees' assistance in solving problems and use assistants when conducting group meetings on certain subjects.
   D. Properly assign responsibilities and give adequate authority for fulfillment of such assignments.

E. Keep employees informed about matters that affect them.
F. Criticize and reprimand employees privately.
G. Be accessible and willing to listen.
H. Be fair.
I. Be alert to detect training possibilities so that you will not miss an opportunity to help each employee do a better job, and if possible with less effort on his part.
J. Set a good example.
K. Apply the golden rule.

II. SOME INDICATIONS OF GOOD MORALE

A. Good quality of work
B. Good quantity
C. Good attitude of employees
D. Good discipline
E. Teamwork
F. Good attendance
G. Employee participation

MOTIVATION

DRIVES

A drive, stated simply, is a desire or force which causes a person to do or say certain things. These are some of the most usual drives and some of their identifying characteristics recognizable in people motivated by such drives:

A. Security (desire to provide for the future)
Always on time for work
Works for the same employer for many years
Never takes unnecessary chances
Seldom resists doing what he is told

B. Recognition (desire to be rewarded for accomplishment)
Likes to be asked for his opinion
Becomes very disturbed when he makes a mistake
Does things to attract attention
Likes to see his name in print

C. Position (desire to hold certain status in relation to others)
Boasts about important people he knows
Wants to be known as a key man
Likes titles
Demands respect
Belongs to clubs, for prestige

D. Accomplishment (desire to get things done)
   Complains when things are held up
   Likes to do things that have tangible results
   Never lies down on the job
   Is proud of turning out good work

E. Companionship (desire to associate with other people)
   Likes to work with others
   Tells stories and jokes
   Indulges in horseplay
   Finds excuses to talk to others on the job

F. Possession (desire to collect and hoard objects)
   Likes to collect things
   Puts his name on things belonging to him
   Insists on the same location

Supervisors may find that identifying the drives of employees is a helpful step toward motivating them to self-improvement and better job performance. For example: An employee's job performance is below average. His supervisor, having previously determined that the employee is motivated by a drive for security, suggests that taking training courses will help the employee to improve, advance, and earn more money. Since earning more money can be a step toward greater security, the employee's drive for security would motivate him to take the training suggested by the supervisor. In essence, this is the process of charting an employee's future course by using his motivating drives to positive advantage.

EMPLOYEE PARTICIPATION

I. WHAT IS PARTICIPATION

Employee participation is the employee's giving freely of his time, skill, and knowledge to an extent which cannot be obtained by demand.

II. WHY IS IT IMPORTANT?

The supervisor's responsibility is to get the job done through people. A good supervisor gets the job done through people who work willingly and well. The participation of employees is important because:

A. Employees develop a greater sense of responsibility when they share in working out operating plans and goals.
B. Participation provides greater opportunity and stimulation for employees to learn, and to develop their ability.
C. Participation sometimes provides better solutions to problems because such solutions may combine the experience and knowledge of interested employees who want the solutions to work.
D. An employee or group may offer a solution which the supervisor might hesitate to make for fear of demanding too much.

E. Since the group wants to make the solution work, they exert pressure in a constructive way on each other.
F. Participation usually results in reducing the need for close supervision.

II. HOW MAY SUPERVISORS OBTAIN IT?

Participation is encouraged when employees feel that they share some responsibility for the work and that their ideas are sincerely wanted and valued. Some ways of obtaining employee participation are:

A. Conduct orientation programs for new employees to inform them about the organization and their rights and responsibilities as employees.
B. Explain the aims and objectives of the agency. On a continuing basis, be sure that the employees know what these aims and objectives are.
C. Share job successes and responsibilities and give credit for success.
D. Consult with employees, both as individuals and in groups, about things that affect them.
E. Encourage suggestions for job improvements. Help employees to develop good suggestions. The suggestions can bring them recognition. The city's suggestion program offers additional encouragement through cash awards.

The supervisor who encourages employee participation is not surrendering his authority. He must still make decisions and initiate action, and he must continue to be ultimately responsible for the work of those he supervises. But, through employee participation, he is helping his group to develop greater ability and a sense of responsibility while getting the job done faster and better.

STEPS IN HANDLING A GRIEVANCE

1. Get the Facts
    a. Listen sympathetically
    b. Let him talk himself out
    c. Get his story straight
    d. Get his point of view
    e. Don't argue with him
    f. Give him plenty of time
    g. Conduct the interview privately
    h. Don't try to shift the blame or pass the buck

2. Consider the Facts
    a. Consider the employee's viewpoint
    b. How will the decision affect similar cases
    c. Consider each decision as a possible precedent
    d. Avoid snap judgments—don't jump to conclusions

3. Make or Get a Decision
    a. Frame an effective counter-proposal
    b. Make sure it is fair to all
    c. Have confidence in your judgment
    d. Be sure you can substantiate your decision

4. Notify the Employee of Your Decision
   Be sure he is told; try to convince him that the decision is fair and just.

5. Take Action When Needed and If Within Your Authority
   Otherwise, tell employee that the matter will be called to the attention of the proper person or that nothing can be done, and why it cannot.

6. Follow through to see that the desired result is achieved.

7. Record key facts concerning the complaint and the action taken.

8. Leave the way open to him to appeal your decision to a higher authority.

9. Report all grievances to your superior, whether they are appealed or not.

DISCIPLINE

Discipline is training that develops self-control, orderly conduct, and efficiency.

To discipline does not necessarily mean to punish.

To discipline does mean to train, to regulate, and to govern conduct.

I. THE DISCIPLINARY INTERVIEW

Most employees sincerely want to do what is expected of them. In other words, they are self-disciplined. Some employees, however, fail to observe established rules and standards, and disciplinary action by the supervisor is required.

The primary purpose of disciplinary action is to improve conduct without creating dissatisfaction, bitterness, or resentment in the process.

Constructive disciplinary action is more concerned with causes and explanations of breaches of conduct than with punishment. The disciplinary interview is held to get at the causes of apparent misbehavior and to motivate better performance in the future.

It is important that the interview be kept on an impersonal a basis as possible. If the supervisor lets the interview descend to the plane of an argument, it loses its effectiveness.

II. PLANNING THE INTERVIEW

Get all pertinent facts concerning the situation so that you can talk in specific terms to the employee.

Review the employee's record, appraisal ratings, etc.

Consider what you know about the temperament of the employee. Consider your attitude toward the employee. Remember that the primary requisite of disciplinary action is fairness.

Don't enter upon the interview when angry.

Schedule the interview for a place which is private and out of hearing of others.

III. CONDUCTING THE INTERVIEW

   A. Make an effort to establish accord.
   B. Question the employee about the apparent breach of discipline. Be sure that the question is not so worded as to be itself an accusation.
   C. Give the employee a chance to tell his side of the story. Give him ample opportunity to talk.
   D. Use understanding—listening except where it is necessary to ask a question or to point out some details of which the employee may not be aware. If the employee misrepresents facts, make a plain, accurate statement of the facts, but don't argue and don't engage in personal controversy.
   E. Listen and try to understand the reasons for the employee's (mis)conduct. First of all, don't assume that there has been a breach of discipline. Evaluate the employee's reasons for his conduct in the light of his opinions and feelings concerning the consistency and reasonableness of the standards which he was expected to follow. Has the supervisor done his part in explaining the reasons for the rule? Was the employee's behavior unintentional or deliberate? Does he think he had real reasons for his actions? What new facts is he telling? Do the facts justify his actions? What causes, other than those mentioned, could have stimulated the behavior?
   F. After listening to the employee's version of the situation, and if censure of his actions is warranted, the supervisor should proceed with whatever criticism is justified. Emphasis should be placed on future improvement rather than exclusively on the employee's failure to measure up to expected standards of job conduct.
   G. Fit the criticism to the individual. With one employee, a word of correction may be all that is required.
   H. Attempt to distinguish between unintentional error and deliberate misbehavior. An error due to ignorance requires training and not censure.
   I. Administer criticism in a controlled, even tone of voice, never in anger. Make it clear that you are acting as an agent of the department. In general, criticism should refer to the job or the employee's actions and not to the person. Criticism of the employee's work is not an attack on the individual.
   J. Be sure the interview does not destroy the employee's self-confidence. Mention his good qualities and assure him that you feel confident that he can improve his performance.
   K. Wherever possible, before the employee leaves the interview, satisfy him that the incident is closed, that nothing more will be said on the subject unless the offense is repeated.